ECONOMIC THEORIES AND THEIR RELATIONAL STRUCTURES

Also by Erwin Klein

MATHEMATICAL METHODS IN THEORETICAL ECONOMICS –
TOPOLOGICAL AND VECTOR SPACE FOUNDATIONS OF
EQUILIBRIUM ANALYSIS

THEORY OF CORRESPONDENCES – INCLUDING APPLICATIONS
TO MATHEMATICAL ECONOMICS (*with Anthony C. Thompson*)

Economic Theories and their Relational Structures

A Model-Theoretic Characterization

Erwin Klein
Professor of Economics
Dalhousie University
Halifax
Nova Scotia, Canada

First published in Great Britain 1998 by
MACMILLAN PRESS LTD
Houndmills, Basingstoke, Hampshire RG21 6XS and London
Companies and representatives throughout the world

A catalogue record for this book is available from the British Library.

ISBN 0–333–68792–2

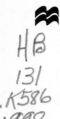

First published in the United States of America 1998 by
ST. MARTIN'S PRESS, INC.,
Scholarly and Reference Division,
175 Fifth Avenue, New York, N.Y. 10010

ISBN 0–312–17458–6

Library of Congress Cataloging-in-Publication Data
Klein, Erwin, 1935–
Economic theories and their relational structures : a model
-theoretic characterization / Erwin Klein.
    p.   cm.
Includes bibliographical references and indexes.
ISBN 0–312–17458–6 (cloth)
1. Economics—Methodology.   I. Title.
HB131.K586 1997
330.1—dc21
                                                            97–1719
                                                              CIP

This book is printed on paper suitable for recycling and made from fully managed and sustained forest sources.

10   9   8   7   6   5   4   3   2   1
07   06   05   04   03   02   01   00   99   98

Printed in Great Britain by
The Ipswich Book Company Ltd
Ipswich, Suffolk

To Estelle

Contents

Preface and Acknowledgements

The intellectual process which now culminates in this book has extended over many years and has developed in very different geographies. It has therefore been influenced mostly by the writings but a few times by the advice of many individuals. I would like to acknowledge the most obvious ones.

So far as tools of analysis are concerned, it is clear that several ideas and approaches used in this book go back to the works of Professors Mario Bunge (McGill) and Patrick Suppes (Stanford). In this connection, I must also acknowledge a most pleasant and useful conversation I had with the late Professor Stig Kanger (Uppsala), several years ago.

Over the years, I have been fortunate enough to be able to discuss various subjects of this book with colleagues. The number of persons is too large and the danger of involuntary omissions too real to provide a list of names here. However, I would like to make one exception and to recall with gratitude an interview with Professor Gerard Debreu (Berkeley, California), in Toronto, also of several years ago. Although that conversation was very influential for my perception of some issues discussed in this book, the interviewee cannot be held accountable for my views on the matter.

The research project behind the book was carried out, in stages, at the Institute of International Economic Studies (Stockholm), the Instituto Torcuato Di Tella (Buenos Aires), the Swedish Collegium for Advanced Study in the Social Sciences, SCASSS (Uppsala) and Dalhousie University (Halifax). Early versions of some of its sections were presented at seminars and a conference in Stockholm, Buenos Aires, Uppsala and Halifax. The Halifax (Nova Scotia) conference was held during 29–31 October 1992.

The final version of the book was written during the two opportunities when I had the privilege of being a fellow of SCASSS, the Spring Term of 1992 and the Fall Term of 1995. I am very impressed by and most thankful to SCASSS for the excellent intellectual environment it provided, its congenial social atmosphere, its comfortable physical facilities, and for generous financial assistance. I would like to thank the Directors of SCASSS for 1992 and 1995. In particular, I wish to express my gratitude to Professor Bo Gustafsson and Professor Björn Wittrock for their steadfast interest and encouragement. All these circumstances made writing the book a very pleasant experience.

An earlier version of the manuscript benefited very much from the constructive criticism of the late Dr Getachew Woldemeskel (SCASSS). Professor Donald W. Katzner (Amherst, Massachusetts), a fellow of SCASSS during the Fall of 1995, was kind enough to read almost the entire manuscript and to offer detailed and helpful criticism as well as advice. Another SCASSS fellow during the same term, Professor Lars Lindhal (Lund), was generous enough to read part of the manuscript and to make most valuable criticism and suggestions for improvement. I am indebted to each of them.

I wish also to express my thanks to the participants of the weekly seminar at SCASSS, many of whom contributed, during and after the session time, useful comments and suggestions. In particular, I would like to express my gratitude to Professor Bo Gustafsson (Uppsala), Dr Alla Frolova (Moscow) and Dr Anna Gomolinska (Warsaw).

Material described in Section 3.3 (pp. 25–6) first appeared in *Erkenntnis* 18 (1982), pp. 65–95 and is adapted with kind permission from Kluwer Academic Publishers.

Tables 8.4.1, 8.4.2 and 8.4.3 first appeared in *European Economic Review*, Vol. 12 (1979), pp. 149–69 and are reprinted here by kind permission of Elsevier Science, NL, Sara Burgerhartstraat 25, 1055 KV Amsterdam, The Netherlands.

Table 9.6.1 and Theorem 9.6.1 are quoted from A. R. Bergstrom 'Monetary Policy in a Model of the UK', which appeared in *Stability and Inflation* (1978), ed. by A. J. L. Catt, M. H. Peston and B. D. J. Silverstone, published by John Wiley & Sons Ltd (Chichester), and are reproduced here by kind permission of the publisher.

Of course, none of the distinguished persons whom I have mentioned in this preface bear any responsibility for my possible mistakes or misinterpretations.

My participation in the actual publication process of this book has been an easy and gratifying task thanks to the high professionalism and understanding of the staff of Macmillan. I would like to express to them my genuine recognition and gratitude.

Last but not least I would like to express my sincere appreciation to Ms Heather Murphy (Halifax) who was in charge of the word-processing of the manuscript. She performed her difficult task with remarkable skill and patience.

ERWIN KLEIN
Halifax, Nova Scotia

Part I   Introduction

1 Overview

This book is a report of research on some aspects of the foundations of contemporary theoretical economics. In turn, this first chapter comments on the main motivation behind the research project, its general aim and its specific research objectives, the scope and method of the investigation, and the organization of the report.

This chapter thus supplies a concise overview of the more important aspects of the originating research project as well as of the arrangement of the ensuing report as contained in the current volume.

The overall goal of the research project was to provide a logical, epistemological and methodological characterization of economic theories which takes into due account some distinctive features of the structures economic theories talk about. The analytical tools used in the study include a general framework and a list of basic concepts both borrowed from that version of formal semantics called model theory, adapted when necessary to the objectives of the study, and a few additional notions which are standard in foundations research.

The overall goal was approached by way of the solutions to three interrelated partial problems. These were, first, the identification of a suitable candidate for a rigorous criterion to characterize the notion *empirical economic theory*; second, the determination of the *epistemological and methodological status* of the many linguistic entities which, though belonging to a well-established class of formal economic theories, would not qualify as empirical theories in terms of the solution given to the first problem; and, third, the design of a *taxonomy of economic theories* consistent with the solutions given to the two preceding problems. For didactic reasons, however, the layout of this report partially reverses the order in which these questions were formulated and answered in the actual research process: the taxonomy is introduced first, the characterization of an empirical theory is attempted next, and the status of the special non-empirical theories is examined last.

In 1.1 we comment on the motivation for this work. This is followed, in 1.2 to 1.7, by an overview of the complete subject of the investigation which includes overall goal, method, subject matter and special objectives. In 1.8 we describe the organization of the book. Finally, in 1.9, as in all other last sections of a chapter, we gather some relevant 'Notes and remarks'.

1.1 MOTIVATION: ON SOME METHODOLOGICAL FEATURES OF ECONOMICS

A moral of this study is that respect for the logical unity of science as expressed by the adherence to the scientific method, on the one hand, and recognition of the need for methodological diversity as imposed by the multifarious character of reality, on the other hand, are not incompatible positions.

In a pure syntactic sense, contemporary theories in economics are not different from theories in any of the formally more developed empirical sciences. Frequently axiomatized within a set-theoretical context, the formal language of an economic theory is, like that of any other theoretical discipline, the language of the branch of mathematics it makes use of. Semantically, in principle, it is also right to claim that economic theories receive their meaning in the same way as other scientific theories.

However, it is argued in the study, when one focuses on the description of the technical aspects that condition the acquisition of empirical meaning by economic theories, it is no longer admissible to ignore the *non-experimental nature* of most economic research. It would seem a natural conclusion, therefore, that the way leading from this admission on to the recognition that this feature might have discernible methodological consequences for the discipline should have been a short one. Such a conclusion would be seriously inappropriate, however.

The last fifteen years or so have borne witness to the rapid growth of a literature devoted to the logical and methodological foundations of economics. This literature includes critical and sometimes normatively inclined accounts of the state of the discipline – see, for instance, Katouzian (1980) – detailed studies in the formal 'reconstruction' of specific economic theories – see, for example, Balzer, Moulines and Sneed (1987) – and more comprehensive, philosophy-of-science type formal investigations into the foundations of economics – see Stigum (1990). Most of these are valuable contributions towards a better understanding of the nature of economics as a science. However, although a few of these works recognize some methodological idiosyncrasies of economics – for example, Händler (1980a), pp. 51–2 – the emphasis seems ordinarily to be placed on those basic traits that are – or in the case of the critical–normative accounts, that 'should be' – common to economics and to other sciences. Actually, while research methods in economics are developed as concrete responses to the non-experimental handicap, there hardly exists a metatheoretical literature of economics which gives to the matter the importance it deserves and, in particular, which solves the three problems enumerated above in a satisfactory manner. This absence has been the main motivation behind the research project reported in this volume.

1.2 OVERALL GOAL

The overall goal of the research reported in this book, concisely formulated, is a suitable logical, epistemological and methodological characterization of economic theories obtained via the help of model-theoretic analytical instruments.

The above paragraph identifies goal, subject matter and method of the investigation. Furthermore, as pointed out in a preceding sentence, achievement of this goal has been attempted via the answers to three related questions. Linguistic considerations dictate, however, that before we focus further on the three objectives the overall goal has been unfolded into – proposal for a taxonomy of economic theories (1.5), characterization of the notion empirical economic theory (1.6), determination of the epistemological and methodological status of a distinguished class of non-empirical economic theories (1.7) – we succinctly introduce the method of approach and the subject matter of the investigation.

1.3 METHOD

As has already been explained – and the title of the book may have suggested – the analytical framework and the principal analytical tools used in this investigation stem from model theory.

As is customary in model theory, a sharp distinction is drawn between the linguistic entity **L**, the 'theory', and the set-theoretical entity(ies) **S**, the 'relational structure(s)' the theory is supposed to talk about. Further usual semantic notions like 'satisfaction', 'validity', 'truth', and especially, 'interpretation' or 'model', and ·'intended or standard interpretation' or 'intended or standard model', are introduced and used in this study.

Modern model theory probably goes back to A. I. Malcev, A. Robinson, T. Skolem and A. Tarski – see, for example, Keisler (1977) – and some of its recent developments and contemporary format owe very much to Robinson (1956, 1963, 1966) who also devoted much of his work to the model-theoretic characterization of mathematical theories.

It was Suppes (1960, 1962, 1967) who, however, most strongly suggested the adaptation and use of model-theoretic concepts to the characterization and reconstruction of scientific theories; he has himself contributed to the axiomatization of important theories within physics and mathematical psychology. This study follows in the steps of Suppes's approach, which is only modified to the extent that this is required (1) to accommodate the overwhelmingly *non-experimental* nature of economic research and (2) to attain a suitable characterization of Suppes's (1962) notion of *model of data*.

On the other hand, the contributions of a recent approach to the analysis of scientific theories that goes back, in its origins, to model theory but which has since followed its own development and formulated its own research agenda – the *structuralist programme of theory reconstruction*; see, for instance, Stegmüller (1978, 1990), and Balzer, Moulines and Sneed (1987) – will not be drawn upon in this study to any substantial degree although some aspects of that approach may be referred to occasionally, in particular in the 'Notes and remarks'. However, it is possible that at least a part of this discussion could have been cast within the structuralist framework and with the help of the language of that point of view.

Finally, with due regard to the importance that the words *scientific experiment* and *experimental method* will acquire in forthcoming arguments in this study, a note of attention is called for at this point. The reader has already found and will continue to find in these pages repeated claims by the author regarding the 'overwhelmingly' or 'predominantly' – other similar qualifications are also used – *non-experimental* nature of economic research. Although a detailed explanation of the author's view on this matter will have to wait until later – when a brief assessment of the self-named *experimental economics* approach will also be offered – the claim may be tentatively understood in the sense that if *scientific experiment* and *experimental method* are assigned the classical restrictive meaning applied in the natural sciences – as opposed to alternative looser meanings – then economics is *experimental* only to an extremely limited extent.

1.4   SUBJECT MATTER AND SCOPE

The subject matter of this study is economic theories, that is hypothetico-deductive systems in economics. The expression 'contemporary theoretical economics' is used to designate the collection of all current economic theories.

An economic theory is defined as a theory that has economic structure(s) as its relational structure(s) (intended realization(s)). Moreover, regarding the determination of what an economic structure is, the conventionalist point of view is adopted that it is possible to agree on a set of rules which permits one to distinguish, within the collection of all relational structures, a subcollection of 'economic structures'.

In a more practical vein, one may, for examples of economic theories, point to the contents of the *Handbook of Mathematical Economics*, the *Handbook of Monetary Economics* and other 'economics handbooks' published by North-Holland Publishing Co. (Amsterdam), including the application chapters of the *Handbook of Econometrics* and the *Handbook of Game Theory with Economic Applications*. The body of theoretical economics we have here in mind includes *explanatory theories* (typically, consisting of descriptive conditional propositions like 'if **a** then **b**' or its negation) and *prescriptive theories* (typically, including normative conditional propositions like 'to get **a** do **b**' or its negation).

Probably, most contemporary economic theories use mathematics as part of their language and many are cast in an axiomatic framework. For the sake of simplicity and without loss of generality, we will assume in this study that all economic theories are mathematical and axiomatic.

Let us make now a summary description of the three research objectives into which the overall goal of the investigation has been decomposed, given here not in the actual sequence of the research development but rather in the order in which they will be dealt with in this volume.

1.5 A TAXONOMY OF ECONOMIC THEORIES

An objective of the investigation has been to come up with a taxonomy realistic enough to take care of differences arising in the actual practice of theory construction in economics and consistent with the results of the other two research objectives previously enumerated.

We begin by noting that reaching this objective presupposed a critical viewpoint of the traditional dichotomy that distinguishes between 'positive' and 'normative' economic theories, and pointed at some common misinterpretations it gives rise to and at its actual limited usefulness. In a more positive sense, it led to two extensions of and one addition to the model-theoretic tools referred to in 1.3, namely the definitions of 'empirical economic structure', 'empirical economic model', and the 'core of empirical claims of a theory' – the 'empirical core', for short. These concepts constitute pivotal analytical tools in the investigations.

Finally, on the basis of a consideration of the epistemological and functional nature of actual economic theories, an alternative taxonomy is proposed based on the combined values of two variables: the theory's epistemological status as *intended* by the theory's author(s) and the theory's *instrumental function*. Development and application of this twofold criterion leads to the identification of four large classes of economic theories: intendedly empirical descriptive theories, intendedly empirical operative theories, non-intendedly empirical descriptive theories and non-intendedly empirical operative theories.

1.6 CHARACTERIZATION OF EMPIRICAL ECONOMIC THEORIES

An important part of the investigation was concerned with empirical economic statements and empirical economic theories. The book offers a description of the process through which an economic theory is given empirical meaning and a characterization of the class of empirical economic statements and theories. To serve this purpose, appropriate frameworks or analytic schemes are developed. These schemes as well as their common centrepiece – the notion of empirical structure – go back to ideas originally proposed some thirty years ago (Suppes, 1962, 1967) to answer some foundational questions of the experimental sciences; here, they are adapted and extended so as to take account of the predominantly non-experimental nature of economic research and to accommodate some of the features resulting therefrom. Thus, model theory continues to provide the basic tools of analysis. In particular, the notions of 'empirical economic model' and 'empirical core', introduced in the context of the design of the taxonomy (1.5), naturally lead to the definition of an 'empirical economic theory'.

Furthermore, a detailed description is offered of the way 'representational theoretical systems and theories' – systems and theories supplying an interpretative explanation of the data (Bunge, 1967b) – and 'phenomenological theoretical systems and theories' – systems and theories supplying a merely subsumptive explanation of the data (Bunge, 1967b) – receive empirical meaning. Illustrative examples are drawn from consumer choice and demand analysis for the case of more complex multi-level representational systems, inter-industry economics and cyclical growth for the case of simpler two-level phenomenological systems, and macroeconometric structural systems as well as vector autoregressive systems (VAR) for the case of what will be called 'phenomenological data-contingent theories'.

1.7 ON THE METHODOLOGICAL FOUNDATIONS OF NON-INTENDEDLY EMPIRICAL ECONOMIC THEORIES

The approach leading to the last objective may be considered an introduction to the methodological foundations of non-experimental economic research. It focuses on the *raison d'être*, the epistemological nature and the instrumental function of non-intendedly empirical theories, an important and large class of theories of the taxonomy (1.5).

As will be argued in Part IV, economics typifies the case of a discipline with 'empirical goals' whose theoretical body consists of a network of theories, a substantial proportion of which are not empirical. First, there is the case of some of the normative or prescriptive theories that have traditionally played an important and accepted role in economics. Second, at the centre of interest for our investigation, there is the case of those theories which have all the appearances of explanatory empirical theories but which cannot be characterized as 'empirical economic theories' in the sense of the proposed characterizing criterion (1.6). Built from the outset without the *intention* of being empirical, a theory of this class may be understood as a theory of a logically possible but non-empirical economic world. What is the cause of and the role for such theories?

The point of view put forward in this study is that the weight of non-intendedly empirical theories within economics is only one methodological response to a fundamental characteristic of economics, possibly shared with other disciplines, namely, its predominantly non-experimental nature.

Furthermore, it is argued that the predominantly non-experimental nature of economics is responsible for three typical methodological results: (1) the invention and growth of econometrics as a special, non-experimental method of empirical research; (2) the development of an approach consisting in the playing of laboratory games, the design and realization of 'token-economy' events and the recording of laboratory exercises with animals directed to the simulation of experiments of economic situations (*laboratory simulation* of experiments) – an interesting and rather recent line of research inaccurately called 'experimental economics' by its practitioners – and (3) the systematic construction of non-intendedly empirical theories, activity assimilated in this study to *analytic simulation* of experiments.

The role of analytic simulation of experiments is further analysed with reference to its part in the process of theory construction and illustrated with examples from general equilibrium analysis. Although appropriate examples could have been chosen from other areas of economics, theories of general economic equilibrium benefit from some important features which tilt the choice in their favour.

With this point of view and without any intention of being exhaustive – an unattainable goal – the text lists analytic procedures, distinguishing those focusing on the relational structures of a theory and/or their properties from those concerned with general matters of language and/or research strategy, and, finally, from those probing into the adequacy of a specific mathematical tool and/or method.

1.8   ORGANIZATION OF THE BOOK

The book is divided into four parts. Part I consists of this 'Introduction', Chapter 2, where we assemble the necessary analytical toolkit we are to borrow from model theory, and Chapter 3, where we delimit the subject of analysis, namely theoretical economics. Part II, which consists of two chapters, is devoted to the 'Taxonomy of Economic Theories'. Chapter 4 discusses the taxonomy principle and then Chapter 5 applies it to classify actual economic theories. In Part III we attempt to describe the way 'Empirical Economic Theories' receive their meaning. Chapter 6 discusses the characterization of an empirical economic theory in very general terms; then Chapters 7 and 8, on the one hand, and Chapters 9 and 10, on the other hand, are devoted to the cases of representational theories and theoretical systems and of phenomenological theories and theoretical systems, respectively. The discussion of Part IV focuses on what we have called, for reasons which will become clearer in Part II, 'Non-Intendedly Empirical Economic Theories'. It consists of Chapter 11, where we comment upon and draw some methodological consequences from the mainly non-experimental character of economic research and discuss the general role of non-intendedly empirical theories, and Chapter 12, where we provide illustrations with a sample of such theories and sort them out according to their particular *analytic simulation-of-experiment* – as opposed to truly and rigorously experimental – function.

1.9   NOTES AND REMARKS

The 'recognition' of the existence of non-empirical theories in economics is easy to find in the literature, although their functions and possible reasons for their presence are usually not discussed. A critical form of this 'recognition' is to be found in Rosenberg (1989) who seems to claim that the whole of (at least, contemporary) economics is only able to make 'generic predictions'. The (at least implicitly) normative nature of his claim may be read from the title of his article: 'Are Generic Predictions Enough?'; in his article on the evolution of economic theories Händler (1982) refers to the existence of 'pure theories', possibly theories without empirical referents.

A considerable effort among 'structuralists' has been devoted to the *logical reconstruction* of economic theories, which mainly consists in re-formalizing a given theory according to the guidelines and conceptual framework of the *programme* recently described by Balzer, Moulines and Sneed (1987). Although these efforts have been pointed in various directions – for instance, Diederich's (1982, 1989) reconstruction of Marxian economic theory, Händler's studies in aggregate market demand and supply functions (1980b) and macroeconomic theories (1982) or Janssen's (1989) reconstruction of classical and Keynesian macroeconomics – the bulk of the work has been devoted to the reconstruction of theories of pure exchange economies. An incomplete list of authors of these sometimes controversial results would include the names of Händler (1980a), Balzer (1982, 1985), Haslinger (1983), Hands (1985), Hamminga and Balzer (1986) and Janssen and Kuipers (1989) – in this connection, see also Requate (1991). Interestingly enough, part of the controversy touches upon the existence or not of *empirical claims* for the economics of pure exchange, arguably one of the less 'empirical' – a qualification that is not to be understood to mean 'irrelevant' or 'useless' – fields of theoretical economic research.

2 Model-Theoretic Toolkit

As was stated in 1.3, the main analytical tools used in this study consist of a general approach and of a list of concepts both borrowed from that version of semantics called *model theory*. These model-theoretic concepts are applied here often in a rather informal way and will be described only for the sake of completeness. One such basic concept is that of a *theory*; another is that of a *model*.

In model theory one sharply distinguishes between the *linguistic entity* **L** – the theory's language – and the *set-theoretical entity(ies)* **S** – the structure(s) the theory is supposed to talk about. We discuss these two notions separately.

2.1 LANGUAGE

A language is a set of symbols – a vocabulary – subject to a set of morphological rules – formation and transformation rules (see, for example, Bunge, 1967a). Application of the morphological rules to the vocabulary leads to the formulas of the language. Since economic-theoretical language is a blend of ordinary language, technical jargon and mathematics, the typical vocabulary of an economic theory consists of ordinary language words, technical–economic words and mathematical and logical symbols subject to morphological rules of ordinary and mathematical languages (with, of course, logic in the background). In what follows we do not distinguish between the notions of a 'theory' and of a 'theory's language'.

A 'well-formed formula' (wff for short) is a formula constructed in strict accordance with the morphological rules. A wff containing free variables (for example, $x > y$) will also be referred to as a 'potential statement', a 'propositional function' or a 'sentential function'. A wff the symbols of which are only constants – that is, which does not contain free variables (for example, $1 > 0$) – will be indistinctly referred to as a 'statement', a 'proposition' or a 'sentence'.

Henceforth by a *theory* **L** we shall understand a set **F** of wffs closed under the operation ⊢ of deduction, meaning that, for any set $\mathbf{B} \subset \mathbf{F}$, if $\mathbf{B} \vdash \mathbf{t}$ then $\mathbf{t} \in \mathbf{F}$. That is, there is a list of rules (logical and mathematical) – rules of inference – that when applied to formulas of **L** produce formulas of **L**.

2.2 SEMI-FORMALIZED LANGUAGES: AXIOMATIC THEORIES

A theory **L** is *axiomatizable* if all its deducible formulas can be derived from a proper subset **A** $\subset$ **F** which will be called the *axiom base* of **L**. A theory constructed or reconstructed in this manner will be called an *axiomatic theory*. Theories axiomatized within a set-theoretical framework, that is by defining a predicate specified in set-theoretical terms – as opposed to first- or higher-order logic – are usually referred to as semi-formalized theories. Contemporary theoretical economics shows many examples of such axiomatization.

Among the sentences of an axiomatic theory one can distinguish three classes: the primitive propositions or 'axioms'; the derived statements or 'theorems'; and an especially helpful though (in principle if not in practice) dispensable class of sentences, the 'definitions'.

An *axiom* **a** is simply a member of the axiom base **A**; formally, a sentence **t** is a *theorem* of **L** if and only if it has a proof in **L**, that is, if and only if it is the last term in a finite sequence of formulas of **L** each of which is either an axiom of **L** or obtainable from preceding formulas in that sequence by the (logical and mathematical) rules of inference of **L**; finally, a *definition* is an operation performed in the language **L** by means of which a new symbol is introduced to **L** in terms of pre-existent symbols of **L**. Definitions are usually required to be 'non-creative' in the sense that they should not make it possible for the theory to generate, with their help, theorems that would not be obtainable in their absence – see, for example, Przelecki (1969). Definitions may thus be regarded as 'non-creative axioms' and counted as members of the axiom base **A**.

Among the symbols that constitute the vocabulary of **L** it is customary to distinguish the *formal symbols*, in our case logical and mathematical ones (for example, '¬' for negation, '$\int$' for integration) from the *extra-formal symbols*, in our case, typically, the economic ones (for example, '>' for preference, '$\mathscr{C}$' for a specific class of economies). Some of these symbols are called *primitive symbols* because they are undefined or at least not defined within the same theory **L**; they denote, in the case of economic theories, the primitive economic concepts of the theory and they are assigned meaning by the primitive sentences or axioms of **L** in a way to be described below in 2.4.

2.3 STRUCTURES

Definition 2.3.1   Let D be a non-empty set, I an index set and Z the set of non-negative integers. By a *relational structure* S it is meant here a pair $\langle D, \langle R_i \rangle_{i \in I} \rangle$ together with a function $\pi: I \to Z$ such that for each $i \in I$, if $\pi(i) = 0$ then $R_i \in D$ and if $\pi(i) > 0$ then $R_i \subset D^{\pi(i)}$. D is the domain of individuals; relation R_i is a *relation of type* $\pi(i)$ that is a subset of the product set $R^{\pi(i)}$; in particular, $R_i \in D$ is an individual and $R_i \subset D$ is a unary relation or property.

The above definition can be easily modified to accommodate those cases in which the set D stands for a whole collection of domains $D_1, \ldots, D_n$ rather than for a single domain.

The set of extra-formal (or economic, in the case of an economic theory) symbols of L consists of a list of constants and a list of variables $V = \{v_i : i \in I\}$. It is assumed that L contains variables corresponding to each of the *types* present in S. In particular, a function $\pi': I \to Z$ defines the variable's type. If $\pi'(i) = 0$, v_i is called an individual variable; if $\pi'(i) > 0$, v_i is called a predicate variable. As stated before, the underived, primitive formulas in A characterize the primitive, extra-formal symbols in V.

The following definition describes how meaning is assigned to the extra-formal symbols of L.

Definition 2.3.2   A set-theoretical structure S is said to be an *assignment* to or a *possible interpretation* or *realization* of L if a one-to-one correspondence $\mu: L \to S$ exists such that variables v of L are assigned relations of the same logical *type* in S.

2.4 MODELS

The following two definitions summarize the semantic notion of truth or validity.

Definition 2.4.1   A *value assignment* for the well-formed formulas of L is a mapping w from L to the set $\{0, 1\}$. The *value* assigned to a sentence α is either $w(\alpha) = 1$ or $w(\alpha) = 0$. The *value* assigned to a well-formed formula having free variables depends on the assignment made to its free variables. If the value is 1 (respectively, 0) for any such assignment one says that the formula is *valid* (respectively, *contravalid*) in **S**; if it is 1 for at least one assignment to its free variables, one says that it is *satisfiable* in **S**.

Definition 2.4.2 A set-theoretical structure **S** is a *model* of the theory **L** if: (1) every axiom of **L** is valid in **S**; (2) if **t** is a wff of **L**, **B** is a set of wffs of **L**, and there is a rule such that **B** ⊢ **t**, then if every formula of **B** is valid in **S**, also **t** is valid in **S**. In particular, **S** is a model of a subset **K** of sentences of **L** if every sentence of **K** is valid in **S**.

The previous paragraph gives a possible characterization of the *logical* notion of a model. It is this notion of a model that will be used predominantly throughout this study. It is thus very important to be able to distinguish clearly this use of the word 'model' from other uses which are most frequent in the empirical sciences (economics in particular): an iconic model, a system of equations or even a theory – for the differences and relations among the various uses of the word 'model' see Suppes (1960). In the few cases in which 'model' is used in this study in a sense other than the logical sense, explicit mention of that fact will be made.

2.5 STRUCTURAL AND PROPER AXIOMS

In Suppes's (1967) view, to axiomatize a theory (using a set-theoretical framework) is *to define a set-theoretical predicate*. This is done by means of a subset of the theory's axiom base, the members of which are called *structural* axioms. For example, in the axiomatization of a mathematical theory of groups one may introduce the predicate 'group' as follows:

Definition 2.5.1 A *group* is a triple ⟨G, **0**, o⟩ where:

A2.5.1 G is a non-empty set.
A2.5.2 **0** ∈ G.
A2.5.3 o is a function from G × G into G.
A2.5.4 $\forall x \forall y \forall z: x \text{ o } (y \text{ o } z) = (x \text{ o } y) \text{ o } z$.
A2.5.5 $\forall x: x \text{ o } \mathbf{0} = x$.
A2.5.6 $\forall x \exists y: x \text{ o } y = \mathbf{0}$.

Thus the structural axioms – in the example A2.5.1 to A2.5.3 – determine the possible or potential models of a theory of groups. The other axioms, often called *proper axioms* – in the example A2.5.4 to A2.5.6 – describe law-like relations within the theory. A model of a theory, of course, must satisfy the structural as well as the proper axioms of that theory. In this context, despite recognizing the philosophical difficulties which beset the notion of 'law-likeness', Balzer, Moulines and Sneed (1987) agree that '[r]oughly, the distinction between actual and potential models is parallel to the distinction between lawlike and non-lawlike axiomatic statements'.

2.6   INTENDED AND NON-INTENDED STRUCTURES AND MODELS

Among the set-theoretical structures which are possible realizations or interpretations of **L**, one characterizes the *intended* or *standard* one(s) as being precisely that (those) set-theoretical structure(s) the theory was originally intended to talk about. The notion of *intended* or *standard* model(s) of a theory immediately follows from that of intended or standard possible realizations or interpretations of the theory.

2.7   AN ECONOMIC EXAMPLE

From Debreu (1959), for instance, the set-theoretical structure 'economy' may be defined as follows.

Definition 2.7.1   An *economy* is a structure $\mathbf{E} = \langle R^l, \langle \mathbf{X}_i, \succcurlyeq_i \rangle, \langle \mathbf{Y}_j \rangle, \omega \rangle$ where:

A2.7.1   for each $i = 1, \ldots, m$ $\mathbf{X}_i$ is a non-empty subset of R^l;

A2.7.2   for each $i = 1, \ldots, m$ $\succcurlyeq_i$ is a complete preordering on $\mathbf{X}_i$;

A2.7.3   for each $j = 1, \ldots, n$ $\mathbf{Y}_j$ is a non-empty subset of R^l;

A2.7.4 ω is an interior point of R^l.

Axioms A2.7.1 to A2.7.4 may be regarded as structural axioms in the sense that they define the set-theoretical predicate 'economy'. In the same cited work one also finds the set-theoretical structure 'private-ownership economy', a special case of the structure of the preceding definition.

Definition 2.7.2   A *private-ownership economy* is a structure $\mathcal{E} = \langle R^l,$ $\langle \mathbf{X}_i, \succeq_i, \mathbf{w}_i, \theta_{ij} \rangle, \langle \mathbf{Y}_j \rangle, \omega \rangle$ where $\langle R^l, \langle \mathbf{X}_i, \succeq_i \rangle, \langle \mathbf{Y}_j \rangle, \omega \rangle$ is an economy **E** and additionally:

A2.7.5   for each i, $\mathbf{w}_i \in R^l$ and $\Sigma_i \mathbf{w}_i = \omega$,

A2.7.6   for each pair (i, j), $\theta_{ij} \geq 0$ and such that $\Sigma_i \theta_{ij} = 1$ for every j.

Now axioms A2.7.1 to A2.7.6 may be said to define the more complex set-theoretical structure 'private-ownership economy'. The informal interpretation of the above symbols is well known: R^l is the *commodity space*; the 4-tuple $\langle \mathbf{X}_i, \succeq_i, \mathbf{w}_i, \theta_{ij} \rangle$ is called the *ith consumer*, made up of the *consumption possibility set* $\mathbf{X}_i$, the *preference-indifference relation* $\succeq_i$, the *initial-endowment vector* $\mathbf{w}_i$, and the *consumer's share in the jth firm* θ_{ij}; finally, $\mathbf{Y}_j$ stands for the *production possibility set of the jth firm*, and ω represents the *total initial resources* of $\mathcal{E}$.

The central problem in Debreu's theory, in the context we are referring to here, is the existence of a *competitive equilibrium* for a structure like $\mathcal{E}$. Without going into technical details here – the reader is referred to Debreu (1959) – *sufficient conditions* for a private-ownership economy $\mathcal{E}$ to have a competitive equilibrium, that is, *sufficient conditions* for a set-theoretical structure $\mathcal{E}$ like the one of Definition 2.7.2 to be a model of Debreu's (1959) *equilibrium existence theory* are given in the following set of additional axioms:

A2.7.7 $\forall i$: $\mathbf{X}_i$ is closed, convex, and has a lower bound for $\leq$;

A2.7.8 $\forall i$: there is no satiation consumption in $\mathbf{X}_i$;

A2.7.9 $\forall i$: $\mathbf{x}_i' \in \mathbf{X}_i$ the sets $\{\mathbf{x}_i \in \mathbf{X}_i: \mathbf{x}_i \succeq_i \mathbf{x}_i'\}$ and $\{\mathbf{x}_i \in \mathbf{X}_i: \mathbf{x}_i' \succeq_i \mathbf{x}_i\}$ are closed in $\mathbf{X}_i$;

A2.7.10 $\forall i$: if $\mathbf{x}_i^1, \mathbf{x}_i^2 \in \mathbf{X}_i$, and if $\lambda \in [0,1]$ then $\mathbf{x}_i^1 >_i \mathbf{x}_i^2$ implies $\mathbf{x}^1 >_i \lambda \mathbf{x}_i^2 + (1 - \lambda)\mathbf{x}_i^1$;

A2.7.11 $\forall i$: $\exists \mathbf{x}_i^0 \in \mathbf{X}_i$ such that $\mathbf{x}_i^0 \ll \mathbf{w}_i$;

A2.7.12 $\forall j$: $0 \in \mathbf{Y}_j$;

A2.7.13 $\mathbf{Y} = \Sigma_{j=1}^n \mathbf{Y}_j$ is closed and convex;

A2.7.14 $\mathbf{Y} \cap (-\mathbf{Y}) = \{0\}$, where $-\mathbf{Y}$ is the negative of $\mathbf{Y} = \Sigma_{j=1}^n \mathbf{Y}_j$;

A2.7.15 $\mathbf{Y} \supset (-\mathbf{\Omega})$, where $-\mathbf{\Omega}$ is the non-positive orthant of R^l.

2.8 NOTES AND REMARKS

For detailed and more rigorous introductions to mathematical logic and model theory see Rogers (1971) and Kopperman (1972), respectively.

In regard to their language set-ups and to their relational structures the degree of complexity of theories varies immensely. With this in mind, one may postulate the existence in 'the limit' of some minimal indecomposable theoretical unit and then understand any actual 'grown up' theory as a more or less complex network of such simplest, indecomposable units. This viewpoint lies at the foundations of the structuralist approach, which makes the minimalistic concept 'theory-element' the centrepiece of its analytic framework and which reserves the name 'theory-net' for more complex decomposable theories.

In structuralist writings, the dichotomy language–structure and the reference to the place and role of statements is not found, as a rule, at the outset of the discussion – in apparent contrast to what is usual in the standard model-theoretic approach – probably due to the elementary linguistic nature of the primitive concept theory-element (see for example Stegmüller, 1990). In the customary structuralist notation, a theory-element is an entity $T = \langle K, I \rangle$ where K, the *core* of T, is of the form $K = \langle M_p, M, M_{pp}, GC, GL \rangle$ and where I is called the set of *intended applications* of T. M_p is the set of *potential models*, that is, the set of structures which satisfy the structural axioms; M stands for the set of *models*, in the usual sense, and is thus included in M_p; a typical M_p consists of four kind of entities: a k-tuple of base sets (the objects the theory talks about), an l-tuple of auxiliary base sets (purely mathematical sets endowed with the appropriate structure), a p-tuple of non-theoretical functions (functions measured in a non-T-dependent way) and a q-tuple of theoretical functions (functions measured in a T-dependent way) – for a detailed discussion of the structuralist notion of *theoreticity* see Balzer, Moulines and Sneed (1987). M_{pp} is called the set of *partial potential models*, and includes the potential models in M_p but after having eliminated from each of them all theoretical terms, that is the terms the measurement of which is T-dependent. Finally, GC is the *general constraint* or set-theoretical intersection of all *single constraints* (a single constraint eliminates a certain combination of potential models) and GL is the *general link* or intersection of all sets of inter-theoretical links of T with other theory-elements. I, the set of intended applications of the theory, is made up of elements of M_{pp}, that is, is contained in the latter. Intuitively, I includes only those empirical structures which satisfy the theory. An economic illustration of the above general concepts will be given in Chapter 3. Finally, for a very detailed exposition of the structuralist view the reader is referred again to Balzer, Moulines and Sneed (1987). A summary version of the approach, the basis of the current note, is the excellent review by Stegmüller (1990).

3 Theoretical Economics

The discussion of this study is confined to 'economic theories' in a restricted sense, namely to *hypothetico-deductive systems* in economics. The emphasis on the 'hypothetico-deductive' nature of the 'system' is meant here to forewarn that a purely descriptive account of a phenomenon, historical or statistical, would by itself not qualify as a theory no matter how important it may be as a potential or actual source or motivation for theoretical activity.

Furthermore, to ease the task in the use of the analytic tools of Chapter 2, it is assumed that the theories to be considered both use mathematics in their languages and have been axiomatized by means of the definition of set-theoretical predicates in the manner discussed in that chapter. They are thus semi-formalized theories in the sense described in Chapter 2. These assumptions will not restrict the generality of the discussion in any serious way, for most of contemporary theoretical economics is formulated in this manner; besides, any 'non-formal' theory could be recast in an axiomatic setting if needed; indeed, in a few instances of our discussion, we do make reference to theories the original versions of which were presented in ordinary language; in such cases we take it for granted that a mathematical axiomatic formulation is either available or can readily be made so.

3.1 ECONOMIC THEORIES AND MODELS

The first question we have to respond to here is the following: when is a theory an *economic* theory? The point of view taken in this study is that an economic theory has – in principle, so far as the intention of its author(s) is concerned – *economic* structure(s) as its intended realization(s). Moreover, regarding the determination of what an economic structure is, the conventionalist point of view is adopted that it is possible to agree on a set of practical rules which allow us to distinguish, within the collection of all set-theoretical structures, a subcollection of 'economic structures'.

Admittedly, the suggested procedure implies that alternative rules may be chosen and thus that a certain degree of arbitrariness in the characterization of what economic structures are is unavoidable. However, there does not seem to be any viable and non-controversial alternative procedure.

Of course, some famous prerequisites which have often been made cornerstones of venerable descriptions (wrongly called 'definitions') of economics – like the (nowadays less fashionable) enumeration of 'production', 'exchange' and 'consumption' as the archetypical economic activities, or the (somewhat more modern) reference to 'systems and processes for the allocation of limited resources to the satisfaction of unlimited wants' – may continue to be used among such pragmatic rules of identification.

A possible list of the economic theories we have in mind would include *abstract* theories – theories referring to wide collections of structures but remote from any specific set of empirical data – as well as *concrete* theories – data-specific and data-contingent theories – in the following fields.

- *Microeconomics*: consumer theories, producer theories; theories of market behaviour; theories of investment; theories of market demand and excess demand; theories of equilibrium: existence, determinacy, stability; temporary equilibrium theories; theories of equilibrium under uncertainty; theories of alternative solution concepts for perfectly competitive and imperfectly competitive economies; theories of social choice; economic information theories; Pareto optimality; economic growth theories; optimal growth theories; second-best theories; theories of incentives for decentralized systems; theories of organization; theories of planning.
- *Macroeconomics*: aggregate demand and supply theories; macroeconomic equilibrium and disequilibrium theories; policy theories.
- *'Applied' special field theories*, like monetary economics theories; international economics theories; public economics theories; development economics theories; resource economics theories.
- *Black box and input–output theories*, including theories of linear economic models; structural and autoregressive econometric systems.

A list like the above one is, of course, by no means exhaustive and it will be the subject of perpetual change over time. Notice moreover that, when we refer to fields of research, we prefer to use the plural expression 'theories' rather than the singular one, 'theory'. This is in accordance with the notion of an axiomatic theory being a hypothetico-deductive system where the theorems are derived from a given axiom base. Thus we may make reference to 'the equilibrium-existence theory for finite economies', 'the equilibrium-existence theory for economies with a continuum of traders and a finite number of commodities', 'the equilibrium-existence theory for economies with infinite-dimensional commodity spaces and a finite number of agents' and so on, when we want to make the point that each of these constructs is by itself a closed hypothetico-deductive system. Of course, this does not deny the possibility of reduction, extension and unification of theories within and between fields. Observe also that this approach is only dictated by the logical view of theories and by the convenience of recognizing analytically the identity of the 'smaller' theoretical elements as elementary wholes and should not be understood as a suggestion that two theories in a particular field are in any way competing (let alone mutually inconsistent) with each other.

In accordance with the point of view just expressed, we use without exception the expression *theoretical economics* instead of the much more frequent but misleading expression *economic theory* to refer to the bulk of *economic theories*. In our sense, theoretical economics may be said to be the collection of all economic theories.

A second and final warning may be useful here. With the exception of those very few cases where we explicitly emphasize the more apparent than real transgression of the adopted rule, mainly to refer precisely to the use made in other contexts by other authors, the word 'model' is always used in this study in the restricted, logical sense – that is, to denote the set-theoretical structure where a theory or sets of sentences is satisfied – and not to denote a theory or a system of equations.

3.2   AN EXAMPLE: THEORY OF CONSUMER CHOICE

There is possibly no controversy among economists that the generic entity called 'individual consumer' is a typical example of an economic structure; and that an *economic theory of individual consumer choice* – see Richter (1966, 1971) – explains mechanisms by means of which a consumer, following some choice criterion or pattern and facing different budget situations, performs choices of commodity bundles. A possible realization of one such theory is a 3-tuple $\langle \mathbf{X}, B, \mathbf{H} \rangle$, where $\mathbf{X}$ is an *a priori* given set of commodity bundles (possible consumptions), B is the family of all possible budget situations, and $\mathbf{H}$ is a dominance relation on $\mathbf{X}$ describing an *ex-ante* choice criterion (consumer's taste) or an *ex-post* (observed) choice pattern. Of course, there are different suitable characterizations of the models of the theory. One possible characterization is the following – compare, for instance, with that given in 2.7:

Definition 3.2.1   A structure $\langle X, B, H \rangle$ is a *consumer*, that is a *model of the theory of individual consumer choice*, if and only if the following axioms are satisfied:

A3.2.1 X is a non-empty set;
A3.2.2 $B = \{ B \subset X : B \neq \emptyset \}$;
A3.2.3 $H \subset X \times X$.

Axioms A3.2.1 to A3.2.3 may be regarded as the structural axioms of a theory of individual consumer choice. Usually, additional axioms would be needed both to put a bit more 'mathematical detail' or 'substance' into the structure – thus also determining in a more precise manner the language of the theory – and to postulate some law-like relations. However, this need not bother us at this point of the discussion.

An important idea for any theory of choice is that of a 'choice function'. Here one may define such a function with help of the dominance relation H as follows.

Definition 3.2.2   A *choice function* h is a map that assigns to every set $B \in B$ a set $h(B) \subseteq B$ defined by $h(B) = \{ x \in B : \forall y \in B : xHy \}$.

One may easily imagine several different dominance relations compatible with A3.2.3. First, we consider a 'transitive-rational' consumer by specifying a suitable choice criterion to which the consumer adjusts her behaviour. This may be done by imposing appropriate assumptions on H. In particular, we say that (1) H is *reflexive* if $\forall x \in X$, xHx; (2) H is *transitive* if $\forall x,y,z \in X$, if xHy and yHz then xHz; (3) H is *complete* if $\forall x,y \in X$ either xHy or yHx.

Definition 3.2.3   If the binary relation H on X is reflexive, transitive, and complete, then the consumer $\langle X, B, H \rangle$ is said to be a *transitive-rational consumer*.

Next one can imagine some observable behaviour pattern by describing some notion of 'revealed preferences'. Such a notion is given here by means of three definitions.

Definition 3.2.4 $xVy \Leftrightarrow \exists B \in B: x \in h(B) \wedge y \in B$.

Definition 3.2.5 $xWy \Rightarrow xVu_1V \ldots Vu_nVy$.

When xVy holds one says that 'x is directly revealed preferred to y'; on the other hand, when for x, y, and a finite sequence (u_k: $k = 1$, $2, \ldots, n$) one has the situation described in 3.2.5, one says that 'x is revealed preferred to y'.

Definition 3.2.6   If H is the relation W of Definition 3.2.5, then the consumer $\langle X, B, H \rangle$ is said to be a *congruous consumer*.

An interesting result of the theory is a theorem asserting the equivalence of the two viewpoints expressed by Definition 3.2.3, on the one hand, and jointly by Definitions 3.2.5 and 3.2.6, on the other – for a proof see Richter (1971).

Theorem 3.2.1   A consumer $\langle X, B, H \rangle$ is transitive-rational if and only if she is congruous.

A brief comment on Theorem 3.2.1: a transitive-rational consumer always shows a congruent behaviour; conversely, a consumer whose observable behaviour is congruent may be thought of as if she chooses following a preference relation like the one of Definition 3.2.3.

To close this section, we wish to raise a question that will concern us later on, in other parts of this study: what is the possible ontological status of the objects in the domain X of the structure of the above theory sketch?

It would seem, in principle, that X could be (1) a subset of some appropriate mathematical space; or (2) an organized set of empirical data resulting from measurement operations performed on a well-determined set of actual commodities; or (3) a bunch of actual commodities. It will be a contention of this study that while structures with domains as in (1) and (2) may qualify as possible models of the theory, case (3) is of such an ambiguous nature that it precludes itself as a potential model. Case (1) is a typical example of the ideal interpretative structure of the theory; case (2) is a possible example of an empirical interpretative structure of the same theory; case (3), in the best of circumstances, may be regarded as a fuzzy, mediate referent of the theory, to which the theory can hardly be matched in any rigorous way.

3.3 NOTES AND REMARKS

We illustrate next the use of the structuralist framework by means of Händler's (1982) recast of the textbook standard closed four-market Keynesian analytic system.

According to the structuralist view, the core **K** of a theory-element **T** = ⟨**K, I**⟩ is given by the system **K** = ⟨**M**$_p$, **M**, **M**$_{pp}$, **GC, GL**⟩ – refer to 2.8. On the other hand, the standard closed four-market Keynesian theory (**TS**) is usually summarized by means of the following equations:

Commodity market:	$Y(N) = C(Y(N)) + I(r) + G$
Labour market:	$N^s(w/p) = N^d(w/p) = N$
Money market:	$M/p = L(Y(N), r)$

where Y (real national income), C (real consumption), I (real invest-ment), L (real liquidity preference), N (employment), N^s, N^d (supply of and demand for labour), N (employment), w (nominal wage rate), r (real interest rate) and p (price level) are the endogenous variables and G (real government spending) and M (nominal money supply) are the exogenous variables.

Specializing the notation and taking account of the fact that **GC** and **GL** are not needed in the present context (see Händler, 1982) we may write **TS** = ⟨**KS, IS**⟩ for the (standard) theory-element and **KS** = ⟨**MS**$_p$, **MS**, **MS**$_{pp}$⟩ for its core. In Händler's (1982) view the relevant structure is here the 16-tuple ⟨$Y, C, I, G, N, M, L, w, p, r, C^*, I^*, Y^*, N^{s*}, N^{d*}, L^*$⟩ where the first ten components are subsets of appropriate numerical sets 'not-**TS**-dependent', that is 'not-**TS**-theoretical' (Händler goes a step further: 'times series of cardinality T'), and where the next six components are '**TS**-theoretical functions'.

Definition 3.3.1   ⟨$Y, C, I, G, N, M, L, w, p, r, C^*, I^*, Y^*, N^{s*}, N^{d*}, L^*$⟩ is a *potential model* of **TS** if and only if:

A3.3.1 $Y, C, I, G, N, M, L, w, p, r$ are subsets of R;
A3.3.2 $C^*, I^*, Y^*, N^{s*}, N^{d*}$, are functions from R to R and L^* is a function from R^2 to R.

It has been already pointed out that in his characterization of a potential model of the theory-element Händler (1982) requires that $Y, C, I, G, N, M, L, w, p$ and r be time series of cardinality T, that is elements of R^T.

Definition 3.3.2 $\langle Y, C, I, G, N, M, L, w, p, r, C^*, I^*, Y^*, N^{s*}, N^{d*},$ $L^* \rangle$ is a *model* of **TS** if and only if it satisfies Definition 3.3.1 and:

A3.3.3	(a) $Y = C + I + G$;
	(b) $M/p = L$;
A3.3.4	(a) $C^*, I^*, I^*, N^{s*}, N^{d*}$, and L^* are twice differentiable;
A3.3.5	(b) $C^{*'} > 0, I^{*'} < 0, Y^{*'} > 0$, and $Y^{*''} < 0$
	$N^{s*'} > 0, N^{d*'} < 0, L_Y' > 0, L_r' < 0$.
A3.3.6	$C_t = C^*(Y_t)$;
A3.3.7	$I_t = I^*(r_t)$;
A3.3.8	$Y_t = Y^*(N_t)$;
A3.3.9	$N_t = N^{s*}(w_t/p_t) = N^{d*}(w_t/p_t)$;
A3.3.10	$L_t = L^*(Y_t, r_t)$.

Since only C^*, Y^*, N^{s*}, N^{d*} and L^* represent here the **TS**-theoretical terms, the set $\mathbf{MS}_{pp}$ of *partial potential models* consists of 10-tuples of the form $\langle Y, C, I, G, N, M, L, w, p, r \rangle$. The set **IS** of intended applications of **TS** is a subset of $\mathbf{MS}_{pp}$.

Part II   A Taxonomy of Economic Theories

4 A Taxonomy of Economic Theories Based upon Intended Epistemological Status and Pragmatic Function

The body of contemporary theoretical economics is made up of an ever-increasing number of more or less interdependent individual theories with differentiated cognitive and operative functions. The main purpose of Part II is to devise and illustrate a classification of economic theories that would serve as a framework tentatively to accommodate the main results of this study to be developed in detail in Parts III and IV. The suggested taxonomy criterion will permit a classification of economic theories according to their intended epistemological status and instrumental roles.

Although the contents of Part II are, in an essential way, a by-product of the original main objectives of the investigation, their presence could be independently motivated by our viewpoint regarding the need for a taxonomy alternative to the customary textbook dichotomy 'positive–normative'. The latter is not only too often misunderstood but it is also, for our purposes, too simplistic a classification for capturing characteristic methodological features of economic-theoretical research.

To classify economic theories is, in itself, not a very exciting endeavour unless it contributes to a better understanding of some of the methodological features that are typical of economic research (or, perhaps more generally, of non-experimental research) as distinct from other branches of scientific research and, in this way, to an appreciation of the place that a particular theory holds within the body of theoretical economics. In this sense, one hopes, a useful taxonomy may help us to understand why economics has come to be what it is, and also to highlight the significance of and the interdependence amongst its individual theories. To understand such issues properly is important, among other reasons, because misunderstandings often lead to unwarranted expectations about the actual explanatory ability, the predictive reliability, or the operative effectiveness of the discipline at a given point in time, and also to misconceptions regarding the causes of the deficiencies in relation to all and each of these three aspects.

It is customary in economics textbooks to distinguish between positive and normative economic theories – according to J. N. Keynes (1955), theories of 'what is', and of 'what ought to be', respectively. The positive-normative classification criterion has a venerable tradition but it is not very satisfactory for a logical, epistemological and methodological appraisal of economics aiming at the objectives set forth in this study. Let us now see why.

The expressions 'positive' and 'normative' are not exactly antonyms, and are thus not adequate as labels of a dichotomic classification. To begin with, what are, in the usual description, positive and normative theories?

We are told that a positive theory is 'a theory of what is', a characterization that in the common scientific positivist interpretation means the same as an empirical theory, that is, informally speaking, a theory of the 'real world'. If this interpretation is accepted as correct, are then all non-empirical theories – let us say, theories without testable propositions – normative?

A normative theory is commonly characterized, following J. N. Keynes, as a theory of 'what ought to be', one may say a theory of 'the best', with respect to some optimality criterion.

However, there are very many economic theories which are clearly not normative but would hardly qualify as 'empirical' theories in any acceptable sense of the term. They are neither theories of 'what is' (empirical) nor of 'what ought to be' (normative) but rather theories of 'what could be'; Händler (1980a, 1980b), recognizing their existence as theories of 'possible worlds', calls them 'pure theories'.

In the current economic literature, the expression 'normative' is far from unequivocal. A perusal of standard textbooks and of research articles and monographs will show that this category has been made to include (a) epistemologically abstract theories – like the neoclassical theory of the firm – see, for instance, Alchian (1950) and Naylor and Vernon (1969); (b) applied policy theories as well as their abstract choice-theoretical foundations – see, for example, Hirshleifer (1984); (c) explanatory as well as policy theories for imaginary economic systems – see, for instance, Koopmans (1957); and finally (d) those theories which supposedly contain value judgements – for example, Quirk and Saposnik (1968) – or value axioms – for instance, Walsh (1970) – thus confusing the motivations of a theory's author (a psychological problem external to the theory) with the consequences of the presence of specific condition statements (a logical problem internal to the theory). The current situation seems to obey the following principle: define first the term 'positive' (resp. 'normative'), and then call 'normative' (resp. 'positive') every theory which does not satisfy the definition. We shall elaborate further on these issues in 4.6, 4.7 and 4.8.

An alternative typology of economic theories can be obtained by using, as taxonomy, the combined values of two variables, namely, the theory's epistemological status as intended by the theory's author(s) and the theory's instrumental function or pragmatic role. This twofold criterion will be developed and applied in this study.

4.1 THE INTENDED MODELS OF A THEORY

We begin with the variable *epistemological status as intended by the theory's author(s)* (shorter: *intended epistemological status*). As we have seen in 2.6, among the set-theoretical structures which are possible realizations or interpretations of a theory L, one distinguishes and singles out the *intended* or *standard* one(s) as being that (those) which the theory's single or collective author wants to talk about. The notion of *intended* or *standard* model(s) of a theory immediately follows from that of intended or standard possible realizations or interpretations of the theory.

In principle and informally, a theory intended to talk about the 'empirical world', that is, a theory whose class of *intended potential* models consists of or includes an empirical structure – notion to be defined in Definition 4.2.1 (see page 33) – or a collection of empirical structures will be called an *intendedly empirical theory*; on the contrary, a theory intended to talk about a 'possible world' other than the 'empirical world', that is, a theory whose *intended* potential models are *not* empirical structures will be called a *non-intendedly empirical theory*. It is important to notice that what is immediately and directly negated here is the adverb (intendedly) rather than the adjective (empirical); in particular, a non-intendedly empirical theory need not be a theory intended to be non-empirical. In a more descriptive but longer formulation, a non-intendedly empirical theory is nothing more and nothing less than a theory which is not intended to be empirical.

4.2 INTENDEDLY EMPIRICAL THEORIES

Moreover, what is an empirical structure? From a *logical* point of view it is not possible to distinguish between a theory of pure mathematics and a theory of mathematical economics. As Suppes (1967) has pointed out in a much broader context, the distinction between pure mathematics and theoretical science (applied mathematics) is spurious. All such theories have set-theoretical entities as their referents. Hence, a deeper insight into the nature of empirical theories – economic theories, in particular – requires that the description of their logical features be complemented with some information regarding the *ontological* and *epistemological* status of the objects which make up the domains of the structure(s) they talk about.

In principle, as we have already suggested in 3.2, the space which constitutes the domain **D** of a referential structure of a theory may consist of (1) some abstract mathematical space – like, say, the Euclidean *l*-space (Debreu, 1959), a Riesz space (Aliprantis and Brown, 1983), an arbitrary topological vector lattice (Mas-Colell, 1986; Jones, 1987; Araujo and Monteiro, 1989) – or subsets thereof, not related to any specific measurement operations but designed nonetheless to portray aspects of the 'actual world' or even of an 'imaginary world'; or (2) an organized set of empirical data, like time series of traded quantities of commodities, prices and expenditures – see, for instance, Barten (1969) – resulting from measurement operations performed on a determinate list of properties selected to portray and to characterize a set of 'actual economic objects'; or (3) the 'actual economic objects' – that is the set of physical commodities and individual agents – on which the just-mentioned measurement operations were performed and to which the resulting empirical data referred. We shall distinguish among these three kinds of referential entities of a theory in this study, by designating them as the (immediate) mathematical or ideal referent, the (immediate) empirical referent, and the mediate (empirical) referent, respectively. The use of the word 'referent', without the qualification 'mediate', will always indicate an immediate (ideal or empirical) referent.

It is sometimes claimed that entities with objects of the third kind above (the mediate referents) are, or at least should be, the relevant relational structures of scientific theories. This view is sometimes echoed in statements that contend, for instance, that the relational structures of empirical theories are, 'intuitively speaking, any fragment of reality which the language can speak about' (see Przelecki, 1969) or that the objects of the domains of the potential model of an economic theory of pure exchange are 'a set of persons or stable group of persons (families, enterprises) . . . a set of kinds of commodities' (see Balzer, Moulines and Sneed, 1987). It may be argued that the remarks just quoted should be understood in a metaphorical sense only and such an assertion is likely to be correct. Nonetheless, there actually exists such a naïve view of the relation theory–data among some philosophers of science as well as scientists. To be sure, it is not that we wish to contest the view that the main aim of science – economic science in particular – is to explain reality, the mediate referents. However, it is necessary to understand that the relation between theory and reality is much more complex and roundabout than such simplistic accounts would have one believe. In the best of cases, a theory is not confronted with 'reality' but with sets of empirical data which are supposed to convey information about a few selected aspects of a rather elusive reality. Moreover, such data already presuppose substantive theories about their generation as well as theories about their collection, processing and suitable organization. Notions like 'reality', 'fragments of reality', or 'the real economy' may have some intuitive appeal in certain contexts, but they are too vague to qualify for the *formal status* of relational structures of economic theories.

Hence, in the actual practice of economic research, one is left with structures having domains of individuals as those described in (1) and (2) in the above paragraph.

As an example of what has been just said, in Definition 3.2.1 the set **X** may be an *abstract* subset of one of the mathematical spaces mentioned three paragraphs above or it may be a *concrete* finite collection of arrays of numbers whose components are measured values, the results of empirical operations. The distinction is not formal but satisfies a pragmatic criterion. In the former case, the domain of the structure consists of ideal mathematical objects; one may call such a structure an *ideal structure*. In the latter case, the domain of the structure consists of objects which satisfy the additional condition of being empirical data.

One need not be concerned here with a rigorous characterization – let alone definition – of the concept *empirical data*. It suffices to take it as a primitive of the current analysis. Intuitively, however, 'empirical data' is the label for a class of signs representing the outcomes of specific empirical operations – observations, experiments and measurements.

Definition 4.2.1   A set-theoretical structure $S = \langle D, \langle R_i \rangle_{i \in I} \rangle$ is an *empirical or observed economic structure* if and only if (1) it is an economic structure; and (2) its domain **D** is a set of empirical data.

The definition relies on two primitives, namely, the notion of *economic structure* introduced in 3.1 and the notion of *empirical data* just commented on. An economic theory is, as agreed in the preceding chapter, the theory of an economic structure or collection of structures (empirical or otherwise).

It is clear that a *sufficient* condition for an economic theory **L** to be an intendedly empirical theory is that the class of intended possible models of **L** contain at least one empirical economic structure. However, for reasons that will be discussed in more detail in Part III, it would seem too strong to make such a condition, in general, also a *necessary* condition. Whereas for theories specifically constructed to explain a concrete system of data – 'data-contingent phenomenological theories' in the language of Chapter 5 – such a characterization may appear to be appropriate, 'general' or more 'abstract theories' would defy such a characterization. In the latter case, one would expect the author(s) of the theory to regard the endeavour as a success when even a short list of selected substantive sentences of the theory, which the author(s) may designate as the 'testable sentences of the theory', is satisfied by an intended empirical structure. We shall refer to this selected set of sentences of a theory **L** as the *core of empirical claims* of **L** (in short, and with a certain abuse of language, the *empirical core* of **L**) and denote it **C(L)**.

Definition 4.2.2   An economic theory **L** is an *intendedly empirical economic theory* if and only if the class *S* of the *intended potential* models of the theory's core of empirical claims or empirical core **C(L)** contains at least one empirical structure.

Summarizing, in a slightly different formulation, intendedly empirical economic theories intend to talk about empirical economic structures and to describe their actual as well as their possible states. The states of a structure – the actual and the possible ones – are characterized by particular value configurations of its variables.

The well-known 1929–52 macroeconometric 'model' of the United States by Klein and Goldberger (1955) (refer to 2.4 for the notion of 'model') is an obvious example of an intendedly empirical theory in the sense of being a theory whose single intended model has a domain consisting of statistical time series for a concrete economy and period. The *linear expenditure system* (see Stone, 1954) is another example of an intendedly empirical theory, this time of a theory whose intended potential models include, possibly, several empirical models of its designated **C(L)**.

4.3 NON-INTENDEDLY EMPIRICAL THEORIES

The body of theoretical economics, when compared with physics, chemistry or biology, has a remarkable trait, namely the very strong presence of a class of mathematically highly formalized theories of which it can hardly be said that they have empirical structures among their *intended* models; on the contrary, the *intended* models or interpretations of these theories, as determined very often by their axioms, are ideal as opposed to empirical structures. Of a theory of this kind it will be said here that it is 'non-intendedly empirical', not so much to emphasize the absence of empirical interpretations of the theory, but rather to emphasize that *it was not the intention* of the theory's author(s) that it should be liable to such interpretations. Clearly, the core of empirical claims or empirical core of a non-intendedly empirical theory is empty because no such core has been designated.

In contrast to Definition 4.2.2 one thus has:

Definition 4.3.1   An economic theory **L** is a *non-intendedly empirical economic theory* if and only if the class **S** of its *intended potential* models does not contain any empirical structure.

While, with reference to a theory of a pure exchange economy, Balzer, Moulines and Sneed (1987) claim 'that a survey of the literature in theoretical economics suggests that theoretical economists are not interested in empirical applications of their abstract concepts', Händler (1980a) describes a mathematical (ideal) structure of a static microeconomic equilibrium theory as the structure of 'a *pure* theory such that the referents are those possible but not actually existing worlds for which the statements are true'. Lind (1990), writing in Swedish, refers to similar abstract structures as 'tänkta economier' – literal English translation: 'thought economies' – an expression which he translates in an English language abstract of his work as (economic) 'models'.

Summarizing the basic idea, non-intendedly empirical economic theories intend to talk about non-empirical ideal economic structures and to describe their possible states. The possible states of a structure, here too, are characterized by particular value configurations of its variables.

By way of a terminological digression, let us compare here the way in which the expression 'logically possible worlds' as opposed to 'the actual world' is routinely used by logicians in their works and the way we have contrasted here the expressions 'empirical world' to 'possible world other than the empirical one' (in 4.1), or 'actual world' to 'imaginary world' (in 4.2), or 'possible world' to 'actual world', and 'possible world' to 'possible but not actually existing world' (quoting Händler, 1980a, in the preceding paragraph).

Since we observe that there is an apparent similarity as well as important differences between the customary logical usage and our terminology, it would seem advisable to pause here, clarify some concepts and adopt the terminology we would like to adhere to for the remainder of this study.

For our purposes, it will be convenient to distinguish the 'economic empirical world' – in each concrete situation represented by an empirical economic structure – from a 'logically possible but non-empirical economic world' (henceforth shortened to 'imaginary economic world') – represented by the ideal mathematical model of a non-intendedly empirical theory. Notice that the reference to the existence of the ideal mathematical model in the latter case is the guarantee that we are talking here about a 'logically possible' albeit non-empirical world.

Furthermore, whereas with respect to the 'empirical economic world' we shall distinguish between its 'actual' and its 'possible states', for an 'imaginary economic world', for obvious reasons, we shall only be able to recognize its (logically) 'possible states'. As in previous descriptions, states of the world are defined by particular value configurations – actual or possible, in the case of the empirical world; possible, in the case of an imaginary world – of the variables of the relational structure in question.

For a very direct example of a non-intendedly empirical theory one may choose here any formalized version of a theory of 'market socialism' or of 'labour-managed economies' – see, for instance, Ichiishi (1977).

In Part IV of this study the existence of non-intendedly empirical theories will be explained as a methodological consequence of the predominantly non-experimental nature of economic research and the claim will be made that the role of such theories must be understood within the body of theoretical economics in the context of other – including empirical – theories.

4.4   INTENDED AND ACTUAL EPISTEMOLOGICAL STATUS

It is perhaps useful to underline once more that the key concept in the theory classification of 4.2 and 4.3 is the *intention* of a theory's author(s). On the one hand, such a classification amounts to no less than a recognition of an outstanding feature of contemporary theoretical economic research. On the other hand, though this is not relevant to the discussion of this chapter, it is clear that the *intended* and *actual* epistemological status of a theory may or may not coincide. It is very easy to think of an intendedly empirical theory that fails empirical tests – that is, a theory that has intended *potential* empirical models but fails to have *actual* empirical models – and it is possible to imagine an initially non-intendedly empirical theory that ends up verified by empirical data – that is, ends up with an empirical interpretation. In the latter case, of course, the originally intended epistemological status of the theory becomes a datum of mere historical interest as the theory will now qualify as an empirical one.

4.5 DESCRIPTIVE THEORIES

In this and in the next section the classification variable *instrumental function* or *pragmatic role* will be briefly analysed.

Economic theories are built with one of two distinct objectives in mind: to describe and explain their referent structures, that is their potential models, or to lay down rules directed at controlling and influencing the behaviour of such structures. Strictly, thus, only theories with the first objective would pre-qualify for the status of 'scientific theories' while those with the second objective – no matter how deeply scientifically grounded, that is, how strongly founded upon descriptive– explanatory theories – would come closer to the sort of disciplines which in other fields are often referred to as technological theories. Of course, a particular instance of actual economic research may combine results which fulfil the objectives of both kinds of theory. However, for analytic purposes, it is assumed here that in those cases the 'theoretical whole' can be adequately decomposed into a theory of the first kind and a theory of the second kind.

According to their instrumental function or pragmatic role it is thus possible to recognize two very distinct kinds of economic theory which will be called here 'descriptive economic theories' and 'operative economic theories', respectively. This section will discuss theories of the first kind.

A descriptive economic theory describes or explains a class of economic structures or predicts outcomes related to them. Its propositions have the general character of nomological statements. At the propositional level, these statements have the form 'if α, then β' or 'if not α, then not β' – see here Bunge (1967b).

It is clear that statements of the above kind may have an empirical structure among their immediate referents (a system of empirical data) or only a purely conceptual structure (an imaginary world).

For an example of a macroeconomic theory with an empirical referent – see for instance, J. B. Taylor (1993) – consider the proposition: 'Changes in the money supply M effect changes in real interest rates R and exchange rates E and, through these changes, temporary changes in real output Y and employment O'. The conditional formulation of this statement is: 'If M changes then R and E change and Y and O change temporarily.' Another illustration of a conditional statement, in a similar context but this time describing a relation between the federal funds rate RS and the stock of money in the USA is the following: 'If $\Delta RS > 0$ (< 0) then $\Delta M < 0$ (> 0).'

For an example of the second kind – an allocation theory for a world other than the empirical one – consider a socialist market economy (see Lange, 1938, and Heal, 1973). A socialist market economy $\mathbf{E}$ may be thought of as a structure consisting of a twice continuously differentiable social utility function $\mathbf{u}$ in l demands $\mathbf{x}_h$ by m consumers, n profit-maximizing labour- or state-owned firms each represented by a twice continuously differentiable production function $\mathbf{f}_j$, a distributor agent h for each final demand h, a Central Planning Board (CPB), and a vector $\mathbf{z}$ of initial resources. In the current context, a characteristic nomological statement would be: 'When there is an equilibrium price vector $\mathbf{p}^*$ for $\mathbf{E}$ and a price-determination process for CPB which converges to $\mathbf{p}^*$ we say that $\mathbf{E}$ has an allocation plan.' The following is a case – expressed in conditional form – in which the allocation problem for a socialist market economy $\mathbf{E}$ has a solution: 'If the social utility function $\mathbf{u}$ and each of the production functions $\mathbf{f}_j$ are strictly concave, then there exists an equilibrium $\mathbf{p}^*$ for $\mathbf{E}$ and a planning process for CPB – called the Lange–Arrow–Hurwicz process (LAH) – which converges to $\mathbf{p}^*$ – see Arrow, Hurwicz and Uzawa (1958) and Heal (1973).

4.6 OPERATIVE THEORIES

An operative economic theory prescribes the norms or rules for operating – in particular, for operating optimally – on members of a class of economic systems. The denomination 'normative economic theory' is thus justified in this particular context.

Operative theories include among their propositions nomopragmatic statements and/or technical operation rules (rules, for short). A nomopragmatic statement – here we follow Bunge (1967b) – has the form of a nomological statement. However, whereas the antecedent of the latter refers to a fact – either 'actual' or 'imaginary' – the antecedent of the former refers to a human operation; hence, we have here too 'if α then β' or 'if not α then not β', but with α specifically referring to an operation. Rules, on the other hand, are statements of the form 'do α to obtain β' or 'do not do α to avoid β'. While rules do not have truth values they have effectiveness values (see for instance Bunge, 1967b).

We give next, as examples, two nomopragmatic statements based on the nomological statement of the corresponding cases of 4.5.

The first is founded on the proposition regarding the relation between changes in the money supply and temporary changes in output and employment and the statement which describes the negative relationship between the volume of money and the level of the federal funds rate in the USA: 'If the Federal Reserve Bank changes the funds rate SR then R and E will change and Y and O will change temporarily.' This statement is clearly the ground for the monetary policy rule

$$RS - RS^* = LP(+4) - LP + a(LP - LP^*) + b(LY - LY^*)$$

where L, P and Y stand for logarithm, price level and GDP, respectively, the asterisk distinguishes a target value, and $P(+4)$ is the rational forecast of the price level made four quarters ahead – for other interesting policy theories which could have served here as examples, see Taylor (1993).

Regarding the example with the imaginary world of the socialist market economy, a nomopragmatic statement founded upon the nomological proposition of 4.5 is the following: 'If in **E** the functions **u** and $\mathbf{f}_j$ $(j = 1, 2, \ldots, n)$ are strictly concave and CPB applies the LAH planning process, then prices will converge to an equilibrium price vector **p***.' This statement is the foundation for the following set of rules, which informally summarize the LAH planning process: '(1) CPB shall announce arbitrary price vector **p** to firms and communicate valuation $\mathbf{u}_h$ to h-distributor for arbitrary $\mathbf{x}_h \geq 0$; (2) each firm shall determine the production plan that maximizes its profit at **p** and inform CPB; (3) distributor h shall adjust consumption of h proportionally to difference $\mathbf{u}_h - \mathbf{p}_h$ respecting a non-negativity constraint and inform CPB; (4) CPB shall revise each price proportionally to corresponding excess demand, subject to a non-negativity constraint on prices; (5) the procedure is reiterated with CPB communicating new prices and valuations to firms and distributors, respectively, and stops when **p*** has been determined' – see Lange (1938) and chapter 4 in Heal (1973).

4.7   VALUE JUDGEMENTS AND VALUE AXIOMS: THEIR PLACE AND FORM

This may be the right place to pause and examine the viewpoint that attributes a special role in normative theories to value judgements and to value axioms. Since the terminology used in the field is far from uniform, it will be convenient to begin by explaining the meaning that the expressions 'value judgement' and 'value axiom' will be given in this study.

By a *value judgement* we shall understand a proposition involving one or two variables and a one- or two-place *ethical* or *aesthetical* predicate, $\mho(x)$, $\mho(x, y)$: 'x is good', 'x is fair', 'x is beautiful', 'x is better than y', 'x is fairer than y', 'x is more beautiful than y', 'x is the best', 'x is the fairest', 'x is the most beautiful'. Moreover, if we suppose that such a proposition makes sense as a member of the axiom base of a theory, then we may elevate the value judgement to the rank of axiom of that theory – to a *value axiom*, to be precise. The view that this latter circumstance is what characterizes a normative economic theory is, we believe, the conventional opinion among economists.

This form of incorporation of a value judgement into the set of sentences of a theory – even if spuriously elevated to the status of value 'axiom' – is rejected in this study as being contrary to the logical structure of theories. On the contrary, our position on this issue will be based on a different, technical meaning that may be given to the expression 'value axiom'. Before discussing it, let us illustrate and comment on the rejected view.

A typical example of the conventional view may be construed from the following passages of a very well-known textbook by Quirk and Saposnik (1968). Using the expression *welfare economics* as the 'generic term for the normative aspects of economics', the quoted authors find that '[T]he *basic assumptions* [our italics] underlying welfare economics ... are value judgements that any economist is free to accept or reject; there is no conceivable manner in which the truth or falsity of these *axioms* [our italics] could be tested.'

It is clear that the expressions 'basic assumptions' and 'axioms' are used here in the sense of value judgements in the axiom base, a line of reasoning we have just rejected. One thus gets the impression that what distinguishes normative theories is the presence of untestable value judgements in the form of axioms of a very special kind. In 'positive economics', on the contrary, 'assumptions as well as conclusions, at least under ideal circumstances, can be subjected to empirical and/or logical test to determine their truth or falsity. . . .' (Quirk and Saposnik, 1968).

The above quotations illustrate what we have already pointed out: the presence of a certain confusion of aspects that, though important in other respects, are *external* to the theory – the motivations (ethical, aesthetic) which triggered and guided the theory's author(s) – with *internal* (logical) features of the theory itself. Factors of the first kind concern the historical, the sociological and the psychological background of a theory inasmuch as they may dictate the nature of the chosen problem and perhaps the approach to it. Specifically, they influence choice of structure (the objects), goals to be pursued with structure, means to be used towards those goals, and conditions that the use of the means will be subjected to.

Let us focus now on a second meaning of the expression 'value axiom', the one we deem acceptable and shall adhere to in this study.

In an adequate operative theory, some axioms will appropriately characterize, at a formal level, the *normative criteria* (for instance, those embodied in a particular social welfare function), the *operation constraints* (for instance, the available resources and the institutional rules) and the *suitable actions* (for example, the available policy mechanisms). These axioms – especially those characterizing the normative criteria – may have been dictated by extra-theoretical motivations (value judgements) and thus deserve the designation 'value axioms'. However, thus understood, the special theory's formulas that we call value axioms and the extra-theoretical motivations belong to two very different spheres. Let us illustrate the point with an example.

The achievement of human equality constitutes an example of a rather constant if controversial ethical goal in modern history; cherished by many and loathed also by many, the value 'human equality' is given very unequal rankings in the value systems of different individuals and groups. To begin with, it is not a simple matter to decide what human equality and the achievement of human equality should precisely mean. However, this is by no means an insurmountable difficulty, for such vague notions can certainly be given (probably many different) precise meanings. Giving to the expressions an economic connotation, an equalitarian would speak, for instance, of 'income equality' and of the 'achievement of income equality', respectively.

Propositions to the effect that equality – or income equality – is intrinsically good (bad) and that equality – respectively, income equality – is intrinsically better (worse) than inequality – respectively, income inequality – naturally belong to philosophical–ethical discourse. It is hard to see, however, how such value judgements could be elevated to the rank of axioms and what they would contribute to the deductive or operative power of a theory. It is much easier to see, however, why a value system underlying such propositions would be the driving force for a researcher of distribution theories and distributive policies. Summarizing, whereas it is true that the value judgements 'income equality is good' and 'income equality is better than income inequality' may encapsulate the motivation for a successful policy research programme, the same propositions, elevated to the rank of 'axioms' of a theory, become spurious and barren.

Passing now from the motivational, extra-theoretical side of the issue to the technical, policy-theoretical one, it is clear that the value judgement 'income equality is better than income inequality' may be the driving force for the design of a policy theory whose centrepiece is a social welfare function which orders Pareto-optimal states with respect to an equality index. Notice that such a function does not postulate the intrinsic goodness of income equality and, in a logical if not psychological sense, it is independent of the value judgement. Actually, whether or not motivated by the value judgement, the axioms which characterize the social welfare function merely establish an ordering or policy criterion to guide policy choices. Their meanings are as objective and clear for those who share as for those who do not share the equalitarian value judgement.

A rather different issue is whether or not or when and when not income equality is 'good', 'bad', 'better', 'worse' in some limited economic sense – as opposed to ethical sense. Answers to such questions would depend on the precise characterization of 'income equality', on the one hand, and of the predicates 'good', 'bad', 'better', 'worse', on the other hand; moreover, crucial for the determination of the answers is the structure within which the problems are to be solved, in particular the constraints and the values of the other variables of the system. Problems of this sort may be the subject of intendedly empirical as well as of non-intendedly empirical economic theories.

Finally, let us turn our attention to the question of the testability of value axioms, both logically and empirically.

Regarding the first kind of tests, we ascertain that every axiom of an operative theory – even those which determine the normative criteria, the operative constraints and the suitable actions and may, possibly, be dictated by extra-theoretical value preferences – can and indeed should be subjected to logical test; such a test, however, can only consist of checking whether the axiom in question, as a sentence, satisfies the rules of sentence-formation of the underlying logical and mathematical background theories, and whether it is consistent with the other axioms of the theory. It should be obvious, however, that the formal acceptance of a set of axioms and of the propositions which logically result therefrom do not commit one in any substantive way to the value system which might have motivated the theory's author(s). In principle, it should always be possible to agree on the logical validity of 'from "α" and from "if α then β" follows "β"', whatever our ethical stand in regard to α or to β.

If the expression 'value axiom' is to be understood with the meaning we have suggested and not in the sense of value judgement, then a 'value axiom' and an 'ordinary axiom' are logically indistinguishable from one another. Predicates must simply have a meaning in the context of the theory where they occur. The same holds regarding propositions derived within the theory. Given the assumptions which underlie Arrow's famous Impossibility Theorem (Arrow, 1951), the conclusion necessarily follows. However, the recognition of this logical necessity does not commit anyone to upholding a particular sociopolitical value system. In a rigorous theory, each assumption has a transparent form and a recognizable meaning. If we accept them – even, in the extreme, if only for the sake of the argument – we must also recognize their logical consequences; but no more than that.

Let us now look briefly at the empirical side of the issue. It is widely held among scientists and philosophers of science that statements of the kind we are discussing here are very resistant to empirical testing. Think, for example, of an axiom characterizing the set of primitives of the theory as allocations belonging to the 'core' of an economy. In some cases – refer to the same example – there would seem even to be something 'intrinsic' that conspires against the possibility of such tests. However, many axioms that presumably nobody would regard as 'value axioms' are not empirically testable either, even if we freely stretch the 'ideal circumstances' for a test. The very common assumption that the individual consumption set of a consumer is convex – a very important linguistic assumption – cannot be tested. Moreover, if we imagine 'ideal circumstances' for the test, I think that for obvious reasons our conclusions would run against the assumption; unless, of course, under 'ideal circumstances' we mean a world very different from ours. However, this would not make the assumption a 'value axiom' or the theory a normative one.

4.8   NOTES AND REMARKS

The view which attaches a 'normative' interpretation to what perhaps most economists regard as a 'positive' theory is not unusual. Defending the neoclassical theory of the firm and with explicit reference to its standard conceptual tools, Alchian (1950) states that 'These are concepts for the economist's use and not necessarily for the individual participant's, who may have other analytic or customary devices, which, while of interest to the economist, serve as data and not as analytic method.' Naylor and Vernon (1969, p. 139) interpret Alchian (1950) thus: 'although business firms may not objectively pursue marginal calculus in making decisions, in the long-run only those firms will survive which make decisions which are consistent with neoclassical theory.' In the same textbook by Naylor and Vernon (1969) – a textbook whose material consists of the standard 'positive' theory of the firm – we find the following purposeful statement (p. 6):

> Throughout this book the problem of the firm will be defined in terms of a decision problem for the managers of the firm. We shall be interested in how managers *should* make decisions (normative economics) in order to achieve particular goals. To the extent that these normative 'models' [our quotation marks] correspond to the real world behavior of firms, we shall be attempting to explain how managers of firms *actually* make economic decisions (positive economics).

This view easily reduces the entirety of theoretical microeconomics to a 'normative' discipline.

Hirshleifer (1984, p. 462) expresses very clearly the stand of those who adopt the dichotomy of a 'theory of what is' (positive analysis) and a 'theory of what ought to be' (normative analysis). Normative analysis thus includes policy theories and their welfare-theoretical foundations. Discussing the interest rate, for instance, he contrasts the *positive* question of 'what interest rates are decision-makers actually employing in their investment decisions?' to the *normative* one of 'what interest rates ought a decision-maker employ in accepting or rejecting an investment project?'

Koopmans (1957) distinguishes between descriptive and normative applications 'of the "model" [our quotation marks] of competitive equilibrium'. As an example of the applications in the normative sense he points out that 'the most clear-cut case of this application is the recommendations by Barone, Lange, Lerner, and others for the operation of a socialist economy through price-guided allocations'. Although this statement is essentially correct, it is useful to recall that a considerable part of the theories of the authors referred to are of the descriptive kind (descriptive of an 'imaginary economy').

The place of value judgements in theoretical welfare economics is emphasized in Quirk and Saposnik (1968, p. 104), though they do not admit to any distinction between the extra-theoretical motivations (ethical and aesthetic beliefs) and the normative propositions (objectives, constraints and rules of action) of an operative theory. For instance, 'a primary objective of welfare economics is to provide a guide for distinguishing between "good" ("desirable") and "bad" ("undesirable") states of the economy. Because of the diversity of opinion, even among "reasonable" men, as to the meaning of these terms, the ultimate validity of much of welfare economics must remain a matter of personal opinion'. Walsh's (1970, p. 99) views are perhaps closer to those exposed in this study although his use of the expression 'value axiom' is somewhat ambiguous, referring sometimes to value judgements and sometimes coming closer to our technical notion discussed in 4.7. This ambiguity is particularly evident in the sentence 'A reformulated Pigovian theory need not be unscientific if it were so axiomatized that the *moral assumptions* [our italics] necessary were explicitly built into the *value axioms* [our italics] and the argument clearly based on them, so that it admittedly followed, *if and only if* one accepted the whole axiom set, including the *value axioms* [our italics].' Whereas the statement distinguishes here between moral assumptions and value axioms, the ambivalence of the latter expression is manifested by the confusion between the need for the acceptance of the 'whole axiom set' in a *logical sense* (a merely linguistic and logical operation) and the acceptance of the 'whole axiom set' in a *moral sense* (tantamount to a declaration of adherence to a certain belief system).

For the detailed theories behind the intendedly empirical descriptive and operative examples of 4.5 and 4.6 the reader is referred to J. B. Taylor (1993). An extensive discussion – with more emphasis on the operative side – of the theories which led to the non-intendedly empirical descriptive and operative counterparts is to be found in Heal (1973).

5 A Taxonomy of Economic Theories: Application

This chapter is an application of the taxonomy developed in Chapter 4. Its objective is to provide in each of the following four sections a few concrete and historically prominent examples of each of the four theory types previously described. Later on, in 5.5, we make a more up-to-date reference to modern economic literature.

5.1 INTENDEDLY EMPIRICAL DESCRIPTIVE THEORIES

An *intendedly empirical descriptive economic theory* is a descriptive or explanatory economic theory, the intended interpretation of which is a specific empirical structure or a class of structures that includes a subclass of empirical structures. If it succeeds in being satisfied by empirical structure(s) in the sense to be discussed later on in Part III, then it can be declared an empirical descriptive economic theory.

From the preceding paragraph it follows that the structural axioms of an intendedly empirical descriptive economic theory may determine that its intended model is a very specific empirical one – that is, they may point at *one* empirical structure as being *the* intended model; or they may determine a larger class of models which will include, alongside pure mathematical models, a subcollection of empirical ones. In Part III we develop analytic systems which distinguish 'data-specific' and 'data-contingent' theories from 'general' theories of various degrees of generality.

Another important distinction that we shall examine further on and build into our analytic systems in Chapter 6 is that between 'representational theories', on the one hand, and 'phenomenological theories', on the other hand. It is characteristic of representational theories to offer *interpretative explanations* of the data as opposed to the merely *subsumptive accounts* provided by phenomenological theories – see, for instance, Bunge (1967b). In an epistemological sense, representational theories are deeper than phenomenological ones for they offer representations – usually including (non-observable) high-level constructs – of the hypothesized mechanisms underlying the empirical facts.

Precisely, phenomenological theories owe their designation to the fact that they are epistemologically shallower, closer to phenomena – Bunge (1967b).

In this study, a phenomenological theory designed from the outset to refer to one and only one empirical structure is said to be 'data-contingent'. Examples of such theories are very frequent in the field of macroeconometrics, and a short list would certainly include *An Econometric 'Model' of the United States 1929–1952* (Klein and Goldberger, 1955), and *An Econometric 'Model' of the United Kingdom* (Klein et al., 1961) (our quotation marks). Although any scientific exercise may be viewed as involving the tests of some general propositions, it seems clear that the primary aim of each of these two theories was to explain and forecast behaviour of two very special concrete economies (empirical structures). In contrast, the expression 'data-specific phenomenological theory' will be reserved to designate the application of a 'generic phenomenological theory' – for instance, the *input–output system of the theory of linear economic models* (see Leontief, 1941; Dorfman, Samuelson and Solow, 1958; Allen, 1960; Gale, 1960 – to a specific empirical structure, for example, Leontief's (1941, 1953) *input–output 'model' of the American economy, 1919–39* (once again, the word 'model' has been placed here in quotation marks to emphasize that its use deviates from the logical meaning defined in Chapter 2, being closer to referring to a 'theory' or a 'system of equations').

Theories of the representational type are rather prominent in the more 'mature' branches of economics. In the field of microeconomics, a case in point is *neoclassical analysis of the firm* – see, for example, Shephard (1970) – with its two remarkable historical developments, *Cobb–Douglas production theory* (Cobb and Douglas, 1928; Douglas, 1976) and *CES-production theory* (Arrow *et al.*, 1961). These are instances of theories of an intermediate albeit different level of generality which point at wide classes of empirical structures as their potential empirical referents. Examples of 'data-specific' representational theories are given by the many applications of one of the various *consumer demand systems* – for instance, the *Rotterdam demand system* (Barten, 1964; Theil, 1965) – to actual data, for example, Theil (1975, 1976).

5.2 NON-INTENDEDLY EMPIRICAL DESCRIPTIVE THEORIES

A perusal of what we call theoretical economics would readily show the conspicuous presence of theories which have the same formal features of descriptive intendedly empirical theories – that is, of 'positive theories' in the usual terminology – and which, yet, have not been constructed to refer directly to empirical structures. While they frequently display a highly formalized language where propositions have the standard form of nomological statements they actually lack – more importantly, they are not intended to have – empirical models.

Non-intendedly empirical descriptive theories are not built to refer immediately to actual empirical data. Their descriptive import for science is indirect and ancillary; they contribute to the understanding of reality to the extent that they are components of larger and more complex systems of knowledge. In physics, perfect gas theory contributes indirectly and in concert with other theories to our understanding of actual gases. However, what this theory directly and in isolation explains are 'perfect gases', and such gases do not form part of physical reality. The situation of many economic theories is similar. Their descriptive role is to provide descriptions, explanations and predictions of 'imaginary worlds', and as such they may be regarded as instances of analytic simulations of experiments. In Part IV of this study the methodological background for these theories as well as their descriptive roles are explored in more detail. A *theory of dynamic market adjustment under 'tâtonnement'* – see for example, Arrow and Hahn (1971) – the *theory of a pure exchange economy with a continuum of agents and infinitely many commodities* – see Bewley (1973) – or the descriptive part of a *theory of market socialism* – for instance, Lange (1938) – are appropriate examples of the theories we have in mind.

5.3   INTENDEDLY EMPIRICAL OPERATIVE THEORIES

We want to assert here that if economics is to have an ultimate operative goal then that goal is surely to influence and to control economic processes in accordance with rational rules and criteria (in particular, optimality criteria). The extent to which and the ways in which economic phenomena might be successfully influenced and controlled depend on these factors: (a) existing knowledge about economic systems (scientific factor); (b) availability of adequate policy theories (operative factor); and (c) sociopolitical philosophy (value motivation factor).

A reasonably strict assessment of the current state of affairs in the development of the discipline might convince us of two facts, namely, that the stage reached in relation to breadth and depth of our knowledge of economic systems still leaves much to be desired; and, consequently, that the existing scientific foundations of policy theories are relatively weak. These circumstances are often invoked – see, for example, M. Friedman (1960, 1962) – in support of 'non-activist' policy prescriptions or to impugn particular policy recommendations. However, we shall take here the view that knowledge about the system makes possible rational actions based on the system's behaviour, and that increase in that knowledge leads to improvement in those actions. Of course, this view does not and cannot entail the refusal to recognize that different sociopolitical philosophies will still condition and determine different attitudes regarding the ethical acceptability of policy goals and policy means.

Within the class of theories of our current concern and focusing for a moment on a theory's relative 'closeness' to actual policy operations, one may further distinguish two different subclasses of theories.

The theories belonging to the first subclass are theories of a *foundational* nature. Their intended role is not so much to assist directly in the actual process of controlling an economic system, but rather to serve as the foundations for applied technical policy theories. A part, at least, of so-called 'theoretical welfare economics' belongs to this class, the outstanding classical example being Arrow's (1951) contribution to *social choice analysis*. Ideally, theories of this kind will themselves be founded upon descriptive theories like those discussed in 5.1.

The second subclass consists of theories of a *technical* nature in the sense that they are more or less detailed descriptions of specific policy operations. As to their generality and levels of abstraction, the landscape here may be as rich and varied as in the case of intendedly empirical descriptive theories. A historically important example of work on operative *macroeconomic policy theories* is Tinbergen (1956).

5.4 NON-INTENDEDLY EMPIRICAL OPERATIVE THEORIES

Policy theories of the class discussed in 5.3 are supposed to lay down operational rules for empirical economic systems, even if some of them may be formulated at a rather high level of abstraction, or to provide the foundations for such theories. The theories we have in mind in this section are, at least formally, similar to intendedly empirical operative theories. They are different, however, in the sense that they refer to 'imaginary' instead of 'empirical' systems.

Besides theories of the foundational type, the current class includes theories which may be regarded as *analytic policy simulations in 'imaginary systems'*. A list of now classical examples would include in this category the policy-theoretical parts of Barone's (1908), Lange's (1938), F. M. Taylor's (1938), and Lerner's (1944) works.

A final comment is in order here. The theories we are referring to in this section have similar formal features to the theories we have described in the preceding section. However, they are operative theories only in the sense that they contain nomopragmatic statements – or that some of their original statements can be legitimately thus reformulated – and/or rules. Since, in principle, they are not intended to refer to actual empirical structures, one can only speak of *analytically simulated policies*. This suggests, however, that these theories pursue actually descriptive goals and are operative in merely a formal sense. They could well be called *operation-simulations theories*.

5.5   NOTES AND REMARKS

The objective of this section is to illustrate the taxonomy discussed in this and the preceding chapter with the help of more recent theoretical contributions. Important reference sources for most of the examples will be the *Handbook of Mathematical Economics*, Vols. II and III, edited by Arrow and Intriligator (1982 and 1986) and Vol. IV, edited by Hildenbrand and Sonnenschein (1991); the *Handbook of Econometrics*, Vol. III, edited by Griliches and Intriligator (1986); and the *Handbook of Monetary Economics*, Vols. I and II, edited by Friedman and Hahn (1990).

Regarding macroeconomic theories, see Mankiw and Romer (1991) for the 'New Keynesian' perspective and Sargent (1987) for the 'New Classical' point of view. The effects of the 'rational expectations revolution' – Muth (1961), Lucas (1972), Lucas and Sargent (1981) – beyond new classical theories and upon new Keynesian analysis can be appreciated in J. B. Taylor (1993).

For a comparison and assessment of some actual intendedly empirical descriptive theories of the phenomenological kind – in this case macroeconometric 'models' of the USA – we refer to the various articles in the volume edited by L. Klein (1991). For the history of the econometric approach to macroeconomic research from its beginnings until the present, the short and very interesting book by Epstein (1987) may be consulted. The non-structural equation systems used in many recent 'Granger causality tests' – see Granger (1969, 1989) – are indeed nothing but the cores of phenomenological theories; the 'vector autoregression system' (VAR), which may be regarded as an extended version of a

Granger-test system, is also a good example of an intendedly empirical descriptive phenomenological theory – see, for rather different examples, Sims (1980a, 1980b), Blanchard and Quah (1989) and Blanchard (1990).

As stated in 5.1, intendedly empirical descriptive theories of the representational kind are more prominent in the older and more 'mature' branches of economics. In the field of microeconomics, some examples of succinct expositions of contemporary theories which include historical notes as well as extensive references to the literature are Barten and Böhm (1982) and Deaton (1986) – general consumer choice theory and econometric demand analysis, respectively – Shafer and Sonnenschein (1982) – theory of market demand and excess-demand functions – and Nadiri (1982) and Jorgenson (1986) – general producer theory and econometric analysis of the firm, respectively.

If intendedly empirical descriptive theories are more prominent in the 'established' areas of economics, non-intendedly empirical descriptive theories are most frequent, for reasons that will become clearer in Chapters 11 and 12, in the frontier areas of economic-theoretical research. The surveys by Debreu (1982) – existence of competitive equilibrium – and Mas-Colell and Zame (1991) – equilibrium theory in infinite dimensional spaces – and the articles by Duffie (1990) – general monetary equilibrium – and Bénassy (1990) – non-Walrasian equilibrium and money – provide some examples of such theories with extensive references to the literature. This class would also seem to be the proper pigeonhole in which to place descriptive theories of optimal behaviour such as theories of optimal growth – see McKenzie (1986).

To the examples referred to in the preceding paragraph it is important to add the cases of descriptive theories of 'alternative economic systems' – Lange's (1938) already mentioned contribution to the theory of socialist market economies is a classical case in point, while general and abstract theories of decentralized resource-allocation mechanisms – see for instance, Hurwicz (1986) – are much more recent examples. Although works in this field usually show, for reasons that are quite obvious, a substantial normative content and a definite operative direction, we have only in mind here, when these exist, their more or less developed descriptive-explanatory theoretical background components. Important references are here Vanek (1970), Meade (1972), Drèze (1974, 1976) and Ichiishi (1977).

The class of intendedly empirical operative theories looks very much like a hierarchy of systems where one finds, at one extreme, abstract theories of a foundational nature (see Sen's (1986) survey on social choice theory); in the middle ground still abstract theories, although of a more specialized content (for example, second-best theories, theories of optimal taxation, and theories of optimal policy and control are discussed by Murata (1982), Mirrles (1986), and Sheshinski (1986), respectively); and, at the other extreme, more or less detailed policy-operation guidelines – for interesting macroeconomic examples and references, see Fischer (1990), B. M. Friedman (1990), Dornbusch and Giovannini (1990) on theories of monetary policies, and J. B. Taylor (1986, 1993) on econometric design and operation of stabilization policies.

For examples of non-intendedly empirical operative theories the reader is referred to the policy sections of the works on the economics of market socialism cited two paragraphs above. An extension of that list must include the contributions of Arrow and Hurwicz (1960), Malinvaud (1967), Heal (1973) and the survey articles by Hurwicz (1986) – on incentives – and by Heal (1986) – on planning. In a different field – overlapping generations 'models' – the article by Brock (1990) discusses non-intendedly empirical theories which include analytical components of the descriptive kind (those ambiguously referred to, by some, as 'positive' and wrongly, by others, as 'normative' systems) as well as of the operative ('normative') kind.

Part III   Empirical Economic Theories

6 General Characterization

In Part III we shall be exclusively concerned with empirical economic statements and with empirical economic theories. More specifically, we shall be interested in providing a description of the process through which an economic theory is given empirical meaning, and then in ways of characterizing the class of empirical economic statements and theories. To do this we continue using our basic model-theoretic tools of analysis.

In 6.2, 6.3 and 6.4 we shall develop two analytic schemes or frameworks which should serve the above purpose. Their design as well as their common centrepiece – the notion of empirical structure – go back to ideas originally proposed by Suppes (1962, 1967) to answer some foundational questions in the context of the experimental sciences; here, these are adapted and extended so as to take account of the predominantly non-experimental nature of economic research and to accommodate some of the features resulting therefrom.

6.1 EMPIRICAL STRUCTURES AND EMPIRICAL THEORIES

Given a theory, a possible realization is simply a set-theoretical structure of the appropriate kind, whereas a model of the theory is a possible realization where all the valid sentences (theorems) of the theory are satisfied. If all the valid sentences are defined as those which are consequences of the axioms, then a possible realization is a model of the theory if it satisfies its axioms – see Suppes (1962). We may also say that a possible realization S of the theory L is a model of a subset K of sentences of L if each sentence $k \in K$ is satisfied in S; a specially relevant example of the latter situation is when the structure S is a model of the subset $C(L)$, the empirical core of L.

The concepts 'economic structure' and 'economic theory' have been discussed in Chapter 3. The notion 'empirical economic structure' has been given in Definition 4.2.1. In Chapter 4, the idea of the empirical core $C(L)$ of a theory L was introduced too. The idea of an 'empirical economic theory' can now be naturally introduced with their help.

Definition 6.1.1 An economic theory **L** is an *empirical economic theory* if and only if the class **M** of the models of the theory's empirical core **C(L)** contains at least one empirical structure.

Notice the difference between the contents of Definition 6.1.1 and those of Definition 4.2.2. Whereas the former introduces the notion of an *actual* empirical theory – hence the reference to models of the empirical core – the latter defines *intendedly* empirical theories – hence the reference to intended potential models.

6.2   ANALYTIC SCHEMES I: HIERARCHIC SYSTEMS OF THEORIES AND MODELS

With these preliminary ideas at hand we can now proceed to describe the way economic theories are given empirical meaning. Intuitively, the operation of empirically testing an economic theory **L** or its empirical core **C(L)** can be naturally understood, in the model-theoretic context, as that of finding out whether empirical economic structures qualify as models of **L** or of **C(L)**, respectively.

The explanation of empirical economic structures is the ultimate cognitive goal of economics as a science, even if it need not be the goal of every single theory, as we have seen in Part II and as we shall discuss again in Part IV.

However, even for intendedly empirical theories, the nature of the relation language–data varies very much from theory to theory. Therefore, to prepare the ground for the construction of the necessary analytic schemes we have referred to above, let us first discuss two basic epistemological issues which should be adequately taken care of by those very analytic schemes. The issues concern the distinctions between 'general' and 'special' theories, on the one hand, and between 'representational' and 'phenomenological' theories, on the other.

In relation to the first issue, one needs to recognize the case of the *general theory*, designed to refer to a possibly very large collection of structures – for example, the generic properties of consumer demand relations – and distinguish it from the case of a *special theory*, constructed to explain a smaller subcollection of structures of the former – for example, the particular properties of the so-called Rotterdam demand system – see Theil (1965).

The adjective 'general' is used here in the sense of 'extensive' or 'comprehensive'. Moreover, the more general a theory, the more abstract it is in the epistemological sense, that is in the sense of the theory's remoteness from concrete experience, or from any specific set of empirical data. Despite the fact that the adjectives 'general' and 'special' are only relative ones – general economic theories are subsumed, in due time and for only a limited period, into a *most* general one (the 'foundations' or 'basic theory') and special theories are further refined and specialized to a set of data (the 'data-specific theory') – they do denote useful concepts for taxonomic purposes.

In relation to the second issue, the distinction between a *representational theory* and a *phenomenological theory*, first introduced in 5.1, has a rather deep epistemological import.

Paraphrasing Bunge (1967b), and partially repeating what was said in 5.1, while scientific theories, representational or phenomenological, all provide subsumptive explanations of the data, what distinguishes a representational theory from a phenomenological one is that the former supplies, in addition, an interpretative explanation of the data.

The expression 'phenomenological theory' is used with several different meanings in the literature, including the one denoting the result of an interdisciplinary approach to the study of a phenomenon; here the expression is only used to designate the opposite of a representational theory, namely a purely subsumptive explanation. From this epistemological viewpoint, it is clear that representational theories are deeper than phenomenological ones.

An explanation of a consumer's demand can be provided, for instance, by relating, via a linear regression vector-equation, two sets of variables of the same structural level, namely, a vector of quantities purchased (the *explanandum*), on the one side of the equation, to a vector of prices and the scalar income (the *explanans*), on the other. This equation is the centrepiece of a phenomenological theory of consumer demand founded upon the empirical generalization 'demanded quantity is a function of relative prices and income'. It may indicate direction and magnitude of the change in some variables following a change in some other variables, but it stops short of describing the relating causal mechanism.

A deeper explanation of a consumer's demand is obtained, however, when we approach the data as the result of an expenditure-allocation decision founded upon the notion of constrained preference satisfaction or utility maximization. This is an example of a representational theory. It relates variables of different structural levels – demanded quantities (the *explanandum*), prices and income, at one level, with preferences or utility at another, deeper level – and it makes use of those inter-level relations to hypothesize the *mechanism* (constrained preference satisfaction or utility maximization) that determines the *modus operandi* (law of demand) of the structure.

Summarizing, as Bunge (1967b) has pointed out – and the above two examples may help to illustrate – phenomenological theories only provide accounts or descriptions of observable relations between variables belonging to the same level as the *explanandum* ('input–output' relations), and without disclosing the mechanism which determines the *modus operandi* of their referents ('black-box' systems). In contrast, representational theories explain relations between variables involving levels other than the level of the *explanandum*. In so doing, and by means, possibly, of non-observable, transempirical concepts – in the above example, the preference relation or the utility function – they supply the hypothesized mechanism (for example, constrained preference satisfaction or utility maximization) and the *modus operandi* (for instance, law of demand) of the structures they talk about. While phenomenological theories remain in their explanations close to the surface, at the level of the phenomena, representational theories penetrate deeper into the structure to offer interpretative representations of the internal mechanisms that may generate the data.

6.2.1 Epistemological levels and logical types

Our next task is to construct the analytic schemes or frameworks to describe how economic theories receive empirical meaning. Our construction rests on the caveat that the relation theory–data is – particularly so in the case of representational economic theories – by no means a simple one. Instead of referring to *the* theory and to *its* class of empirical models, a satisfactory general account requires the recognition and description of a whole hierarchy of theories and models of different logical types. At each level of this hierarchy, whose extremes are the most general theory with its abstract mathematical model and the data-specific theory with its structure of organized empirical data, respectively, there may be theories of their own with their characteristic classes of models. In Suppes's (1962) words, 'theory at one level is given empirical meaning by making formal connections with theory at a *higher level*' – our italics; see 6.6.

The preceding paragraph suggests that, in the general case, beyond dealing with isolated individual theories and models, we have to consider vertical multi-level hierarchic systems associating theories and models of different logical types.

This circumstance must thus be reflected in our general analytic schemes which will themselves account for configuration and details. At the bottom, there will be the more general and abstract theory of the system with its ideal interpretations or models; at the top, there will be the more concrete and special theories of the system with their empirical interpretations, or structures of data. Moreover, the distinction between a representational and a phenomenological theory will be extended to the notions of a system of representational theories (representational theoretical system) and a system of phenomenological theories (phenomenological theoretical system), respectively.

On account of the far greater complexity of representational theories and theoretical systems over phenomenological theories and theoretical systems, we have chosen a four-level scheme to describe a typical theoretical system of the former kind and a two-level as well as a single-level scheme to describe two instances of the latter kind, respectively. We shall also refer to them as 'semantic systems' since what is at the centre of the discussion is precisely the question of meaning.

Although we have to caution that there is nothing essential about this choice of the number of levels, such schemes do come close, in our opinion, to what is practice in actual economic research. Here, they will facilitate the task of providing a detailed description of rather general situations, by allowing us to single out in an orderly fashion, at each level, distinctive features of the corresponding theories and models. The single-level theoretical system corresponds, of course, to the case of an isolated phenomenological theory.

We focus first on the description of the representational theoretical system and then turn our attention to the phenomenological theoretical system which, if only in a purely formal sense, may be regarded as a special case of the former.

At level one, the bottom of the semantic scheme of a representational system of theories, we find what we shall name the *foundations theory*, *general theory* or *basic theory* with its very abstract mathematical models; climbing up the vertical chain we encounter, at level two, usually more than one instance of what we shall call a *general-class theory*, each with its mathematical interpretations; next, at level three, there may be several specimens of what we shall refer to as a *special-class theory*, each with its strongly particularized, satisfying set-theoretical structures; finally, at level four, the top of the semantic scheme, we find *data-specific theories*, each with its unique (up to isomorphism) empirical structure which we shall call the *primal* model of data. Since, in an intuitive sense, the theory of level four constitutes a conformation of a level-three theory to conditions determined by the data, we shall also refer to it as the *concrete (data-conform)* theory.

In our ideal design of the multi-level analytic scheme we associate, with theories at each level, their corresponding primitives, axiom bases and sets of theorems so that no superposition of the formulas of theories at two different levels may occur.

Observe that, in practice, a primitive object of a level-two or general-class theory – for example, a utility function – may have already occurred as a derived object of the level-one or general theory; or a primitive object of a level-three or special-class theory – for instance a transcendental logarithmic utility function – may have already occurred as a derived object of a level-two or general-class theory; and so on.

The observation of the last paragraph and the desideratum of the one preceding it point to two consequences. First, there will usually be more than one choice for the status of primitives and axiom base for some of the theories in a multi-level system like the one we are currently discussing. Second, the arrangement of a list of actual theories into such a hierarchic system may require the reconstruction of the axiom base of some of them. This will become evident in the examples to be developed in Chapter 7 and, in particular, in Chapter 8.

We now turn our attention to the much simpler case of the phenomenological economic theoretical system, a scheme of 'input–output' or 'black-box' theories where relations merely involve variables of the same structural level as the *explanandum*. We begin by recognizing two possible instances.

In the first instance we shall approach the issue with a two-level scheme where at the bottom we find a general theory to be designated the *generic theory* – to avoid confusion with other 'general theories' met in the preceding paragraphs – and at the top, once again, a *data-specific* (phenomenological) *theory. Mutatis mutandis*, we may stretch out the conclusions of our preceding observations regarding primitives, axiom base and distinction of logical types for the four-level scheme to the simpler scheme of a two-level phenomenological theoretical system.

In the second instance there is, strictly speaking, no generic theory. Indeed, rather than the application of a generic theory to a specific empirical situation, what one finds in the single-level case is an *ad hoc*, data-dependent theoretical construct which consists in a more or less complicated mesh of hypotheses stemming from different fields of theoretical economics and other disciplines, empirical generalizations, stochastic assumptions and even educated hunches. The dependence of theory on data appears to be far more direct here than in the case of a data-specific phenomenological theory – the application of a concrete (data-conform) version of a generic phenomenological theory to a specific structure of data – and justifies the stronger qualification as a *data-contingent theory*.

From now on, it will be convenient to denote by L_ι, $C(L_\iota)$, and S_ι, $\iota = 1, 2, 3, 4$, the ι-level theory (language), the empirical core, and an ι-level relational structure of a representational theoretical system, respectively. Similarly, L_ι, $C(L_\iota)$, and S_ι, $\iota = 1, 2$, will denote the ι-level theory (language), the empirical core, and an ι-level relational structure of a phenomenological theoretical system, respectively.

6.2.2 Logical types and cores of empirical claims

In the above description, we have systematically made reference to 'an ι-level theory' and its corresponding 'ι-level model(s)'. This is consistent with the logical hierarchy of theories and models upon which our semantic scheme is based. However, when our task is to explain the actual means by which economic theories of different levels receive empirical meaning, such a description is not enough. It must be completed with a description of the actual inter-level links of theories and models. One must know, for instance, whether the level-two model qualifies as a model of the level-one theory or a subset of its propositions; whether a level-three model qualifies as a model of the level-two and/or level-one theories or subsets of their propositions; in particular, it is of crucial interest whether a level-four model (a model of data) qualifies as a model of the empirical cores of the level-three, level-two and level-one theories.

We conclude the description of our analytic schemes by summarizing the nature of the relation of meaning among the various epistemological levels. As usual, we first focus on the larger, four-level representational system and then briefly adapt the results to the simpler, two-level phenomenological cases.

To begin with, the theory of level one is intendedly empirical for, despite its extreme generality, it has been devised to refer, even if remotely, to empirical data – for instance, the determinants and the most fundamental properties of a consumer's demand relation. A theory of level two, on the other hand, is intendedly empirical for, despite its still apparent generality, it has been constructed to explain, within the universe of the basic theory, an extended class of empirical phenomena – for instance, the determinants and the general properties of a transitive consumer's demand functions. A theory of level three offers a special mathematical formulation – embodying a suitable parametric representation – within the formal confines determined by the general-class theory. It is intendedly empirical for its aim is to lay down the basics of one special system – for example, demand functions of translog type – and of the testing, directly, of some special properties – for example, separability of the hypothesized utility function – and, indirectly, even of some foundational properties – for instance integrability of the derived demand relations. Finally, the theory of level four is one actual empirical instance of the theory of level three in the sense of being a theory of a structure of data admissible under the special class theory.

In the context of the hierarchic scheme, the empirical structure S_4 at level four must be a model of the theory of the same level – L_4, as the concrete, data-conform version of L_3 – and, at least, a model of the empirical core $C(L_3)$ if the special-class theory is to qualify as empirical theory. Notice that the first part of the preceding sentence implies the assumption that, for a level-four theory, its core equals the set of all its valid sentences. Although this latter assumption is not the essence of the matter – we could have adopted the view that, under some circumstances, $C(L_4)$ is properly contained in L_4 – it seems a rather natural one and it will be adopted throughout this study.

On the other hand, being S_4, in general, a structure of a different logical type from the typical structures of a level-one, level-two and even level-three theory, will usually not satisfy one or more axioms and theorems of the latter three theories. However, if the special-class theory is empirical, that is, if S_4 satisfies $C(L_3)$, then S_4 may also satisfy $C(L_2)$ since the level-three theory is a special case of the general-class theory; moreover, in the latter case, the structure S_4 may also be a model of the basic theory, that is, it would satisfy $C(L_1)$.

Focusing still on the structure of data S_4, it becomes apparent that as we move step by step from the 'concreteness' of level four to the 'abstractness' of level one, the reference relations become more and more remote. With respect to properties of a general nature, one may find persistence throughout all levels – for example, homogeneity of degree zero in prices of a level-four supply function (that is, of an estimated empirical supply function) is an instance of confirmation of homogeneity of degree zero for the very abstract supply correspondence of level one; on the other hand, with respect to much more specific properties, their presence at the top of the scheme only points to an instance of one of (perhaps) several possibilities at lower levels of the scheme – for example, integrability of demand at level four points to the existence of a utility function and thus constitutes an instance of transitivity of preference, one of two possibilities, at level one.

Before continuing the discussion, it would seem convenient to caution against too optimistic an expectation regarding a possible inclusion relation involving the empirical cores of all different levels. In particular, the above result should not prompt the conclusion that we can satisfy, in general, a relation of the form $C_1 \subseteq C_2 \subseteq C_3 \subseteq C_4 = L_4$. Indeed, linguistic differences as well as the differences of logical type that we encounter across levels will often conspire against such a possibility. As an example of the latter kind of differences – still within the context of consumer's choice analysis – one may find in a level-one theory the primitive 'preference correspondence' as a variable for which the predicate 'asymmetric and negatively transitive' (a sufficient condition for the existence of a utility function) is only one of a range of possible values while, in a level-two theory, the primitive 'direct utility function' is a variable for which the predicate 'transcendental logarithmic' is also only one of a range of possible values; and similarly for level three and level four of the theoretical system.

Although satisfaction of a nested inclusion relation by the empirical cores of all levels is a desirable situation, it may not be possible to satisfy it under all circumstances. Moreover, the fact that we have designed our examples in Chapters 7 and 8 to try to satisfy such an inclusion relation should not be construed as a general statement to that effect.

In the cases of phenomenological systems, systems which in a formal though surely not epistemological sense may be regarded as special cases of representational systems, what we have is an 'upward collapse' of the four or more levels into two and even one level. In the context of the two-level hierarchic scheme, if the generic theory is to qualify as empirical theory, then S_2, the empirical model of the level-two theory, must be a model of the concrete (data-conform) level-one theory and a model of the empirical core $C(L_1)$. In the case of the one-level system, on the other hand, the core becomes indistinguishable from the theory as a whole (that is, $C(L) = L$) so that a model of the core is simply a model of the theory.

6.3 ANALYTIC SCHEMES II: LEVEL-SPECIFIC FEATURES OF THEORIES AND MODELS

In what follows we list and comment on some distinct features of theories and models corresponding to the different levels of the analytic schemes. In all instances we discuss first the four levels of the representational system before turning our attention to the case of phenomenological theories.

6.3.1 The features of the axiom base

Of the axioms of a level-one theory, some are devoted to the formal characterization of non-observable primitives, typically, the preference-indifference relation $\geqslant$ in a theory of consumer choice, which includes the detailed specification of mathematical properties – for example, '$\geqslant$ is convex, continuous, non-satiated' – while others postulate properties of observables which, while essential at the formal, analytical level, may have no counterparts in the empirical data – for example, 'the production possibility set of the firm, Y, is closed and convex'. Such formal properties are reflections of the foundational as well as of the general nature of the theory and manifest a 'preceptive' intent to the extent that they establish necessary and/or sufficient conditions for the applicability of a particular kind of mathematical argument.

A situation similar to that commented on in the preceding paragraph is to be found among level-two theories, especially among those showing greater generality and mathematical sophistication. At this level, mathematical properties without verifiable empirical counterparts may be attributed to non-observables – for example, in consumer demand theory, 'the utility function u is Borel-measurable' – as well as to observables – for instance, in production theory, 'the production function f is twice differentiable'.

At level three, the axiom bases of many theories are devoted to the characterization of observable primitives – for example, in production theory, data on the quantities of outputs and on the quantities of inputs, and a complete description of the functional form of the production function including a detailed specification of the random disturbance. However, the axiom bases of several actual theories, which in the current description would properly belong to the third level of the hierarchic scheme, do indeed incorporate characterizations of non-observable primitives – for instance, direct or indirect utility functions in the translog consumer choice theory (compare with 6.2.1 above) – to buttress the very special theoretical support of their distinctive observable and testable derivates (for example, the indirect or direct translog demand system).

Preservation of the overall consistency of a hierarchic scheme as well as methodological parsimony suggest that when a characterization of non-observables – for example, the description of the direct or indirect translog utility function of the preceding illustration – is present in the actual versions of two theories of successive levels, one may remove such characterization from the higher-level theory to incorporate it instead, as a special chapter, into the theory of the preceding level. Such a limited reconstruction of the axiom base of the higher-level theory – confining it to the level of the observables – is an approach to be followed later on, in Chapter 8, with respect to the example of an L_3.

One typical feature of the axiom base of an L_3 thus constructed or reconstructed is that instead of referring to some smooth property – for instance, continuity of functions, convergence of infinite sequences, local convexity in some well-behaved mathematical space – of ideal objects, it describes generic (abstracted) properties – for instance, discreteness, finiteness, non-negativity – of a class of data – for example, in consumer demand analysis, time series of a finite length or a finite cross-section sample of observations in quantities, prices and expenditures.

Finally, at level four, the axioms point to sets of actual empirical data (and to potential empirical isomorphic instances) – for example, in demand analysis, time series of measurements of the quantities bought of each commodity from a list of actual commodities, of their corresponding prices, and of total expenditures, for a determinate period of time. They may describe in detail the estimated concrete (data-conform) system – for instance, still in demand analysis, a concrete set of numerical translog demand functions, the coefficients of which have been computed on the basis of the methods prescribed at level three and applied, at level four, to the just-mentioned array of statistical data; and they lay down the 'maintained hypothesis' to be tested, a detailed description of the application and of the results of the tests contemplated at level three (including all the relevant restrictions such tests may impose upon the maintained hypothesis), with due mention of the required limits of statistical tolerance regarding estimation, tests and, possibly, projections.

So much for the four-level scheme. On the one hand, in a purely formal sense, there is no reason to expect differences between the characteristics of the axiom bases of a level-three representational theory axiomatized (or re-axiomatized) on the basis of the observables and those of a generic phenomenological theory, or between the axiom bases of a level-four representational theory and their data-specific and data-contingent phenomenological counterparts, respectively. One may want to emphasize, however, that whereas the axiom bases of data-specific theories of either class point to specific sets of data which are special realizations of the structure of the theory which precedes them in level, the axiom base of a data-contingent theory lacks such foundation. Moreover, in an ontological and epistemological sense – more on this in 6.3.3 – the differences between the axiom bases of representational and phenomenological theories will reflect the substantial differences in depth that are characteristic of these two types of theory.

6.3.2   The cognitive goals and scope of the theory

The goal of the basic or general theory L_1 is to serve as the ultimate groundwork as well as to set the outermost confines for the collection of general-class theories in a field of theoretical economics research. In this respect, the basic theory may be said to have a 'paradigmatic' or 'preceptive' role in so far as it determines the collection of admissible general-class, that is, level-two theories. Regarding scope, it thus follows that a basic theory is the most general theory of the field in question (for example, production or consumer choice analysis) and the foundations of level-two theories.

The goal of a general-class theory L_2 is to focus on and to explain a wide subfield (for instance, theory of demand of the transitive-total consumer, theory of the non-increasing returns to scale firm) of the foundations or general theory. General-class theories, as the name suggests, have also a very general scope: each general-class theory determines the confines and the basis of a whole collection of level-three theories, that is of special-class theories.

Within the scheme, a special-class theory L_3 has as its goal to supply, within the confines of a general-class theory, a special parametric formulation – for example, linear expenditure demand system, Rotterdam demand system, Cobb–Douglas production function, linear activity analysis production function – of a system proper of the class; this may allow, for instance, the estimation of the parameters of the system and make possible the tests of propositions of the general-class theory. On the one hand, a special-class theory always offers a strongly specified version of a system; on the other hand, in so far as it refers to a 'special class', it offers a summary, generic formulation of important empirical specifications the level-four theories must satisfy. In this latter sense, in relation to level-four theories, the scope of a special-class theory is still 'general'.

A theory L_4 is the adaptation of the parametric formulation and the generic empirical specifications of the level-three theory to the requirements of a structure of concrete empirical data. In the context of the special examples given above for levels one, two and three, the possible goals of a level-four theory may include the statistical estimation of a system of supply or demand equations for actual empirical data – of, say, the Federal Republic of Germany for the period 1950–70 – to provide tests of the propositions parametrized in the concrete, data-conform version of L_3, to determine properties specific to the data and to the system that generated it and, finally and very often, to serve as a tool for economic projections. It should be pointed out, however, that whatever its mediate relations to the lower levels of the scheme – providing confirmations or falsifications of hypotheses – the scope of the level-four theory is, at least initially, specific to the data organized in its primal model.

Shifting the focus now to the case of the two-level phenomenological system and except for what was said in relation to epistemological depth – absence of representational hypotheses – generic theories usually share with general theories properties regarding goal, and with special-class theories properties regarding scope. On the other hand, in the two-level and single-level schemes, phenomenological data-specific and data-contingent theories share goal and scope with representational data-specific theories.

6.3.3 The ontological and/or epistemological assumptions and hypotheses

The first and most important aspect to emphasize and to keep in mind in the present context is that the decisive distinction between representational and phenomenological theories consists in the fact that while theories of the former kind make use of observables and/or non-observable constructs (epistemological aspect) which 'occur in hypothetical "mechanisms" which underlie the facts referred to by the theory (ontological aspect)' (Bunge, 1967b), theories of the latter kind do not.

The second aspect that attracts our attention here concerns the deterministic versus stochastic nature of a theory. With the actual practice of economics in mind, it is interesting to observe these features as they relate to the level occupied by a theory within a hierarchic theoretical system.

We focus first on the four-level scheme. Current economic theories of levels one and two are very often, though not always, deterministic – for example, in Chapter 7 we discuss the case of a stochastic theory of consumer demand which, given its characteristics, belongs to our general-class category. On the other hand, theories of level three are usually formulated within the econometric methodology and thus are stochastic in nature. Finally, level-four theories are most of the time statistical, for they encompass the performance of sets of statistical operations and include the presentation and evaluation of the corresponding results.

Turning our attention to phenomenological theories, many but not all generic theories are formulated within a stochastic framework – for instance, in Chapter 9, we use as illustration of a level-one phenomenological theory a non-stochastic linear input–output system. Finally, as one would expect, data-specific and data-contingent theories are ordinarily statistical systems.

6.3.4 The characterization of observables: place and specification

Let us, once again, begin with the four-level scheme. At the foundations or general-theory level the observables are often derived constructs (for example, in consumer choice theory, demand correspondences) rather than primitives, and the specification of their properties is weak and most general (for instance, in consumer demand theory, 'the demand correspondence $d(p, m)$ is compact-valued . . . and homogeneous of degree zero in p and m').

At the general-class theory level, observables may be derived concepts (for instance, in consumer demand theory, the demand functions are derived from budget-constrained maximization of the utility function) or primitives (for example, in production theory, the production function). The specification of the properties of observables is still general but less than at level one since we deal here with classes within the set of observables of level one (for example, in production theory, 'the production function f is continuous, non-decreasing, quasiconcave . . .'; in consumer demand theory, 'the demand function d is continuous, homogeneous of degree zero, has a symmetric, negative semidefinite Slutsky matrix . . .').

Keeping in mind our reservations regarding the axiomatization of level-three theories as expressed in 6.3.1, and following a possible axiomatic reconstruction, the observables of a systemic version of an L_3 are primitives rather than derived constructs and the specification of their properties, although generic, is complete, mathematically very detailed (for example, in production theory, 'the nested CES production function is $y = \Sigma_s(\alpha_s z_s^{-\rho})^{-1/\rho}$ where $z_s = [\Sigma_{i \in N_s}\beta_i^s(x_i^s)^{-\rho^s}]^{-1/\rho^s}$, where $s = 1, 2, \ldots, S$ and $\ldots$'; in consumer demand theory 'the Rotterdam-system demand function for the ith commodity is $w_i d \ln x_i = \alpha_i d \ln x + \Sigma_j \pi_{ij} d \ln p_j + \epsilon_i$ where $\ldots$') and given in parametric form – for instance, in the case of the CES production function, '$\alpha_s > 0, -1 < \rho = (1 - \sigma)/\sigma < \infty, \beta_i^s > 0, -1 < (1 - \sigma_s)/\sigma_s <$'; in the case of the Rotterdam-system ith demand equation, 'homogeneity imposes $\Sigma_j \pi_{ij} = 0$, symmetry imposes $\pi_{ij} = \pi_{ji}$ for all $(i, j), \ldots$'.

At the level of the data-specific theory, the observables are the sets of organized empirical data and, possibly, the estimated relations – continuing the preceding examples, numerical CES production function or numerical Rotterdam-system demand functions; the sets of statistical data and, when available, the estimated econometric equations, constitute concrete empirical instances of those corresponding entities so thoroughly, precisely and yet still generically described by the preceding theory of level three.

Turning to phenomenological theories, the striking difference we find is the absence of non-observables. While level-one and level-two representational theories may explicitly include non-observables among their primitives (for instance, preference relations, utility functions) as components of the hypothesized mechanisms (for instance, constrained preference satisfaction, utility maximization) which explain the observables (for example, demand), level-three and level-four representational theories infer the existence of non-observables (for example, utility functions) from successful statistical tests regarding relevant properties (for instance, integrability) of observables (for instance, demand functions). In contrast, phenomenological theories confine their function to the description of 'input–output', 'black-box' relationships between observables.

6.3.5 The overall linguistic features

The mathematical language of economic theory L_1 is, almost as a rule, very abstract, responding to analytic modalities imposed by the theory's cognitive goals and scope; not surprisingly, it often stems from one or more of the foundation disciplines of mathematics. In the cases of those branches of economics we are using here as examples – static theories of the firm and consumer behaviour – those disciplines include, among others, formal logic, set theory, abstract algebra, general topology, algebraic topology, measure and integration theory.

At level two the mathematical language is far less abstract. Analytic requirements impose, instead, a finer and more discriminating instrument. In the case of our two illustrative branches the mathematics is borrowed from, among others, linear algebra, game and programming theory, differential topology, differential equations, theory of probability.

The language of a level-three theory is, as one might expect, strongly influenced by the presence of the econometric methodology. In the case of the static theories of the firm and consumer behaviour one should mention linear algebra, differential and integral calculus, optimization, and mathematical statistics.

Finally, at level four, the formal language is very much that of arithmetic and applied statistics. Actual estimations of systems of equations, measurements and other empirical procedures, the execution of a variety of tests together with the presentation of their results and possibly projection operations are, at this level, the decisive factors which determine the choice of language.

Whereas most generic phenomenological theories share the linguistic characteristics of level-three representational theories, data-specific and data-contingent phenomenological theory languages do not differ in any fundamental ways from what is standard among level-four representational ones.

6.3.6 The characteristics of structures and models

It is at the level of the foundations or general theory L_1 where one finds a definition of S_1, the most extensive and comprehensive set-theoretical predicate of the hierarchic system. In general production theory this is a structure $\langle C, Y, \ldots \rangle$, where the *production possibility set* Y, a subset of some infinitely or finitely dimensional topological vector space, the commodity space C, embodies the technology of the firm; in basic consumer choice theory one meets a structure $\langle C, X, >, \ldots \rangle$ where $X \subseteq C$ is called the *consumption possibility set* and the non-observable $>$ the consumer's *preference relation*.

General-class theories define set-theoretical predicates S_2 which are special cases of and finer instances than the structures of level one. In a relational structure $\langle Y, f, \ldots \rangle$ of a level-two production theory, the technology of the firm is depicted by the *production function* $f \subset Y$, summarizing the efficient productions vectors y in Y. As an example of a level-two theory the relational structures of which include a non-observable – the real-valued function u of $\langle X, u, \ldots \rangle$ – we mention the case of a consumer demand theory based on a utility function **u** with domain **X**.

Special-class theories have as referents narrowly defined set-theoretical predicates S_3 which, in principle – see 6.3.1 – may or may not include non-observables among the primitives. In a level-three production structure $\langle Y, f, \ldots \rangle$, Y refers to a set of finite data with well-specified properties and **f** is now a fully specified functional form (for example, Cobb–Douglas). In a data-conform level-three consumer demand theory, that is, one axiomatized or axiomatically reconstructed at the level of the observables (see, again, 6.3.1 and Chapter 8), S_3 would certainly include a specific system of demand equations – for example, the indirect or direct translog demand system. In actual research practice, the decision to choose the utility function **u** – or indirect utility function **v** – as opposed to the demand function **d** for a primitive would probably be influenced by whether the 'theoretical' or the 'empirical' aspect of the question is being accentuated. To emphasize the systemic aspect of our discussion, as explained before, we shall follow the latter approach when illustrating the two highest levels of the hierarchic scheme in Chapter 8.

Finally, at level four, the definition points straight to a single empirical instance (and to its possible empirical isomorphic transformations) of the predicate definition of level three. In particular, the domain(s) of actual data of level four constitute(s) embedding(s) in the sub-structure of domain(s) of generic data of level three. For instance, the set of actual production data or demand data of level four is an actual realization of the set of generic data on production or demand of level three, respectively.

Regarding phenomenological theories, it suffices to point out that whereas structures of the generic theory level share the characteristics of special-class theories, phenomenological data-specific and data-contingent theories are of the same type as level-four representational theories. Of course, whereas the empirical structure of a data-specific theory is always regarded as a possible realization of a structure of level three, the empirical structure of a data-contingent theory is only data-subordinate in the sense that there is no reference to any level-three theory or structure.

6.3.7 Methodological features

In the context of representational systems, theories of level one and two do not usually include estimable propositions, that is, relations expressed in parametric form. Moreover, they are only indirectly testable, namely when one of their possible parametric representations of level three is subject to estimation and tests at level four. Level-one and level-two theories are thus independent of any particular estimation or testing method.

A theory of level three constitutes a theory of a special parametric representation of economic-theoretical constructs developed at level one and specially at level two. It includes assumptions regarding the generation of the empirical data (for example, '... the actual observations constitute a multivariate random drawing from a normal distribution ...'), a determination of the applicable estimation method(s) and the detailed rules of the testing procedures – including the blueprint of the restrictions to be imposed upon the 'maintained hypothesis'.

When estimation is at stake, the level-four theory particularizes one specific estimation method; moreover, it particularizes the generic testing rules determined at level three to the concrete (data-conform) version of the parametric representation of the special-class theory.

L_4 sets the margins of statistical tolerance for the tests and, if relevant, for estimation and for projections. In this connection, it summarizes the results of the estimation of parameters and of the testing of the empirical validity of the set of its propositions. To the extent that the latter include level-one and level-two propositions in the parametric representation of level three, these procedures amount to tests of the empirical cores of level one and level two within the strong specification determined at level three.

In the context of phenomenological theories, generic theories, on the one hand, and data-specific and data-contingent theories, on the other, share very much the characteristics of level-three and level-four representational theories, respectively, provided the two latter have been axiomatized – or their axiom bases have been recast – at the level of the observables (see 6.2.1).

6.4 ANALYTIC SCHEMES III: THE GENERAL CASE

We conclude this section with an adaptation of Definition 6.1.1. Since we have stated that the number of levels is not the essence of the problem – the choice of four and two levels was dictated by considerations which combine descriptive requirements with the convenience of approximating the actual state of theoretical economics – we shall here extend the scheme to an arbitrary though finite number of levels, namely n.

Definition 6.4.1   In an *n*-level semantic system of economic theories, the level-ι theory $\mathbf{L}_ι$ or $L_ι$, $ι = 1, 2, \ldots, n$, is said to be an *empirical economic theory* if and only if $\mathbf{S}_n$ or S_n, the empirical model of the level-*n* theory, is a model of $C(\mathbf{L}_ι)$ or $C(L_ι)$, that is, a model of every formula in $C(\mathbf{L}_ι)$ or $C(L_ι)$.

In the above definition we have taken the view, already advanced in 6.2.2, that $\mathbf{L}_n = C(\mathbf{L}_n)$. Once again, although not indispensable, such an assumption would seem to fit neatly with the overall empirical role of a theory $\mathbf{L}_n$.

Finally, extending an observation made in 6.2.2, a nested inclusion relation involving all the successive empirical cores ($ι = 1, 2, \ldots, n$) of an *n*-level system of theories would constitute an ideal, very desirable situation most unlikely to hold, unfortunately, as a general rule.

6.5   MODELS AND PROJECTIONS

A very important cognitive function of data-specific and data-contingent economic theories consists in their service as tools for scientific projections regarding the future or past behaviour of a system – predicting or forecasting and retrodicting or aftercasting. A projection, as understood here, is a statement regarding the future or past values of some variables of the system (*projectandum*) made *conditional* on specific assumptions regarding the values of some other variables of the system (*projectans*) – see Bunge (1967b). Besides its cognitive function, it is clear that scientific forecasting also has an important role as a test procedure for a theory (methodological function) and as a guide-post for action (policy function). In economics, quantitative retrodictions – often also called '*ex-post* projections' or, putting emphasis on the methodological aspect, 'validations' – are used among the initial tests of the explanatory adequacy of theories, while quantitative predictions have become the main output of specialized public and private forecasting agencies.

In different parts of this chapter we have referred to the 'uniqueness' (up to isomorphism) of the empirical model of a data-specific or a data-contingent theory, and we have called this model the primal model. The primal model is here the structure of data the theory has been primarily designed to explain and also the empirical source material with whose help the formal statements of the theory have been estimated and initially tested. Besides this 'primogenital' character, the primal model has a certain canonical role in so far as it summarizes the common formal properties of all other empirical isomorphic, that is, admissible structures.

From the model-theoretic point of view, to predict successfully may thus be understood as projecting accurately, that is, within the tolerance limits determined by the axioms of the theory, the values of the unknown variables of isomorphic empirical models of the theory. If in a data-specific or data-contingent theory '$y = f(x)$' we choose for example a theoretically admissible but otherwise arbitrary – in the sense of 'non-empirical' – set of numerical values for the *projectans* x, we obtain a consistent set of numerical values for the *projectandum* y. These numerical values of x and y clearly constitute a numerical model of '$y = f(x)$', isomorphic to the primal model; however, this model is by no stretch of the imagination an empirical model. Instead, in scientific economic forecasting, one would compare the actual y generated by the economy for the actual x with the projected $y°$, computed by the projecting device for the same, actual, y. If the difference $y° - y$ is within the limits established in the relevant axioms, then the new data structure is an empirical model of the theory, isomorphic to the primal one.

6.6   NOTES AND REMARKS

The vertical scheme proposed by Suppes (1962) as a semantic paradigm 'descends' from the more abstract theory with its ideal models, at the top, to the more concrete theory with its 'model of data', at the bottom. On our part, having chosen to call 'basic theory' or 'foundations theory' the theory of maximal generality of the scheme, and striving to be consistent with standard linguistic usage, our paradigm 'ascends' from the more abstract theory with its ideal models, at the bottom, to the data-specific theory, with its empirical structure, at the top. Thus, when quoting Suppes (1962), we have replaced his 'lower level' by our italicized '*higher level*'. See also Suppes (1967) and the interesting discussion of his views in Rolleri (1983).

The concept of a 'representational theory', expounded by Bunge (1967b), has been extended to that of a 'representational theoretical system' or 'system of representational theories', in conformity with the idea of a hierarchic multi-level semantic system. The current usage of the expression 'phenomenological theory' has been borrowed from Bunge (1967b) too.

As pointed out in previous paragraphs, the description of two- and one-level phenomenological systems as special cases of (that is, 'upward-collapsed') four-level representational systems is formally although not epistemologically correct. As we shall see in Chapters 7 and 8, in contrast to Chapters 9 and 10, theories L_3 and L_4 (that is, the special-class and the data-specific theory), since they are themselves representational theories, have higher explanatory powers – are deeper in their explanations – than the accounts of one- or even two-level phenomenological theories.

For the economic examples mentioned in this chapter, the reader may consult the article by Nodiri (1982), the article by Christensen, Jorgenson and Lau (1973), the book by Conrad and Jorgenson (1975), and the article by Conrad and Jorgenson (1977) on production analysis; and the books by Powell (1974), Deaton and Muellbauer (1980), and Theil and Clements (1987), and the article by Barten (1977), on demand systems.

A detailed discussion of scientific projections from a philosophy of science point of view can be found in Bunge (1967b). The terminology used in 6.5 has been mainly borrowed from that work although the model-theoretic interpretation of the projecting operations, so far as we know, is ours.

A summary version of the main ideas developed in this chapter was first presented in Klein (1992).

7 Representational Theories and Theoretical Systems (I): Basic or General Theory and General-Class Theory

A representational theory is a theory which includes representational hypotheses; and a representational hypothesis, in contrast to a merely phenomenological one, provides an interpretative explanation of the object it refers to. Such an explanation goes beyond the description of the outward relations between two sets of variables – the *explanandum* and the *explanans* – to supply a representation of the hypothesized inward mechanism which determines the working of the referent; see Bunge (1967b).

This chapter will serve to illustrate, with some detailed examples, the two lower levels of the scheme developed in Chapter 6 for the case of a system of representational theories. In relation to the two types of theories to be considered, we first reintroduce and extend the discussion on the characterization of languages and structures initiated in 6.3 and then go on to investigate some actual theory cases.

7.1 BASIC OR GENERAL THEORY: LANGUAGE AND MODELS

We stated in 6.3.2 that the cognitive goal of a basic, foundations or general theory is to serve as the ultimate groundwork of a representational theoretical system and as the outermost confines for the collection of general-class theories in a field. This is, of course, a static perspective because the status of being at the bottom of a system is hardly a lasting one, but changes with the evolution of the system itself. Rather frequently, what was yesterday a basic theory is today a general-class theory and will perhaps become tomorrow a special-class case. It serves to compare, for example, the places taken up at birth and a few decades later by the succeeding theories of consumer behaviour from Walras (1874) to Hicks (1939), Samuelson (1947), Debreu (1959) until, say, Kim and Richter (1986).

Because of its position at the basis of the system, the basic or general theory is, in scope, the most general of all the theories that make up the system, thus playing a unifying role; it brings together the common, essential properties of diverse sections of a field; it embodies the most general principles, that is, the theoretical foundations of a field at a point in its history and bears for this reason a kind of preceptive function.

Having to deal with most general, common properties, the language of a basic theory in economics is abstract, itself frequently borrowed from the foundation branches of mathematics – set theory, general topology, and measure and integration theory are typical examples for the language of contemporary consumer choice analysis.

Level-one structures consist of ideal, mathematical objects, far removed from empirical data – in analysis of consumer behaviour, for instance, subsets of and relations on subsets of spaces of real vectors, real bounded sequences, bounded measurable functions – and possess properties which have no counterparts in empirical data – the cardinality of the continuum, convexity of sets; Lebesgue-measurability, τ-continuity of relations and functions.

It has already been pointed out that there is no formal distinction between a structure that is a possible realization of a theory of pure mathematics and one that is a possible realization of a theoretical science. This, which is true at any level of the hierarchic scheme, is most easily perceived at the level of a basic theory of mathematical economics.

A level-one model of a basic theory of mathematical economics – in contrast with the level-four empirical model of its empirical core $C(L_1)$ – is usually a complicated algebraic, topological, functional-analytic and perhaps, measure-theoretic system. It is 'economic', and as such 'different' from the systems which interest the pure mathematician, only in a pragmatic sense: the pieces of the system and its final set-up, although belonging to basic branches of mathematics and obeying their rules, have been chosen by motivations and objectives which are not the standard ones of the pure mathematician, but rather those of the economist. To construct a level-one structure in economics means to invent, within mathematics, a system capable of mirroring selected traits of economic phenomena, the mediate and elusive referents. It is also necessary to choose, at the same time, the appropriate mathematical language. The latter choice, of course, automatically determines a list of properties of the structure, some of which, in the context of the theory, will have a mainly linguistic or technical significance.

7.2 A BASIC OR GENERAL THEORY: CONSUMER CHOICE IN R^l

To show an instance of the class of theories we had in mind in our preceding discussions, we choose here a theory we have already met in 3.2, namely, the theory of individual consumer choice, although focusing this time on a different set of aspects of the theory. This theory of consumer choice is the foundation of the level-two theory to be described in 7.4 as well as of other general theories of demand. For the preparation of this section we have used as main references Barten and Böhm (1982) and Weddepohl (1984) – more detailed references are given in the 'Notes and remarks' section of this chapter (7.5).

To follow in the footsteps of Chapter 3, we first identify a consumer with a triple $\langle X, B, H \rangle$. Although in determining the properties of X we can choose the commodity space from a rather wide variety of candidate mathematical spaces – in Chapter 3 we merely required X to be a non-empty set – we shall confine ourselves to the case when the consumption set X is the non-negative orthant of the l-Euclidean space R^l. Furthermore, we shall require the relation H to be a correspondence from X to X, that is, H will have as its domain the whole of X.

With the above restrictions, the set X immediately satisfies the properties of being *closed* in the usual topology (it contains the limit points of all its convergent sequences of points), *bounded from below* (by 0, the smallest of its vectors), and *convex* (it contains the segment joining any two of its different points). The preference correspondence H assigns to every commodity bundle $x \in X$ the set of preferred consumptions $H(x)$. We gather next some properties of H that will be used, directly or indirectly, in the sequel. Some of them may also serve – for example, strict convexity or transitivity – to narrow down, that is to specialize, the scope of the theory. The expression nbd(x) will denote throughout the study an *open neighbourhood* of the point $x \in X$.

Definition 7.2.1   Let H be a preference correspondence on the consumption set X. H is said to be:

(1) *reflexive* if: $\forall x \in X, x \in H(x)$
(2) *irreflexive* if: $\forall x \in X, x \notin H(x)$
(3) *transitive* if: $x \in H(y), y \in H(z) \Rightarrow x \in H(z)$
(4) *negatively transitive* if: $x \notin H(y), y \notin H(z) \Rightarrow x \notin H(z)$
(5) *symmetric* if: $x \in H(y) \Rightarrow y \in H(x)$
(6) *asymmetric* if: $x \in H(y) \Rightarrow y \notin H(x)$

(7) *complete* if: $\forall x, y \in X, \, x \in H(y)$ or $y \in H(x)$

(8) *locally non-satiated* if: $\forall x \in X$ and $\forall nbd(x) \, \exists y \in nbd(x) \cap X$ such that $x \notin H(y)$

(9) *continuous* if: $x, y \in X$ and $y \in H(x)$ then $\exists nbd(x)$, $nbd(y)$ such that $y' \in nbd(y)$ and $x' \in nbd(x) \Rightarrow y' \in H(x')$

(10) *convex-valued* if: $\forall x \in X$, $H(x)$ is a convex set.

For the case of a convex-valued preference correspondence it will be useful to distinguish between two cases. Using the well-known symbols for strong preference '>' and for indifference '~', we shall say that the preferences are *convex* if $\forall x, y \in X$ and $\lambda \in [0, 1]$ if $x > y$ then $\lambda x + (1 - \lambda)y > y$; and *strongly convex* if $\forall x, y \in X$ and $\lambda \in [0, 1]$ if $x \sim y$ then $\lambda x + (1 - \lambda)y > y$.

Let us use $p = (p_1, \ldots, p_l)$ to represent an l-component price vector and m the consumer's income. With the help of these two concepts we can now give a more definite form to the notion of budget situation introduced at a more abstract level in 3.2. If P and M represent the set of price vectors and of incomes, respectively, a typical budget set may be introduced by definition as $B(p, m) = \{x \in X: p \cdot x \leq m$ for $p \in P$ and $m \in M\}$. This way, we may eliminate the class B from the list of primitives of the theory. It will be useful at this point to compare the following characterization of 'a model of the theory of individual consumer choice' with the content of Definition 3.2.1. For ease of reference, we index from now on with the numerals 1, 2, 3 and 4 those primitives appearing in two or more of the level-one, level-two, level-three and level-four structures, respectively. For instance, X_1, X_2, X_3 and X_4 will stand for the 'domain of commodity bundles' of the structure at level one, level two, level three and level four, respectively (the choice of 'domain' is here a matter of convenience, dictated by the need to facilitate inter-level comparisons; one may argue that, in a stricter sense, the actual 'domain' is the whole commodity space).

Definition 7.2.2 A system $S_1 = \langle X_1, P_1, M_1, H \rangle$ is a *model of the theory of individual consumer choice in R^l* if and only if it satisfies the following axioms:

A7.2.1 $X_1 = \{x \in R^l: x_i \geq 0; \, i = 1, \ldots, l\}$.

A7.2.2 $P_1 = \{p \in R^l: p_i > 0; \, i = 1, \ldots, l\}$.

A7.2.3 $M_1 = \{m \in R: m > 0\}$.

A7.2.4 H is a preference correspondence from X_1 to X_1.

A7.2.5   **H** is irreflexive, convex-valued, continuous and locally non-satiated.

The 'individual consumer' may be identified here with the primitive objects $X_1 \subset R^l$, $H \subset X \times X$ and $M_1 \subset R$. The structure is then completed with the 'environmental' component $P_1 \subset R^l$. Axioms A7.2.1 to A7.2.4 are the structural axioms, whereas A7.2.5 is an additional assumption required in the proof of the following proposition (see, for instance, Weddepohl, 1984, on the existence of at least one maximal element for **H** in the budget set). Precisely, for given **p**, **m** the consumer is supposed to choose a maximal element among the set of affordable bundles.

Theorem 7.2.1   Every budget set **B(p, m)** has a maximal element **x*** for **H** such that $p \cdot x^* = m$.

Under certain conditions, preferences are representable by numerical functions. The behaviour of the consumer consists then in choosing a utility-maximizing bundle subject to the budget constraint.

Definition 7.2.3   A utility function is a continuous function $u: X_1 \to R$ such that $y \in H(x) \Leftrightarrow u(y) > u(x)$.

Sufficient conditions for the existence of a utility function **u** as a representation of the preference correspondence **H** are the subjects of the following proposition.

Theorem 7.2.2   If the preference correspondence **H** of S_1 of Definition 7.2.2 is asymmetric and negatively transitive, then it can be represented by a utility function **u**.

The introduction of a utility function would thus narrow down the theory to a 'theory of individual *transitive* consumer choice', a special case. Note, however, that the presence of a utility function is a sufficient condition for transitivity.

We use two possible properties of utility functions to characterize the corresponding properties of representable preferences.

Definition 7.2.4   Let $\{A, B, \ldots, Z\}$ be a partition of the index set $I = \{1, 2, \ldots, l\}$ and denote by $x_A, x_B, \ldots, x_Z$ the corresponding subvectors of $x = (x_1, \ldots, x_l)$. Then the utility function **u** is said to be *groupwise separable* if it can be written $\mathbf{u} = \mathbf{f}[\mathbf{u}_A(\mathbf{x}_A),\ \mathbf{u}_B(\mathbf{x}_B),\ \ldots,\ \mathbf{u}_Z(\mathbf{x}_Z)]$. The preferences $\mathbf{H}$ are said to be *groupwise separable* if and only if they are representable by a groupwise separable utility function $\mathbf{u}$.

Definition 7.2.5 The utility function $\mathbf{u}$ is said to be *additive* if it can be written $\mathbf{u} = \mathbf{f}[\Sigma_i \mathbf{u}_i(\mathbf{x}_i)]$. The preferences $\mathbf{H}$ are said to be *additive* if and only if they are representable by an additive utility function $\mathbf{u}$.

A useful concept which is closely related to the notion of a utility function is that of the 'indirect utility function', intuitively a function that gives the maximum utility achievable by the consumer at given $\mathbf{p}$ and $\mathbf{m}$. We define it next.

Definition 7.2.6 Assume a utility function $\mathbf{u}$ exists. Then the function $\mathbf{v}: \mathbf{P}_1 \times \mathbf{M}_1 \to R$ such that $\mathbf{v}(\mathbf{p},\ \mathbf{m}) = \max \mathbf{u}(\mathbf{x})$ is called the *indirect utility function*.

We give for the indirect utility function properties that parallel the properties of the utility function of the preceding definitions.

Definition 7.2.7 Let $\{A, B, \ldots, Z\}$ be a partition of the index set $I = \{1, 2, \ldots, l\}$ and denote by $\mathbf{p}_A, \mathbf{p}_B, \ldots, \mathbf{p}_Z$ the corresponding subvectors of $\mathbf{p} = (\mathbf{p}_1, \ldots, \mathbf{p}_l)$. Then the indirect utility function $\mathbf{v}$ is said to be *groupwise separable* if it can be written $\mathbf{v} = \mathbf{g}[\mathbf{v}_A(\mathbf{p}_A,\ \mathbf{m}), \mathbf{v}_B(\mathbf{p}_B,\ \mathbf{m}), \ldots, \mathbf{v}_Z(\mathbf{p}_Z,\ \mathbf{m})]$.

Definition 7.2.8 The indirect utility function $\mathbf{v}$ is said to be *additive* if it can be written $\mathbf{v} = \mathbf{g}[\Sigma_i \mathbf{v}_i(\mathbf{p}_i,\ \mathbf{m})]$.

Separability and additivity of preferences – which could have been alternatively and directly defined as primitive concepts – have been introduced here with the help of the utility function. For completeness, we relate the properties of the direct and indirect utility functions.

Theorem 7.2.3 The utility function $\mathbf{u}$ is groupwise separable (respectively, additive) if and only if the indirect utility function $\mathbf{v}$ is groupwise separable (respectively, additive).

Let us return for a moment to our more general context and focus again on the budget sets. It is useful to extend the notion of a family of budget sets to that of a budget correspondence.

Definition 7.2.9   The mapping **B** from $P_1 \times M_1$ to **X** such that $(p, m) \rightarrow B(p, m) = \{x \in X: p \cdot x \leq m\}$ is called the *budget correspondence* of S_1.

Two important results follow. The first guarantees that the budget correspondence is sufficiently 'smooth' and, for the sake of completeness, we characterize first three notions of continuity that are relevant in this context. A correspondence **f** from **X** to **Y** is said to be (1) *lower semi-continuous* if for every $x \in X$ and every net $(x_n: n \in D)$ in **X** which converges to **x**, and every open set **G** in **Y** with $f(x) \cap G \neq \varnothing$, $f(x_n) \cap G \neq \varnothing$ for all sufficiently large n; (2) *upper semi-continuous* if for every $x \in X$ and every net $(x_n: n \in D)$ in **X** which converges to **x**, and every open set **G** in **Y** with $f(x) \subset G$, $f(x_n) \subset G$ for all sufficiently large n; (3) *continuous* if it is both lower and upper semi-continuous. We move on to the first result.

Theorem 7.2.4   The budget correspondence **B** of S_1 is convex-valued, compact-valued and continuous on X_1.

The second result is a main building block for the theory of demand in the absence of 'money illusion' and is a direct consequence of the fact that we have restricted the possible 'budget situations' to only those that satisfy the inequality $p \cdot x \leq m$.

Theorem 7.2.5   The budget correspondence **B** of S_1 is homogeneous of degree zero, that is for any scalar $\lambda > 0$ $B(\lambda p, \lambda m) = B(p, m)$.

At the centre of individual choice theory stands, of course, the concept of individual demand. It captures the essence of preference or utility maximization in a notion whose key attributes are observable. At the level of abstraction and generality of a level-one theory, this is best taken care of by the concept of a demand correspondence.

Definition 7.2.10   The mapping **d** from $P_1 \times M_1$ to X_1 such that $d(p, m) = \{x \in X: H(x) \cap B(p, m) = \varnothing\}$ is called the *demand correspondence* of S_1.

The demand correspondence assigns to every pair (p, m) the set of maximal elements in the corresponding budget set and thus summarizes the choice behaviour of the consumer. As was the case with the budget correspondence, the basic assumptions guarantee the necessary smoothness and the homogeneity of the demand correspondence. The latter property easily follows from Theorem 7.2.5. Note also that, taking its values on X_1, the individual demand correspondence is non-negatively valued.

Theorem 7.2.6   The demand correspondence **d** of S_1 is compact-valued and upper semi-continuous over the consumption set X_1. If **H** is transitive and complete **d** is also convex-valued.

Theorem 7.2.7   The demand correspondence **d** of S_1 is homogeneous of degree zero, that is for any scalar $\lambda > 0$ $\mathbf{d}(\lambda\mathbf{p}, \lambda\mathbf{m}) = \mathbf{d}(\mathbf{p}, \mathbf{m})$.

The following result immediately follows from preference satisfaction or utility maximization and is commonly referred to as summability or the adding-up property of demand.

Theorem 7.2.8   For every $\mathbf{x}^* \in \mathbf{d}(\mathbf{p}^*, \mathbf{m}^*)$, $\mathbf{p}^*\mathbf{x}^* = \mathbf{m}^*$.

The individual consumer's demand correspondences of structure S_1 may be aggregated over sets of commodities, leading to individual demand correspondences for composite commodities. On the other hand, if instead of focusing on the individual consumer we extend our attention to the whole set of consumers who constitute the 'consumption sector' or structure $\langle\langle X_{1q}, M_{1q}, H_q\rangle_{q \in Q}, P_1\rangle$ we can aggregate over Q, the finite or infinite index set of consumers, obtaining the market demand correspondence. The appropriateness of aggregation over commodities is closely related, as one would expect, to the 'separability' properties of preferences – some of which have been characterized in Definitions 7.2.4, 7.2.5, 7.2.7 and 7.2.8. Regarding aggregation over consumers, more will be said in 7.4 and 8.2 below.

Let us return to individual choice and, once again, narrow the scope of the theory of individual consumer choice to focus on another important special case – the case when demand behaviour may be summarized by means of a function.

Theorem 7.2.9   If **H** of S_1 is strongly convex-valued, the individual demand correspondence **d** is a function, that is the image of $(\mathbf{p}, \mathbf{m})$ under **d** is a single consumption bundle, namely the first element of $\mathbf{B}(\mathbf{p}, \mathbf{m})$ for **H**.

To complete the sketch of the level-one theory as exposed so far let us try to answer the following question: from the several propositions examined in this section, which ones should be included in $\mathbf{C}(\mathbf{L}_1)$, the empirical core of L_1? So long as we consider the theory in its general scope, a restrictive answer seems to suggest itself. Since the kernel of the theory is the hypothesis of constrained preference satisfaction, homogeneity and summability of the derived demand relation appear, if not as the sole, at least as the main candidates for empirical claims. Claims involving, for instance, transitivity, the existence of a utility function, or properties of the utility function would relate rather to special cases contemplated by the theory and would be better gathered in the core $C(L_2)$ of a level-two theory.

To keep the issue as simple as possible on account of the mainly illustrative character of the example, let us define $C(L_1) = \{d(R): d(HO) \wedge d(SU)\}$, which may be read 'd is a demand relation which is homogeneous and summable'.

7.3   GENERAL-CLASS THEORIES: LANGUAGE AND MODELS

Within the maximal extension of a field, as determined by the scope of a (historically) given basic or general theory, the aim of a level-two general-class theory is to cover one of the field's well-defined, wide, homogeneous classes. This amounts to identifying (in terms of some uniformity criterion) and explaining (by means of a list of common characterizing features) a wide-reaching category of economic phenomena. Hence, within the confines of a class, the language of level two strives for maximum scope and generality of its propositions.

Compared with the basic theory, a level-two theory is narrower in scope and less general in its claims. Compared with a special-class theory, however, a level-two theory is wide in scope and general in its statements. The relative broadness in scope is achieved at the expense of specificity, while the generality of theorems is a consequence of the relative weakness of the assumptions.

Tracing different general-class theories back to their origins in their common basic theory, it is not unusual to detect among them conspicuous differences in their development levels, a consequence of historical priorities as well as the different difficulties associated with the subjects. At level one, for example, the 'classical' theory of consumer choice – transitive, complete or total preferences – and the 'non-classical' theory of consumer choice – non-transitive, non-total preferences – have both strong theoretical foundations, the latter being, of course, more general than the former: see, for instance, Sonnenschein (1971), Shafer (1974), Kim and Richter (1986). At level two, on the other hand, there is much less in the 'non-classical' line when compared with the much older and developed 'classical' theory of consumer demand.

Relational structures of level-two theories are usually richer in detail than relational structures of the underlying basic theory. Regardless of whether these structures include non-observables or only observables among the primitives, functions replace sets as the main mathematical entities for the description of economic concepts. For the latter reason, properties of and operations with functions take the place of properties of and operations with sets in the analytic core of the formal language.

7.4 A GENERAL-CLASS THEORY: STOCHASTIC THEORY OF TRANSITIVE CONSUMER DEMAND

To serve as an illustration of the current discussion we have chosen a version of a stochastic theory of demand in relation to which the principal reference has been Katzner (1970) and, to a much lesser extent, Barten and Böhm (1982) – for more detailed references see the 'Notes and remarks' section at the end of this chapter (7.5).

Although stochastic in nature, interpreted as a theory of the 'average demand function', the theory sketched in this section is founded upon the abstract choice-theoretical framework of level one. It is sufficiently general for our purposes and, at the same time, it constitutes a special case of the theory examined in 7.2. Furthermore, it has the distinct advantage that it will be easy to relate, later on, to relevant theories at levels three and four.

The aim of the theory is to explain demand behaviour of individual consumers when confronted with an exogenously determined and varying price–income situation. A consumer is represented by a set X_2 of all alternative commodity bundles of the form $x = (x_1, \ldots, x_l)$, the so-called 'consumption possibility set', over which she has an appropriate utility function μ which represents her preferences. As opposed to standard deterministic theories, utility does not only depend on the vector of commodities $x \in X_2$, but also on the random disturbance ϵ drawn from a sample space E_2. We shall denote by ν_2 a probability measure on E_2.

As in the level-one theory introduced in 7.2, let $B(p, m)$ be the budget set containing the affordable bundles for the price–income situations (p, m), where $p = (p_1, \ldots, p_l) \in P_2$ and $m > 0$. The theory asserts that for every $\epsilon \in E_2$, and given a pair (p, m), the consumer chooses that commodity bundle x which maximizes $\mu(\cdot, \epsilon)$ on the budget set $B(p, m)$.

Since a consumer's preferences are subject to random shocks, it is correct to speak of the 'average preference ordering' of the consumer. On the other hand, for given (p, m, ϵ) one speaks of the demand $\delta(p, m, \epsilon)$. Using Lebesgue integration, one then obtains the concept of the 'average demand' by setting $d(p, m) = \int_{E_2} \delta(p, m, \epsilon) dv_2$.

An important task of the stochastic theory of demand is to deal with the existence, and furthermore, characterization of the demand function $\delta:(p, m, \epsilon) \to x$, and of the average demand function $d:(p, m) \to x$. We shall return to this point soon.

With the above notation, and continuing with the practice of indexing the primitives which occur in the structures of two or more levels, a possible realization of the stochastic theory of demand is a 5-tuple $\langle X_2, P_2, M_2, (E_2, v_2), \mu \rangle$. We characterize next the models of the theory. Note that, following standard usage, C^o and C^n, will denote the space of continuous functions and n-times continuously differentiable functions (defined over the same domain), respectively, and that a probability measure v_2 on a space E_2 is defined as a countably additive set function from a σ-algebra of subsets of E_2 to $[0, 1]$.

Definition 7.4.1   A system $S_2 = \langle X_2, P_2, M_2, (E_2, v_2), \mu \rangle$ is a *model of the stochastic theory of demand* if it satisfies the following axioms:

A7.4.1 $X_2 = \{x \in R^l: x_i \geq 0; i = 1, \ldots, l\}$.

A7.4.2 $P_2 = \{p \in R^l: p_i > 0; i = 1, \ldots, l\}$.

A7.4.3 $M_2 = \{m \in R: m > 0\}$.

A7.4.4 (E_2, v_2) is a connected probability space, that is E_2 is a connected sample space and v_2 is a probability measure on E_2.

A7.4.5 $\mu: X_2 \times E_2 \to R_+$ is defined as follows: for some $r > 0$ $\exists \phi^k \in C^o$, $k = 1, 2, \ldots, r$ and an appropriate function υ such that:

(a) For all $x \in X_2$, $\mu(x, \epsilon) = \upsilon(x, \phi^1(\epsilon_1), \ldots, \phi^r(\epsilon_r))$, whenever $\epsilon_k = \epsilon$ for all $k = 1, 2, \ldots, r$.

(b) For all $x \in X_2$, $\int_{E_2} \mu(x, \phi(\epsilon)) dv_2 = \upsilon(x, \int_{E_2} \phi(\epsilon) dv_2$ where $\phi(\epsilon) = (\phi^1(\epsilon_1), \ldots, \phi^r(\epsilon_r))$.

(c) For each $(\epsilon_1, \ldots, \epsilon_r)$:

(c1) over int X_2, $\upsilon \in C^2$; and over X_2, $\upsilon \in C^o$ when it is finite;

(c2) over int $\mathbf{X}_2$, $v_i' > 0$ for all $i = 1, 2, \ldots, l$;

(c3) over $\mathbf{X}_2$, v is strictly quasiconcave.

The 'individual consumer' may now be identified with the primitive objects $\mathbf{X}_2 \subset R^l$, $\mathbf{M}_2 \subset R$, and $\mu \subset \mathbf{X}_2 \times \mathbf{E}_2 \times R$. The probability space $(\mathbf{E}_2, v_2)$ and the set $\mathbf{P}_2$ introduce the 'environmental components' for the consumer in the structure. Axioms A7.4.1 to A7.4.4 are straightforward. In that order, they identify the consumption set and the price vectors set as the non-negative and the positive orthant of the Euclidean l-space, respectively, require that income **m** be a strictly positive real number, and describe the mathematical environment of the stochastic element of the model (imposing the topological condition that $\mathbf{E}_2$ consist of 'one single piece'), respectively. A7.4.5 is both technical in nature and a description of how random disturbances affect preferences. In particular, clause (c) imposes rather standard conditions in neoclassical utility theory: (c1) requires the continuity of v on $\mathbf{X}_2$, when finite, and the existence of continuous second-order partial derivatives of v on int $\mathbf{X}_2$, the set of interior points of $\mathbf{X}_2$; (c2) means that, for given $\epsilon \in \mathbf{E}_2$, 'larger bundles are always preferred to smaller ones' (v_i' denotes here the first-order partial derivative of v with respect to the ith argument); finally, (c3) requires strong convexity of preferences, and is thus a condition which guarantees the uniqueness of the utility-maximizing bundle for given ϵ.

This level-two theory of demand is in many respects less general and possesses a much finer constitution than the level-one foundational theory sketched in 7.2. For instance, consumers possess preferences which are not only transitive and complete but also representable by utility functions which are smooth to a much higher degree. The strict quasiconcavity of the latter will lead to demand functions instead of demand correspondences. The presence of the stochastic element may appear as an exception to what we say. However, to the extent that at a certain point of its discourse the theory turns its attention away from the concepts of 'stochastic utility function' and 'stochastic demand function' to focus on its 'expected' or 'average' counterparts, this exception is at most perhaps only a minor one.

Using the stochastic utility function μ one can define the 'expected utility function' **u** as follows.

Definition 7.4.2 $\mathbf{u}(\mathbf{x}) = \int_{E_2} \mu(\mathbf{x}, \epsilon) dv_2.$

The expected utility function **u** is a core piece of the theory, since the 'average demand functions' may be derived directly from it by utility maximization. By construction, the stochastic utility function μ inherits from υ the properties (c1), (c2) and (c3). The following proposition extends these properties to u.

Theorem 7.4.1 u has the following properties:

(1) $u \in C^2$ on int X_2; and $u \in C^0$ whenever $u(x) < \infty$ on X_2.
(2) $u_i'(x) > 0$ for $i = 1, \ldots, l \; \forall x \in$ int X_2.
(3) u is strictly quasiconcave.

Summarizing, the expected utility function possesses itself all the properties of a well-behaved function as was required from μ. Here u_i' denotes the first-order partial derivative of u with respect to the ith argument. We may now define 'average demand' in terms of the expected utility function.

Definition 7.4.3 $\forall B$: $x = d(p, m) \Leftrightarrow u(x) > u(y) \; \forall y \in B, \; x \neq y$.

Next we single out two special cases of separable and of additive utility functions, properties introduced in Definitions 7.2.4 and 7.2.5.

Definition 7.4.4   Let $\{A, B, \ldots, Z\}$ be a partition of the index set $I = \{1, 2, \ldots, l\}$ and denote by $x_A, x_B, \ldots, x_Z$ the corresponding subvectors of $x = (x_1, \ldots, x_l)$. Then the utility function u is said to be *explicitly groupwise separable* if it can be written $u = \Sigma_k u_k(x_k)$ where $k = A, B, \ldots, Z$.

Definition 7.4.5   The utility function u is said to be *explicitly additive* if it can be written $u = \Sigma_i u_i(x_i)$ for $i = 1, 2, \ldots, l$.

The existence (in an appropriate region) of a solution to the utility-maximization problem in terms of the expected utility function u is the subject of the following proposition.

Theorem 7.4.2   Let $\Phi = \{(p, m): p \in P_2, m \in M_2\}$. Then there exists a positive function λ on an open subset $\Phi' \subset \Phi$ such that $x = d(p, m)$ if and only if $u_i'(x) = \lambda(p, m) \cdot p_i, \; i = 1, \ldots, l$, and $p \cdot x = m$.

The difference between the sets Φ and Φ' involves technical considerations that are not relevant to our current discussion and will not concern us here – the reader is referred to Katzner (1970). Observe, instead, that the equations $u_i'(x) = \lambda(p, m)p_i$, where λ is the Lagrange multiplier, are the standard first-order conditions for (deterministic) utility maximization subject to the constraint $p \cdot x \leq m$.

We remind ourselves of the concept of indirect utility function first introduced in 7.2 and then define the notion of expenditure function.

Definition 7.4.6 The function $v: \Phi' \rightarrow R$ such that $v(p, m) = \max u(x)$ is called the *indirect utility function*; the function $e: P_2 \times R_{++} \rightarrow R_{++}$ defined by $e(p, u^*) = \min p \cdot m$ such that $u(x) \geq u^*$ is called the *expenditure function*.

Theorem 7.4.3 The indirect utility function v is:

(1) continuously differentiable on Φ';
(2) homogeneous of degree zero in p and m;
(3) increasing in m;
(4) non-increasing and quasiconvex in p.

The expenditure function e is:

(1) continuously differentiable on $P_2 \times R_{++}$;
(2) homogeneous of degree one in p, that is, for $\lambda > 0$, $e(\lambda p, u^*) = \lambda e(p, u^*)$;
(3) increasing in u;
(4) non-decreasing and concave in p.

In Theorem 7.4.3, properties (1) to (3) of the indirect utility function v are straightforward; so is the first part of (4); regarding the second part of (4), we note that a function $f: X \rightarrow R$ is said to be *quasiconvex* if and only if for all x_1, x_2 in X and $\lambda \in [0, 1]$, $f[\lambda x_1 + (1-\lambda)x_2] \leq \max[f(x_1), f(x_2)]$. Properties (1) to (4) of the expenditure function e are, again, straightforward.

Definition 7.4.7 Let $\{A, B, \ldots, Z\}$ be a partition of the index set $I = \{1, 2, \ldots, l\}$ and denote by $p_A, p_B, \ldots, p_Z$ the corresponding subvectors of $p = (p_1, \ldots, p_l)$. Then the indirect utility function v is said to be *explicitly groupwise separable* if it can be written $v = \Sigma_k v_k(p_k, m)$ for $k = A, B, \ldots, Z$.

Definition 7.4.8 The indirect utility function v is said to be *explicitly additive* if it can be written $v = \Sigma_i v_i(p_i, m)$ for $i = 1, 2, \ldots, l$.

The following proposition, known for its author as 'Roy's identity' – Roy (1942) – concerns the derivation of individual demand functions from indirect utility functions.

Theorem 7.4.4   On Φ' $d_i(p, m) = -[\partial v(p, m)/\partial p_i]/[\partial v(p, m)/\partial m]$, $i = 1, 2, \ldots, l$.

The function $d(p, m)$ of our preceding discussion is often called the *ordinary* or *Marshallian demand function*. A related, non-observable object is the *Hicksian* or *compensated demand function* $h(p, u)$. The latter is constructed by varying prices and simultaneously varying income in a 'compensating' way so as to keep the consumer at the given fixed level of utility. The following proposition relates the Hicksian demand function h to the expenditure function e.

Theorem 7.4.5   On $P_2 \times R_{++}$ $h_i(p, u) = \partial e(p, u)/\partial p_i$, $i = 1, 2, \ldots, l$.

It is a well-known result of demand theory that the effect of a change in the price p_j on the demand of the ith commodity (the Slutsky or substitution term s_{ij}) can be decomposed as the sum of a pure substitution and a pure income effect. Using Hicksian demand to represent the pure or income-compensated substitution effect, one obtains the following relationship.

Theorem 7.4.6   Let x^* maximize u at (p^*, m^*) and let $u = u(x^*)$. Then $s_{ij}(p, m) = \partial d_i(p, m)/\partial p_j = \partial h_i(p, u)/\partial p_j - [\partial d_i(p, m)/\partial m] \cdot d_j(p, m)$.

The relation of Theorem 7.4.6 is the well-known Slutsky equation. Arranging in matrix form all s_{ij} for i, j $= 1, \ldots, l$ one obtains the 'Slutsky matrix'.

Definition 7.4.9

$$S = S(p, m) = \begin{pmatrix} s_{11}(p, m) & \ldots & s_{1l}(p, m) \\ \vdots & & \vdots \\ s_{l1}(p, m) & \ldots & s_{ll}(p, m) \end{pmatrix}$$

It is now possible to extend this sample of stochastic demand theory with a summary characterization of the average demand function derived from the expected utility function u, and to establish a link between **d** and δ. The first four theorems which follow are fundamental results of demand theory, deterministic or stochastic; here, of course, referred to the function **d**.

Theorem 7.4.7 On Φ′ **d** is continuously differentiable (continuous differentiability).

Theorem 7.4.8 On Φ′ **d** is homogeneous of degree zero, that is, **d(p, m)** = **d**(λ**p**, λ**m**) when λ > 0 (homogeneity).

Theorem 7.4.9 On Φ′ **d(p*, m*)** · **p*** = **m** (summability).

Theorem 7.4.10 On Φ′ s_{ij}(**p, m**) = s_{ji}(**p, m**) (symmetry).

Theorem 7.4.11 On Φ′ the matrix **S** = **S(p, m)** is negative semi-definite, that is, **zSz′** ≤ 0 if **z** ≠ 0 (monotonicity).

Theorems 7.4.7 to 7.4.11 characterize the individual demand function as the product of constrained utility maximization. Strictly speaking, continuity or differentiability are mathematical properties not directly observable in empirical data but rather technical conditions whose presence in the functions is required for analytic–linguistic (mathematical) reasons. The economic interpretation, however, is that 'small and smooth changes' in the arguments of **d**, that is **p** and **m**, are always followed by 'small and smooth changes' (not 'catastrophic' or even 'kinky' jumps) in the choice decisions. Homogeneity, summability of the value of the demanded quantities or value shares, and the symmetry and negative semi-definiteness of the matrix **S** are properties of an observable, the individual consumer's demand function. It is therefore natural to consider the last four theorems as testable propositions of the theory that should be included in its core of empirical claims.

A problem of great theoretical and empirical import within individual consumer's demand analysis is the 'integrability' of the set of commodity demand functions. In other words, what properties characterize demand functions as the result of constrained utility maximization? Suppose we start with a set of *l* functions – think, for instance, of a set of *l* numerical functions which, we are told, are the measured demand functions of an individual household – and try to answer one or both of the following two strongly related questions: are these relations demand functions in the sense of the theory of individual consumer demand, that is, are they the result of constrained utility maximization? Alternatively, if these functions are 'actual' demand functions in the sense of representing observed and measured empirical choice actions, have they been generated by a utility-maximizing behaviour? There is a clear link between the problem of recovering the generating utility function from the given demand functions and the issue of the validity of the main propositions of the theory of individual consumer demand. An answer to the integrability problem is summarized in the following theorem.

Theorem 7.4.12   Let the l-vector valued function $\mathbf{d}(\mathbf{p}, \mathbf{m})$ from Φ' to $\mathbf{X}_2$ be continuously differentiable and satisfy the following conditions:

  (1) homogeneity of degree zero in $\mathbf{p}$ and $\mathbf{m}$;
  (2) summability;
  (3) symmetry of its matrix $\mathbf{S}$;
  (4) negative semi-definiteness of its matrix $\mathbf{S}$ (monotonicity).

Then there exists a utility function $\mathbf{u}$ defined on the range $\mathbf{d}(\Phi')$ of $\mathbf{d}$ such that the value $\mathbf{x}$ of $\mathbf{d}$ at $(\mathbf{p}, \mathbf{m})$ maximizes uniquely $\mathbf{u}$ over the budget set $\mathbf{B}(\mathbf{p}, \mathbf{m})$.

Theorem 7.4.12 may be regarded as a converse of the combined results of Theorems 7.4.7 to 7.4.11. The latter characterized a demand function as the result of constrained utility maximization. The former guarantees the recoverability of the utility function from a continuously differentiable vector function with the characterizing properties. In the literature it is frequent to require, in addition to the four properties listed in Theorem 7.4.12, the condition $\mathbf{d}(\mathbf{p}, \mathbf{m}) \geq 0$ for all $(\mathbf{p}, \mathbf{m})$. Note that this is made unnecessary here for our choice of $\mathbf{X}_2$.

As we did in 7.2, let us briefly comment on the *theory of aggregate demand*, in particular on the *theory of market demand*. In line with what we said in 7.2, individual demand functions may be aggregated over commodities, defining individual demand functions for composite commodities, or over consumers, defining market demand functions for single commodities, or over both. The conditions under which aggregation is admissible and the integrability properties of demand functions are preserved are the object of aggregation theory. It follows from the comment made in 7.2 that the conditions for aggregation over commodities refer to specific properties of the utility function or the indirect utility function generically known as 'separability' properties, a few of which have been met above in this section and in 7.2. The problem of aggregation over consumers has, in a way, a less satisfactory answer. For instance, it is known that besides continuity, among the integrability properties of individual demand functions only homogeneity and summability are also properties of market demand functions in the general case – see, for instance, Sonnenschein (1973, 1974), Debreu (1974), Mantel (1974) and Shafer and Sonnenschein (1982). More about the latter will be said below in 8.2.

Again, as we did in 7.2 for the level-one theory, we should ask ourselves here about the propositions of the expounded level-two theory which should be lifted in the core $C(L_2)$. A restrictive answer suggests the properties (of the demand relation) homogeneity, summability, being a function, symmetry, negative semi-definiteness and monotonicity as appropriate candidates. The central hypothesis of the theory is, after all, constrained utility maximization. With this point of view, claims regarding, for example, the mathematical form of the direct or indirect utility function generating the demand functions are more properly taken care of in $C(L_3)$, the core of a level-three theory.

Continuing the example initiated in the last paragraph of 7.2 and with the same aim we expressed then, we now define $C(L_2) = \{d(R): d(HO) \wedge d(SU) \wedge d(FU) \wedge d(SY) \wedge d(NS) \wedge d(MO)\}$, which reads 'd is a demand relation which is homogeneous, summable, a function, symmetric, negative semi-definite and monotonic'. Of course, we have chosen the example carefully to obtain the special and very desirable situation $C(L_1) \subseteq C(L_2)$. Note too that whereas theory L_2 is a special case of theory L_1 the empirical core of L_1 is contained here in the empirical core of L_2.

7.5 NOTES AND REMARKS

As we have already discussed in Chapter 6, the point in the discourse where the basic theory of individual choice ends and the general-class theory of transitive consumer demand begins does not belong to the essence of the problem for there are alternative ways to axiomatize a theory. The choice made in this chapter is only one of many possibilities and has been dictated by the wish to underline the complexity of some semantic systems and the different roles played by different theories and models within such systems. This will become even more evident in Chapter 8 where we deal with theories L_3 and L_4.

In contrast to what was done in Chapter 3, we did not discuss here the relation between the line of reasoning which derives demand relations from preference satisfaction or utility maximization and the 'revealed preferences approach'. To follow these connections from the foundations level on, the reader is referred to the already mentioned articles by Richter (1971) – for the theory of the transitive, complete consumer – and Kim and Richter (1986) – for the theory of the non-transitive, non-total consumer.

Examples to illustrate levels one and two of our scheme could have been chosen from other fields of theoretical economics, in particular the analysis of production. For example, one could put together a foundations or general theory of the firm on the basis of Debreu (1959) and parts of Nadiri (1982), and a general-class theory using parts of Nadiri (1982) and Shephard (1953, 1970).

8 Representational Theories and Theoretical Systems (II): Special-Class Theory and Data-Specific Theory

In this chapter we shall complete the illustration of the scheme developed in Chapter 6 for the case of a system of representational theories by focusing on its two upper levels. Proceeding in a fashion similar to that of Chapter 7, we give for each of the two types of theories a summary characterization of language and structures followed by a detailed example from the actual practice of economic science. Section 8.5 will then re-examine the question of inter-level theoretical links.

8.1 SPECIAL-CLASS THEORIES: LANGUAGE AND MODELS

At level three of the hierarchy we find a testable theory, in the sense of being an economic theory which incorporates in its body not only a set of substantive economic propositions in a formulation which is suitable for tests (parametric representation), but also the pertinent norms that govern testing and/or estimation procedures plus the generic assumptions which determine the admissibility of the data. It is most likely to be a mathematic–statistical theory or, using the terminology which is standard in economic research and which emphasizes both the substantive and the methodological aspects of the problem, an econometric theory.

Level three of the analytic scheme, we believe, corresponds to what Suppes (1962) has in mind when he speaks of 'the theory of the experiment'. We avoid using this terminology here on the grounds that, to an overwhelming extent, empirical procedures in economic research are of a non-experimental nature. To parallel Suppes's (1962) characterization, one could perhaps make use of the denomination 'theory of the testing and/or estimation procedure', a name that would include 'experiment' among the possible 'testing procedures'. For reasons that, we hope, will become clear in this section, we could also refer to it as the 'theory of observable–estimable structures'.

The goal of a level-three economic theory is, within our scheme, to set the ground rules for the testing of a set of well-determined propositions – possibly including the estimation of a list of parameters – by means of very concrete testing operations and for structures of empirical data with well-specified properties. This determines, in turn, some of the main characteristics of the theory.

The general formulations of the theory of level two find their counterpart, at level three, in a much finer specification. Appropriately formulated – or, if need be, its axiom base systemically reconstructed (see 6.3.1 and 7.5) – L_3 does not speak of general properties of non-observables (for example, 'twice continuously differentiable utility functions') but rather of a much more narrowly defined functional form of an observable (for instance, 'transcendental logarithmic demand function').

It is clear that a strong, detailed specification of a functional form definitely narrows the scope and generality of a theory. If generality and broad scope are features of level-two economic theories, then specificity and narrow scope characterize economic theories at level three. In this sense, the economic theory of level three is a special case, so far as its substantive content is concerned, of the economic theory of level two.

The detailed specification of functional forms is also related in several respects to the availability of testing procedures, their particular conditions, and the generic characteristics of the data. A particular testing procedure usually imposes further restrictions on the choice of functional forms, something that may go far beyond the simple need of specificity. Special functional forms that would be admissible with regard to the requirements of the general-class theory may not be acceptable in terms of the available testing and estimation methods. Quite often, even 'approximations' become indispensable. Finally, it should be pointed out that the properties of the data, those of a generic nature (for instance, finiteness, discreteness) as well as some more circumstantial attributes (for example, length of time series, presence of multicollinearity) further increase the need for strong specification.

The theory of level three also contains a detailed formal account of the (econometric) estimation and/or testing procedure and possibly of projection techniques. Problems of identification are typical of this level; problems of degrees of freedom are too. For instance, in this latter respect, the insufficient length of the actual time series is often mentioned as a typical difficulty. A common procedure to gain degrees of freedom in such circumstances is to use some results from the level-two theory as restrictions on the equations to be estimated. It is clear that the arbitrary imposition of such a method may improve the estimates (assuming the restrictions are valid) but may hardly be acceptable when what is at issue is precisely the test of the empirical validity of such theoretically founded restrictions. More sophisticated procedural rules have to be followed in such cases and it is a task for the theory to spell them out.

The data, finally, present their own problems in relation to theoretical presuppositions. For instance, and very commonly, where the theory speaks of individual commodities, individual prices, or individual behaviour, the data only refer to added-up groups of commodities, average prices for sets of goods, and aggregate behaviour. The theory of aggregation thus becomes a component of a level-three theory inasmuch as it lays down conditions the data must satisfy.

The language of the theory of this level, as opposed to that of level two, will originate in the more computation-oriented branches of mathematics, like calculus, linear algebra and applied mathematical statistics.

A structure S_3 is in an important way different from a structure S_2 since it must satisfy conditions which, in a sense, reflect some basic features of actual data (for instance, finiteness and discreteness). Yet the structural axioms of L_3 do not point to any actual set of empirical data but, somewhat from a distance, to collections of structures the domains of which consist of empirical data satisfying well-prescribed generic properties. Indeed, carrying the argument further, it will not be the special-class theory that will be directly and immediately confronted with the structure of data of level four but, instead, that adapted linguistic entity which we have been calling the concrete (data-conform) theory.

8.2. A SPECIAL-CLASS THEORY: THE DIRECT TRANSLOG DEMAND SYSTEM

In empirical economics research much effort has been devoted to testing the empirical validity of some of the main propositions of the (abstract) theory of demand and to the estimation of 'complete' systems of demand functions – for a survey, see Deaton (1986). Studies of this kind have consisted in the construction of alternative level-three theories of individual demand, several of which are consistent with – and may actually be regarded as special cases of – the level-two stochastic theory of demand.

To illustrate the case of level-three and level-four theories we shall choose here examples involving the 'direct transcendental logarithmic (or translog) demand system' (DTLDS for short). For reasons commented upon earlier, we avoid the frequently used expression 'model' to designate this and other theories of this level and use instead the words 'system' or 'theory'. The main references for our exposition in this section are the seminal articles by Christensen, Jorgenson and Lau (1975), Jorgenson and Lau (1979), and Jorgenson, Lau and Stoker (1982) and the book by Amemiya (1986) – a few additional references are given in the 'Notes and remarks' section (8.6).

The notation we use here is basically similar to that of 7.4. Additionally, the following concept is useful. If $\mathbf{p}$ is a price vector, $\mathbf{x}$ a commodity bundle, and $\mathbf{m}$ income (or, more strictly, expenditure $\mathbf{p} \cdot \mathbf{x}$), then the following vector is called, for obvious reasons, the vector of 'value shares' or 'budget shares':

$$\begin{pmatrix} \mathbf{w}_1 \\ \vdots \\ \mathbf{w}_l \end{pmatrix} = \begin{pmatrix} \mathbf{m}^{-1} \cdot \mathbf{p}_1 \cdot \mathbf{x}_1 \\ \vdots \\ \mathbf{m}^{-1} \cdot \mathbf{p}_l \cdot \mathbf{x}_l \end{pmatrix} \qquad \text{with } \Sigma_i \mathbf{w}_i = 1.$$

The DTLDS is a system of demand (share) equations which explains the allocation of the individual consumer's income (or total expenditure) among a finite number of commodities. Standard explanatory variables are the l commodity prices $\mathbf{p}_i$ and the consumer's income (or total expenditure) $\mathbf{m}$. In the particular version of the DTLDS that we have adopted here and in 8.4, preferences are time-dependent and thus a time variable $\mathbf{t}$ enters each demand function. In more refined versions of the theory – see, for instance, Jorgenson, Lau and Stoker (1982) – each demand function also incorporates variables that allow us to identify the characteristics of the individual consumers.

Before we go into some of the details of the theory, a few remarks regarding axiomatization and interpretation seem desirable.

Let us begin by commenting on the axiomatic version chosen for this example. As we pointed out in the preceding pages – especially in the context of the discussion of 6.3.1 and in 7.5 – there is usually more than one choice for the status of primitives and axiom base for the intermediate and higher-level theories of a multi-level theoretical system. We have chosen here a version of DTLDS which includes among the primitives the observable demand function $\mathbf{d}$ and not the non-observable utility function $\mathbf{u}$. Consistently, the axiom base of our chosen version of DTLDS is formulated at the level of $\mathbf{d}$ instead of $\mathbf{u}$.

This choice should not be construed to mean that one cannot found the DTLDS upon the notion of direct utility or indirect utility. Indeed, in particular, it is perfectly legitimate to postulate the existence of an indirect (translog) utility function as the primitive, and to obtain from it the derived notion of an average vector demand function. Given our target, however, we shall follow here the opposite direction, that is, to take the average vector demand function as primitive and then, by pointing to its integrability, to claim the existence of an indirect utility function (or class of functions). The latter is also a very frequent practice in applied research – see Jorgenson and Lau (1979) and Conrad and Jorgenson (1979). Later, in 8.4, we shall take a similar approach when selecting our example of a level-four theory.

Now to the question of interpretation. Although the demand functions of the DTLDS represent individual demand functions, the system is usually estimated using aggregate per capita data on consumption and then tested for integrability. The latter is sometimes justified with reference to the convenience of having at one's disposal restrictions on the system of aggregate demand functions.

From a strictly theoretical viewpoint, one might argue that it does not make much sense to interpret the demand functions as aggregate demand functions and to subject them to tests that are only relevant at the individual demand level. As pointed out in 7.4, and excluding the exceptional case of homothetic preferences and income distribution independent of prices, from the properties of individual demand functions that constitute sufficient conditions for integrability – the recoverability of the generating direct or indirect utility function – only homogeneity and the budget condition are inherited by aggregate demand functions (Sonnenschein, 1973, 1974; Debreu, 1974; Mantel, 1974; and, Shafer and Sonnenschein, 1982). For instance, as a case in point, there is no theoretical ground for the Slutsky matrices of aggregate demand functions to be at all symmetric.

However, it should be also pointed out that if the aggregate demand functions do satisfy the integrability (and some other) conditions, then there exists a 'community utility function' that generates them and that is consistent with utility maximization at the individual level as well.

There is still a further possible interpretative position. Indeed, one may take the view that when the l individual scalar functions of a DTLDS – and similar arguments would apply to alternative level-three demand theories – are estimated and tested with aggregate per capita variables, they should be interpreted as the demand functions for a list of (usually, composite) commodities by a *representative consumer* and, when they pass all integrability tests, do point to the existence of a direct or indirect utility function of this representative consumer. The notion of a representative consumer – in general, of a *representative agent* – is far from free of controversy in the economic literature and is a topic of discussion in the theory of aggregation. Here, given the characteristics of the theory and keeping in mind the primarily illustrative purposes of the discussion, the representative consumer interpretation would seem to fit our objectives acceptably well. We may add, in passing, that a much more elaborate translog aggregate demand theory, based on a more sophisticated notion of a representative consumer or, perhaps better stated, of a *set* of representative consumers for consumer classes, is described in Jorgenson, Lau and Stoker (1982). However, to expose the latter would unnecessarily lengthen and complicate this chapter.

A possible realization of the DTLDS is a structure $\langle \mathbf{X}_3, \mathbf{P}_3, \mathbf{M}_3, (\mathbf{t} = 1, 2, \ldots, T), (\mathbf{E}_3, \mathbf{v}_3), \mathbf{d} \rangle$ where the number of commodities has been fixed, say at l, and the number of observations in the variables has also been fixed, say at T. $\mathbf{X}_3$ is now the set of all finite sequences of length T of vectors $\mathbf{x}_t$ of l commodities; $\mathbf{P}_3$ is the set of all finite sequences of length T of l-component price vectors $\mathbf{p}_t$; $\mathbf{M}_3$ is the set of all finite sequences of length T of budgets $\mathbf{m}_t = \mathbf{p}_t \cdot \mathbf{x}_t$; $\mathbf{t}$ is a trend; $\mathbf{E}_3$ is a sample space of random disturbances ϵ_t; $\mathbf{v}_3$ is the distribution for the ϵ_t; and $\mathbf{d}$ is the vector demand function that maps a 4-tuple $(\mathbf{p}_t, \mathbf{m}_t, \mathbf{t}, \epsilon_t)$ into a commodity bundle $\mathbf{x}_t$.

Compared with a possible realization of the 'stochastic theory of transitive consumer demand of Definition 7.4.1 – or with the alternative axiomatizations of the DTLDS just referred to – one notes that the current set-theoretical structure $\mathbf{S}_3$ includes among the primitives the demand function $\mathbf{d}$ and not the utility function $\mathbf{u}$.

As in the case of other level-three demand theories, the aim of the DTLDS is to specify a suitable functional form for $\mathbf{d}$ which is compatible with the general theory, specifying, in particular, parametric conditions under which testable properties of the level-three demand function will parallel properties of the level-two demand function, and to lay down stochastic assumptions for ϵ and to determine, accordingly, an admissible estimation procedure. We first define the models of the econometric DTLDS and then sample a few of its propositions.

Definition 8.2.1   The structure $\mathbf{S}_3 = \langle \mathbf{X}_3, \mathbf{P}_3, \mathbf{M}_3, (\mathbf{t} = 1, 2, \ldots, T), (\mathbf{E}_3, \mathbf{v}_3), \mathbf{d} \rangle$ is a *model of the DTLDS* if and only if it satisfies the following assumptions:

A8.2.1 $\mathbf{X}_3$ is the set of all finite sequences $(\mathbf{x}_t: t = 1, 2, \ldots, T)$ of real l-component vectors of the form $\mathbf{x}_t = (\mathbf{x}_{1t}, \ldots, \mathbf{x}_{lt})$ where $\mathbf{x}_{it}$ represents the per capita consumption by the individual representative consumer of the ith commodity during the tth period.

A8.2.2 $\mathbf{P}_3$ is the set of all finite sequences $(\mathbf{p}_t: t = 1, 2, \ldots, T)$ of real l-component vectors of the form $\mathbf{p}_t = (\mathbf{p}_{1t}, \ldots, \mathbf{p}_{lt})$ where $\mathbf{p}_{it}$ represents the price of the ith commodity during the tth period.

A8.2.3 $\mathbf{M}_3$ is the set of all finite sequences $(\mathbf{m}_t: t = 1, 2, \ldots, T)$ of scalars of the form $\mathbf{m}_t = \mathbf{p}_t \cdot \mathbf{x}_t$, denoting the per capita total expenditure of the individual representative consumer during the tth period.

A8.2.4 $\mathbf{E}_3$ is the set of all finite sequences $(\epsilon_t: t = 1, 2, \ldots, T)$ of random vector disturbances of the form $\epsilon_t = (\epsilon_{1t}, \ldots, \epsilon_{lt})$.

A8.2.5 $\mathbf{d}$ is a function that maps each 4-tuple $(\mathbf{p}_t, \mathbf{m}_t, \mathbf{t}, \epsilon_t)$ in $\mathbf{P}_3 \times \mathbf{M}_3 \times \mathbf{t} \times \mathbf{E}_3$ into a vector $\mathbf{x}_t$ in $\mathbf{X}_3$ according to the formula:

$$\mathbf{d}_{it} = \mathbf{w}_{it} = \mathbf{p}_{it} \cdot \mathbf{x}_{it}/\mathbf{m}_t$$

$$= \frac{\alpha_i + \Sigma_j \beta_{ij} \ln(\mathbf{p}_{jt}/\mathbf{m}_t) + \beta_{it} \cdot t}{-1 + \Sigma_j \beta_{mj} \ln(\mathbf{p}_{jt}/\mathbf{m}_t) + \beta^i_{mt} \cdot t} + \epsilon_{it},$$

$$i = 1, 2, \ldots, l.$$

A8.2.6   The random disturbance vectors $(\epsilon_{1t}, \ldots, \epsilon_{lt})$ are distributed according to the normal distribution $\mathbf{v}_3$ such that

$$\Sigma_i \epsilon_{it} = 0$$
$$E(\epsilon_{it}) = 0$$
$$E(\epsilon_{is}\, \epsilon_{jt}) = \sigma^2 \quad \text{if } s = t$$
$$E(\epsilon_{is}\, \epsilon_{jt}) = 0 \quad \text{if } s \neq t.$$

A8.2.7   The equations system A8.2.5 is identified.

Note that the 'individual representative consumer' is now characterized by the primitive objects $\mathbf{X}_3 \subset R^l$, $\mathbf{M}_3 \subset R$ $\mathbf{t}$ and $\mathbf{d} \subset \mathbf{P}_3 \times \mathbf{M}_3 \times \mathbf{t} \times \mathbf{E}_3$ where $\mathbf{d}$ has taken the place of μ or $\mathbf{u}$. The probability space $(\mathbf{E}_3, \mathbf{v}_3)$ and the set $\mathbf{P}_3$ define the 'environmental components' for the consumer in the structure.

We now comment briefly on the axiom base. Assumptions A8.2.1 to A.8.2.3 determine the sets of admissible data, namely, sequences of real numbers referring to the demands of a finite number (l) of consumption commodities, the prices of these commodities and the total expenditures occurring during a finite number of periods (T). Hence, they may be regarded as the structural axioms of the theory at this level. Once A8.2.4 has introduced the non-observable random disturbance vector ϵ_t, A8.2.5 describes in detail the postulated relations between the l explained variables (relative share of each commodity in the consumer's expenditure) and the $l + 2$ explanatory variables (l prices, total expenditure and the variable time), that is the DTLDS. It is worthwhile to compare this mathematically very specific system of demand functions with the sparsely described demand functions of the level-two theory and with the even more abstract constructs (for instance, correspondences) of the level-one theory.

Axiom A8.2.6 lists the stochastic specifications. It is required in this particular example that the vector disturbances ϵ_t be normally distributed, have zero expectation and a covariance matrix which admits contemporaneous correlation while excluding both heteroscedasticity and autocorrelation. Furthermore, note that the condition $\Sigma_i \epsilon_{it} = 0$ is a consequence of the fact that the actual commodity shares in the consumer's budget must add up to unity. The laying down of the stochastic assumptions is most important for the determination of the appropriate estimation and testing procedures. Note too, in this context, that to the extent that a system like the one described in A8.2.5 above might be consistent with more than one set of alternative stochastic specifications, different alternative estimation and testing procedures might be singled out as the appropriate ones. In other words, we may face, even here, rather than a unique theory, a whole class of theories from which we need to select one – each member of the class associated with a different stochastic specification and thus with a different estimation and testing procedure. Finally, A8.2.7 requires the system to be identified.

The theory formulated here has been founded upon a set of observable primitives, namely the individual representative consumer demand functions for single or composite commodities (or, what is equivalent, the average vector demand function) that constitute the DTLDS. As pointed out before, this formulation is frequent in empirical studies – see Conrad and Jorgenson (1979) and Jorgenson and Lau (1979) – and is particularly well suited to illustrate levels three and four of our analytic scheme. The standard alternative consists in postulating as primitive a direct or indirect translog utility function – see Christensen, Jorgenson and Lau (1975) – and obtaining from it the l demand functions (that is, the l-vector function) via Roy's identity, as pointed out in 7.4. The following result summarizes the properties of the demand functions – see Jorgenson, Lau and Stoker (1982).

Theorem 8.2.1 The DTLDS of S_3 (see A8.2.5) satisfies the following properties:

(1) homogeneity: $\forall i$: w_i is independent of total expenditure for given normalized prices;
(2) summability: $\Sigma_i w_i = 1$;
(3) symmetry: $\forall i$: the matrix of compensated own- and cross-price effects is symmetric;
(4) non-negativity: $\forall i$: $w_i \geq 0$;
(5) monotonicity: $\forall i$: the matrix of compensated own- and cross-price effects is negative semi-definite.

Due to (1), (2) and (3) in Theorem 8.2.1 the DTLDS can be generated as the solution to a constrained utility maximization problem. Conversely, and focusing this time on the indirect utility function, let us now establish a few links between indirect utility and demand in the very specific context of the DTLDS. Two important results follow.

Theorem 8.2.2 An indirect utility function **v** generating the DTLDS **d** of A8.2.5 can be represented in the functional form $\ln \mathbf{v} = \ln \mathbf{v}$ $(\mathbf{p}_1/\mathbf{m}, \ldots, \mathbf{p}_l/\mathbf{m}, \mathbf{t})$ called the indirect translog utility function (ITLUF) **v**.

Theorem 8.2.3 A local second-order approximation to the ITLUF **v** is the quadratic function in the ratios $\mathbf{p}_i/\mathbf{m}$, $i = 1, 2, \ldots, l$, $\ln \mathbf{v} = \alpha_o + \Sigma_i \ln(\mathbf{p}_i/\mathbf{m}) + (1/2)\Sigma_i\Sigma_j\beta_{ij} \ln(\mathbf{p}_i/\mathbf{m}) \cdot \ln(\mathbf{p}_j/\mathbf{m}) + (1/2) \beta_{tt}t^2$.

We are now ready to formulate the integration problem in the concrete case of the DTLDS. Since it should be clear that we assume that the equations system satisfies homogeneity, summability and symmetry as demanded by the relevant axioms, we do not need explicitly to list these properties in the definition which follows.

Theorem 8.2.4 The DTLDS can be generated as the solution of the system of partial differential equations $\partial \ln \mathbf{v}/\partial(\mathbf{p}_j/\mathbf{m}) = \mathbf{w}_j\Sigma_i\partial \ln \mathbf{v}/\partial \ln(\mathbf{p}_i/\mathbf{m})$, $j = 1, 2, \ldots, l$, defining a family of ITLUF **v**.

To be precise, it is properties (1), (2) and (3) of Theorem 8.2.1 that guarantee integrability. Furthermore, because of (4) and (5), these indirect utility functions can be obtained from one another by means of monotonically increasing transformations.

Parallel to what was done in 7.2 and 7.4, we define notions of groupwise separability and additivity in the context of the DTLDS. In our example we shall use two rather strong forms of these properties, namely, 'explicit groupwise separability' and 'explicit additivity'.

Definition 8.2.2 Let $\{A, B, \ldots, Z\}$ be a partition of the index set $I = \{1, 2, \ldots, l\}$ and denote by $\mathbf{p}_A, \mathbf{p}_B, \ldots, \mathbf{p}_Z$ the corresponding subvectors of $\mathbf{p} = (\mathbf{p}_1, \ldots, \mathbf{p}_l)$. Then the ITLUF $\mathbf{v}$ is said to be *explicitly groupwise separable* in $A, B, \ldots, Z$ if it can be written $\ln \mathbf{v} = \Sigma_k \ln \mathbf{v}_k(\mathbf{p}_k/\mathbf{m}, \mathbf{t})$, for $k = A, B, \ldots, Z$.

Theorem 8.2.5 A necessary and sufficient condition for the ITLUF $\mathbf{v}$ to be explicitly groupwise separable in $A, B, \ldots, Z$ is that the ratios of budget shares for $\mathbf{x}_k$, $k = A, B, \ldots, Z$ be independent of $\mathbf{p}_h$, $h = A, B, \ldots, Z$ when $k \neq h$.

Definition 8.2.3 The ITLUF $\mathbf{v}$ is said to be *explicitly additive* if it can be written $\ln \mathbf{v} = \Sigma_i \ln \mathbf{v}_i(\mathbf{p}_i/\mathbf{m}, \mathbf{t})$ for $i = 1, 2, \ldots, l$.

A sound methodological rule suggests that the empirical testing of the theory – that is, in our case and up to this point, of the five properties of Theorem 8.2.1 – should be done in successive steps by first estimating a larger and more general system than the DTLDS and then, after imposing on this system the restrictions implied by the properties to be tested, re-estimating and performing the corresponding tests. The wider system is defined next.

Definition 8.2.4 The unrestricted DTLDS (UDTLDS) associated with the DTLDS of Definition 8.2.1, A8.2.5, is the system

$$\mathbf{f}_{it}(\mathbf{w}_t, \mathbf{z}_t, \gamma_i) = \mathbf{w}_{it} = \mathbf{p}_{it} \cdot \mathbf{x}_{it}/\mathbf{m}_t$$

$$= \frac{\alpha_i + \Sigma_j \beta_{ij} \ln(\mathbf{p}_{jt}/\mathbf{m}_t) + \beta_{im} \ln \mathbf{m}_t + \beta_{it} \cdot \mathbf{t}}{-1 + \Sigma_j \beta^i_{mj} \ln(\mathbf{p}_{jt}/\mathbf{m}_t) + \beta^i_{mm} \ln \mathbf{m}_t + \beta^i_{mt} \cdot \mathbf{t}}$$

$$+ \epsilon_{it}; \quad i = 1, 2, \ldots, l, \ t = 1, 2, \ldots, T,$$

where $\mathbf{w}_t$ is the l-vector of endogenous variables, $\mathbf{z}_t = (\mathbf{p}_t, \mathbf{m}_t, \mathbf{t})$ is the $(l + 2)$-vector of exogenous variables, γ_i is the $(5 + 2l)$-vector of unknown parameters $(\alpha_i, \beta_{i1}, \ldots, \beta_{il}, \ldots, \beta^i_{mm}, \beta^i_m)$ of the ith equation and ϵ_{it} is the random disturbance described in A8.2.4 and A8.2.6. For the purpose of statistical tests, the UTLDS is designated as the *maintained hypothesis*.

We focus now on a few essential econometric–statistical statements of the theory. To begin with, the following proposition determines a possible estimation method.

Theorem 8.2.6 Let $\mathbf{f}_{it}(\mathbf{w}_t, \mathbf{z}_t, \gamma_i) = \epsilon_{it}$ $(i = 1, 2, \ldots, l)$, $(t = 1, 2, \ldots, T)$ be the UDTLDS of Definition 8.2.4 and let $\Gamma = (\gamma_1', \ldots, \gamma_l')$ be the matrix of its unknown parameters. Then:

(1) the non-linear full information maximum likelihood (shorter, ML) estimator of the unknown parameters of the UDTLDS is the value $\underline{\Gamma}$ of Γ that maximizes the concentrated log likelihood function

$$\mathbf{L} = \Sigma_t \log\|\partial\mathbf{f}_t/\partial\mathbf{w}_t'\| - (T/2)\log|(1/T)\Sigma_t\mathbf{f}_t\mathbf{f}_t'|;$$

(2) because of A8.2.6, the ML estimator of Γ in the complete UDTLDS is equivalent to the estimator obtained by dropping one equation, estimating the remaining $l - 1$ equations by ML, and then deriving the estimates of the omitted equation from the $l - 1$ equations not omitted;

(3) the ML estimator of Γ is consistent and asymptotically normal.

The following proposition determines the methodology that, beginning with the UDTLDS, finally leads to the consumer-theory conform DTLDS.

Theorem 8.2.7 ML estimates of the DTLDS are obtained by re-estimating the UDTLDS under the following restrictions.

(1) Homogeneity:

$$\beta_{1m} = \ldots = \beta_{l-1m} = \beta_{mm}^1 = \ldots = \beta_{mm}^{l-1} = 0$$

(2) Summability:

$$\beta_{m1}^1 = \ldots = \beta_{m1}^{l-1} = \beta_{m1} \qquad \beta_{mn}^1 = \ldots = \beta_{mn}^{l-1} = \beta_{mn}$$

$$\beta_{m2}^1 = \ldots = \beta_{m2}^{l-1} = \beta_{m2} \qquad \beta_{mt}^1 = \ldots = \beta_{mt}^{l-1} = \beta_{mt}$$

$$\cdots \quad \cdots \quad \cdots \quad \cdots$$

$$\beta_{ml}^1 = \ldots = \beta_{ml}^{l-1} = \beta_{ml}$$

and

$$\Sigma_i \alpha_i = -1 \qquad \Sigma_i \beta_{i1} = \beta_{m1}$$

$$\Sigma_i \beta_{im} = \beta_{mm} \qquad \cdots \quad \cdots \cdots$$

$$\Sigma_i \beta_{it} = \beta_{mt} \qquad \Sigma_i \beta_{il} = \beta_{ml}$$

(3) Symmetry:

$$[\beta_{ij}] = [\beta_{ij}]'$$

(4) Non-negativity:

$$\alpha_i \geq 0 \quad I = 1, 2, \ldots, l-1; \qquad \alpha_l = -1 - \alpha_1 - \alpha_2$$
$$- \ldots - \alpha_{l-1} \leq 0$$

(5) Monotonicity:

$$y'[\beta_{ij}]y \leq 0 \text{ for all } y \neq 0.$$

Strictly speaking, the above formulation of the theoretical restrictions imposed on the UDTLDS is no more than a sketch designed to suggest the procedure to be followed in the estimation of the DTLDS. A more detailed and technical formulation of these restrictions is not necessary here, given the illustrative purposes aimed at and will be omitted – the reader is referred, instead, to Jorgenson, Lau and Stoker (1982). A frequent practice in the estimation of the DTLDS has been first to impose homogeneity and summability restrictions on the UDTLDS and then to re-estimate the homogeneity- and summability-constrained system after additionally imposing on it the other restrictions, for instance symmetry. The next step is, accordingly, the test of the theoretical restrictions. The estimates of the UDTLDS and of the restricted system are then used in at least three of these tests (homogeneity, summability and symmetry).

Let $\lambda = \max \mathbf{L}_\omega / \max \mathbf{L}_\Omega$ be the likelihood ratio, that is the ratio of the maximum value of $\mathbf{L}$ for the restricted system ω to the maximum value of $\mathbf{L}$ for the unrestricted system Ω, and let $|\mathbf{S}_\omega|$ and $|\mathbf{S}_\Omega|$ be the determinant of the restricted and of the unrestricted estimator, respectively, of the variance–covariance matrix. A standard statistic to test hypotheses that take the form of equality restrictions (homogeneity, summability and symmetry) is the likelihood ratio test statistic $-2 \ln \lambda = n(\ln |S_\omega| - \ln |S_\Omega|)$.

Theorem 8.2.8 Under the null hypothesis $-2 \ln \lambda = n(\ln |S_\omega| - \ln |S_\Omega|)$ is distributed asymptotically as χ^2 with a number of degrees of freedom equal to the number of restrictions to be tested.

A standard statistic to test hypotheses which take the form of inequality restrictions (non-negativity and monotonicity) is the ratio $r_\gamma = \gamma/\sigma_\gamma$ of each inequality-constrained estimate to its standard error using a one-sided critical region.

Theorem 8.2.9 For normally distributed disturbances, the statistic r_γ is distributed asymptotically as a standard normal random variable.

So far we have gathered a number of results which parallel properties of the abstract theory of level two, determine the estimation procedure, and disclose the characteristics of a number of relevant tests. The next step is to specialize the theory to the dimensions of a specific array of organized data, by giving numerical values to l and to T, for instance 3 and 24, respectively – the figures chosen here correspond to the data of the illustration discussed below in 8.4. This is an example of what we have been calling the concrete (data-conform) version of a level-three theory. Note that a model of this concrete (data-conform) theory is simply a structure $S_3 = \langle X_3, P_3, M_3, (t = 1, 2 \ldots, 24), (E_3, v_3), d \rangle$ that satisfies Definition 8.2.1 and where $l = 3$ and $T = 24$. By specializing the level-three theory to a specific array of data, we leave level three of our system to walk the first step into its fourth and final level.

Which of the propositions discussed thus far are suitable candidates to be included in $C(L_3)$, the core of the level-three theory? Again, a restrictive answer would point to homogeneity, summability, symmetry, negative semi-definiteness and monotonicity. Moreover, aspects of the mathematical form and the stochastic specification of the demand equations in the DTLDS (denote them by **TL** and **PR**, respectively) are immediately and directly – and of the mathematical form of the generating utility function mediately and indirectly – empirical claims included in the $C(L_3)$. On the other hand, some further properties of the direct or indirect utility function which refer to 'special case' situations

– for example, groupwise separability or additivity – may be better dealt with at the fourth level of the scheme.

Following in the steps of the example initiated in the last paragraph of 7.2 and extended to level two at the end of 7.4, we introduce the definition: $C(L_3) = \{d(R): d(HO) \wedge d(SU) \wedge d(FU) \wedge d(SY) \wedge d(NS) \wedge d(MO) \wedge d(TL) \wedge d(PR)\}$, which is to be read '**d** is a demand relation which is homogeneous, summable, a function, symmetric, negative semi-definite, monotonic, transcendental logarithmic and with such and such stochastic properties'. Here too, the example has been chosen to satisfy the special case of the nested inclusion $C(L_1) \subseteq C(L_2) \subseteq C(L_3)$. Notice, on the other hand, that while L_2 is a special case of theory L_1, L_3 is a special case of theory L_2.

8.3 DATA-SPECIFIC THEORY: LANGUAGE AND MODEL

We have now reached level four of the hierarchic scheme, the level of the data. It corresponds to what Suppes (1962) calls the 'model of data' and, by analogy, the 'theory of the model of data'. The theory of level three includes parallel testable formulations for some otherwise abstract parallel propositions of the level-two and, more remotely, level-one theory, while, at the same time, laying the ground rules for estimation, for specific testing procedures and possibly for projection exercises. The theory of level four is now to determine, for a concrete system of empirical data, whether that testing procedure has been properly run.

The main issues that the level-four theory has to determine can be summarized in a list of tests regarding the data and the adequacy of the data with respect to the prescribed testing procedures. In an economic context, this list customarily includes tests for aggregation, quality of index numbers, goodness of fit – which in turn may itself include more than one testing procedure – and possibly tests for statistical properties of the estimated residuals. Finally, prescriptions for projection procedures may be included.

It is important to emphasize that the goal of the data-specific theory is not so much to decide about the intrinsic merits of the substantive theoretical claims of levels one and two as to determine whether or not the specific data under examination satisfy those claims. This function includes the decision regarding the correct application of the testing procedure to the concrete situation.

In Definition 4.2.1 we have given a characterization of the notion of empirical or observed economic structure, namely, an economic structure whose domain(s) consist(s) of empirical data. The interdependence of the level-three and the level-four theories is here manifest, since, in many ways, it is the former which will determine the basic formal characteristics of the 'observed structure'. Indeed, we always have an 'observed structure with respect to a level-three theory' in the sense that it is precisely the testing procedure decided upon at level three that provides the outline for an adequate organization of the data.

The determination of the conditions that make an observed structure a model of the level-four theory is here, as at any other level, a function of the appropriate theory. As has been pointed out by Suppes (1962), 'the answer requires a detailed statistical theory of goodness of fit'. Having agreed upon a list of tests and a corresponding list of levels of significance, one will declare that the structure is a model of the level-four theory – for the testing procedure predetermined at level three – if it passes the list of tests at the prescribed levels of significance.

Does the model-theoretic characterization of an empirical theory – as summarized in the preceding paragraph – conflict with the common-sense view that asserts that empirical theories only provide inaccurate or approximate explanations of their referents? It does not, in our view, if we are able to keep conceptually separate the *immediate referent*, that is, the empirical structure that qualifies as a possible realization (or potential empirical model) of the theory, and the *mediate referent*, that is, that section of reality which the empirical structure is supposed (partially and imperfectly) to mirror. Without committing ourselves to a full-fledged 'approximation theory' – for which the reader is referred to Balzer, Moulines and Sneed (1987) – we note that, first, the prerequisites for an empirical structure to be a model of a theory are set up by the theory itself (scientific progress is tantamount to systematic tightening of those prerequisites) and, second, the conditions which qualify an empirical structure as an acceptable reflection of reality are functions of ever-changing substantive and methodological criteria. In a dynamic as opposed to a static perspective, the connections between theory and empirical model and between empirical model and mediate referent are in a permanent state of flux.

Let us now have a final word regarding the language of level four. As was pointed out in Chapter 6, the formal language of a level-four theory is very much that of arithmetic and applied statistics; this is fully consistent with the nature of its reference structure and its cognitive function.

8.4   A DATA-SPECIFIC THEORY: AN APPLIED DIRECT TRANSLOG DEMAND SYSTEM

This section brings to an end the sequence of examples from 'individual choice and demand theories' initiated in 7.2. The point of departure for the level-four theory is the concrete (data-conform) version of the level-three theory. Therefore, it is clear that if our level-three theory has been axiomatized (in so far as substantive economic concepts are involved) at the level of the primitive 'translogarithmic demand functions', the level-four theory ought to be axiomatized at the level of the same primitives, that is, at the level of the 'transcendental logarithmic demand functions' of the concrete (data-conform) version of the theory. Of course, a different choice regarding the formalization (or axiomatic reconstruction) of L_3 would immediately impinge on the axiomatic formulation of L_4.

Whereas the generic properties of the data have been defined in the special-class theory, in our example the DTLDS, the specific characteristics of the data structure are recognized in and stated by the concrete (data-conform) version of the level-three theory, in this case by the DTLDS with l and T set equal to 3 and 24, respectively. In the example we have chosen, the DTLDS, consisting of demand functions for three composite commodities ($l = 3$), is to be applied to time series for the Federal Republic of Germany for the period 1950–73. The series thus consist of 24 observations ($T = 24$) in each of two empirically recorded variables, x_{it} and p_{it}, the product m_t of these, and the time trend $t = 1, 2, \ldots, 24$. In other words, we now have a 'three-equation 24-observation DTLDS for the FRG for 1950–73'. Our example of a level-four theory will essentially consist in a report – cast within the framework of the analytic scheme we intend to illustrate – of a few selected aspects of a most interesting empirical research project carried out by Conrad and Jorgenson (1978 and 1979); more detailed references can be found in the 'Notes and remarks' section (8.6).

An admissible structure is now a triple $S_4 = \langle X_4, P_4, M_4, (d_i, i = 1, 2, 3) \rangle$ where X_4 is a sample of 24 different observations of per capita purchases of three different composite commodities; P_4 is a sample of different observations of composite prices corresponding to each of the just-mentioned three composite commodities; M_4 is a sample of 24 different total per capita expenditure values and d_1, d_2, d_3 are three demand functions, that is, binary relations on subsets of the Cartesian product $X_4 \times P_4 \times M_4 \times t$ of observations and the time variable. In contrast, the level-four structure does not include an analogue of the space $(\mathbf{E}_3, \mathbf{v}_3)$ in the preceding structure of the hierarchy, for no such empirical space can be observed. In the same context, the random variables ϵ_{it}, necessary components of the theoretical demand functions of level three, do not appear as terms of the estimated equations of level three. Only their estimates e_{it} will be computed as residuals from the estimated equations. Similarly, since $\mathbf{t}$ is not an empirical variable, it does not occur in $\mathbf{S}_4$. Finally, note that the class of admissible structures includes the primal structure – the one dated 1950–73 – as well as isomorphic empirical structures – in particular, those resulting from projection operations.

In the light of the current example, it is interesting to account for the different but related objectives of a level-four pursuit. First and directly, the researchers are trying to explain the organized data they confront, thereby testing the suitability of the three-equations 24-observations DTLDS in the adopted concrete version (note that this pursuit may also include the use of the estimated system for projection purposes); second and less directly, they are testing the suitability of the DTLDS as a special-class theory of individual consumer demand; third and indirectly, they are testing the validity of the main propositions of stochastic theory of transitive consumer demand regarding properties of individual demand functions; and fourth and very indirectly, they are evaluating the plausibility of some foundational precepts of a level-one theory.

Definition 8.4.1 The empirical structure $\mathbf{S}_4 = \langle \mathbf{X}_4, \mathbf{P}_4, \mathbf{M}_4, (\mathbf{d}_i; i = 1, 2, 3) \rangle$ is the *primal model of the three-equations 24-observations DTLDS for the FRG 1950–73* if and only if $\langle \mathbf{X}_3, \mathbf{P}_3, \mathbf{M}_3, (\mathbf{t} = 1, 2, \ldots 24), (\mathbf{E}_3, \mathbf{v}_3), (\mathbf{d}_i; i = 1, 2, 3) \rangle$ is a model of the DTLDS, and the following conditions are satisfied:

A8.4.1 $\mathbf{X}_4$ is a possible empirical realization of $\mathbf{X}_3$ (in this specific case, the sequence $(x_{it}: i = 1, 2, 3; t = 1, 2, \ldots, 24))$ of observations of personal consumption in per capita terms of the composite commodities 'non-durables', 'durables' and 'energy', respectively, in the Federal Republic of Germany (FRG) during the period 1950–73. *Source*: Conrad and Jorgenson (1975, 1979).

A8.4.2 $\mathbf{P}_4$ is a possible empirical realization of $\mathbf{P}_3$ (in this specific case, the sequence $(p_{it}: i = 1, 2, 3; t = 1, 2, \ldots, 24))$ of observations of prices of the composite commodities 'non-durables', 'durables' and 'energy' in the FRG corresponding to the period 1950–73. *Source*: *idem*.

A8.4.3 M_4 is a possible realization of M_3, namely the sequence $(m_t: t = 1, \ldots, 24)$ obtained from the empirical sequences X_4 and P_4 in accordance with the formula $m_t = \Sigma_i p_{it} \cdot x_{it}$.

A8.4.4   The *maintained hypothesis* is formalized by the two equations in unrestricted form $(i = 1, 2; \mathbf{t}; t = 1, 2, \ldots, 24)$ of the UDTLDS defined by

$$d_{it} = w_{it} = p_{it} \cdot x_{it}/m_t$$

$$= \frac{\alpha_i + \beta_{i1} \ln(p_1/m_t) + \beta_{i2} \ln(p_2/m_t) + \beta_{i3} \ln(p_3/m_t) + \beta_{im} \ln m_t + \beta_{it} \cdot \mathbf{t}}{-1 + \beta^i_{m1} \ln(p_1/m_t) + \beta^i_{m2} \ln(p_2/m_t) + \beta^i_{m3} \ln(p_3/m_t) + \beta^i_{mm} \ln m_t + \beta^i_{mt} \cdot \mathbf{t}}$$
$$+ \, e_{it}$$

(where the estimates of the random disturbances ϵ_{it}, namely the residuals e_{it}, satisfy the condition $\Sigma_i e_i = 0$ at every t and are normally distributed with $E(e_{it}) = 0$, $E(e_{is} \, e_{jt}) = \sigma_{ij}$ if $s = t$ and $E(e_{is} \, e_{jt}) = 0$ if $s \neq t$, $(i = 1, 2)$), whose maximum likelihood (ML) parameter estimates $\underline{\alpha}_i$ of α_i $(i = 1, 2)$, $\underline{\beta}_{ij}$ of β_{ij} $(i, j = 1, 2)$, $\underline{\beta}_{im}$ of β_{im} $(i = 1, 2)$, $\underline{\beta}^i_{mj}$ of β^i_{mj} $(i, j = 1, 2)$, $\underline{\beta}^i_{mn}$ of β^i_{mn} $(i = 1, 2)$ and $\underline{\beta}_{it}$ of β_{it} $(i = 1, 2)$ are displayed in Table 8.4.1 (1) with their standard errors in parentheses.

A8.4.5   The DTLDS is a three-component vector function $\mathbf{w}$ that maps each triple $(p_t, m_t, \mathbf{t})$ in $P_4 \times M_4 \times \mathbf{t}$ into a vector x_t in X_4 according to the formula:

$$d_{it} = w_{it} = p_{it} \cdot x_{it}/m_t$$

$$= \frac{\alpha_i + \Sigma_j \beta_{ij} \ln(p_{jt}/m_t) + \beta_{it} \cdot \mathbf{t}}{-1 + \Sigma_j \beta_{mj} \ln(p_{jt}/m_t) + \beta^i_{mt} \cdot \mathbf{t}} + e_{it},$$

$$i = 1, 2, 3,$$

where $\mathbf{t} = 1, 2, \ldots, 24$.

A8.4.6   The *null hypothesis* of homogeneity of aggregate demand – which is formalized by the two homogeneity-constrained equations $(i = 1, 2)$ of the DTLDS

$$w_i = \frac{\alpha_i + \beta_{i1} \ln(p_1/m) + \beta_{i2} \ln(p_2/m) + \beta_{i3} \ln(p_3/m) + \beta_{it} \cdot \mathbf{t}}{-1 + \beta^i_{m1} \ln(p_1/m) + \beta^i_{m2} \ln(p_2/m) + \beta^i_{m3} \ln(p_3/m) + \beta^i_{mt} \cdot \mathbf{t}}$$

$$i = 1, 2,$$

Table 8.4.1   Estimates of the parameters of the direct translog demand system

Parameters	(1) Unrestricted		(2) Homogeneity		(3) Summability	
α_1	−0.148	(0.001)	−0.147	(0.001)	−0.147	(0.001)
β_{11}	−0.050	(0.189)	−0.049	(0.128)	−0.083	(0.158)
β_{12}	0.042	(0.160)	0.032	(0.172)	0.152	(0.128)
β_{13}	0.098	(0.072)	0.083	(0.069)	0.074	(0.055)
β_{1m}	0.065	(0.173)	−		0.029	(0.139)
β_{1t}	−0.003	(0.012)	−0.0002	(0.008)	0.001	(0.01)
β^1_{m1}	0.151	(1.14)	0.551	(0.588)	0.065	(0.98)
β^1_{m2}	0.684	(1.33)	0.844	(1.36)	1.79	(1.07)
β^1_{m3}	0.373	(0.412)	0.279	(0.397)	0.171	(0.323)
β^1_{mm}	−0.235	(1.18)	−		−0.33	(1.00)
β^1_{mt}	0.091	(0.078)	0.086	(0.054)	0.125	(0.065)
α_2	−0.803	(0.001)	−0.803	(0.001)	−0.803	(0.001)
β_{21}	−0.446	(1.03)	0.42	(0.428)	0.139	(0.782)
β_{22}	0.879	(1.29)	1.17	(1.25)	1.57	(0.917)
β_{23}	0.071	(0.315)	0.007	(0.30)	0.122	(0.258)
β_{2m}	0.887	(1.07)	−		−0.359	(0.833)
β_{2t}	0.108	(0.072)	0.081	(0.053)	0.123	(0.053)
β^m_{m1}	−0.655	(1.29)	0.350	(0.583)	0.065	(0.98)
β^2_{m2}	0.968	(1.53)	1.27	(1.49)	1.79	(1.07)
β^2_{m3}	0.075	(0.403)	0.003	(0.384)	0.171	(0.323)
β^2_{mm}	−0.971	(1.30)	−		−0.33	(1.0)
β^2_{mt}	0.105	(0.089)	0.077	(0.067)	0.125	(0.065)

Source: Table A.2 of Conrad and Jorgenson (1979, p. 167).

and whose ML parameter estimates are displayed in Table 8.4.1 (2) with their standard errors in parentheses (see also Table 8.4.3) – cannot be rejected at the 0.05 significance level.

A8.4.7   The *null hypothesis* of summability of aggregate demand – which is formalized by the three summability-constrained equations of the DTLDS

$$w_i = \frac{\alpha_i + \beta_{i1}\ln(p_1/m) + \beta_{i2}\ln(p_2/m) + \beta_{i3}\ln(p_3/m) + \beta_{im}\ln m + \beta_{it}\cdot t}{-1 + \beta^i_{m1}\ln(p_1/m) + \beta^i_{m2}\ln(p_2/m) + \beta^i_{m3}\ln(p_3/m) + \beta^i_{mm}\ln m + \beta^i_{mt}\cdot t}$$

with $\beta^1_{m1} = \beta^2_{m1} = \beta_{m1}$, $\beta^1_{mm} = \beta^2_{mm} = \beta_{mm}$,
$\beta^1_{m2} = \beta^2_{m2} = \beta_{m2}$, $\beta^1_{mt} = \beta^2_{mt} = \beta_{mt}$,
$\beta^1_{m3} = \beta^2_{m3} = \beta_{m3}$,

Table 8.4.2   Estimates of the parameters of the direct translog demand system

Parameters	(1) Homogeneity and summability	(2) Symmetry
α_1	-0.147 (0.001)	-0.148 (0.001)
β_{11}	-0.107 (0.093)	-0.197 (0.029)
β_{12}	0.195 (0.123)	0.016 (0.097)
β_{13}	0.059 (0.052)	-0.007 (0.016)
β_{1t}	0.003 (0.006)	-0.012 (0.005)
α_2	-0.804 (0.001)	-0.803 (0.001)
β_{21}	0.413 (0.327)	0.016 (0.097)
β_{22}	1.96 (0.839)	0.607 (0.767)
β_{23}	0.041 (0.246)	0.015 (0.031)
β_{2t}	0.117 (0.034)	0.045 (0.034)
α_3	-0.048 (0.0008)	-0.049 (0.0007)
β_{31}	0.009 (0.035)	-0.007 (0.016)
β_{32}	0.082 (0.049)	0.015 (0.031)
β_{33}	-0.027 (0.023)	-0.046 (0.012)
β_{3t}	0.001 (0.002)	-0.003 (0.003)
δ_1	-0.017 (0.045)	
δ_2	0.644 (1.54)	
λ_{21}	-4.93 (8.51)	
λ_{31}	1.13 (4.12)	
λ_{32}	-0.872 (2.08)	

Source: Table A.2 of Conrad and Jorgenson (1979, p. 167).

and $\alpha_1 + \alpha_2 + \alpha_3 = -1$, $\quad \beta_{11} + \beta_{21} + \beta_{31} = \beta_{m1}$,
$\beta_{1m} + \beta_{2m} + \beta_{3m} = \beta_{mn}$, $\quad \beta_{12} + \beta_{22} + \beta_{32} = \beta_{m2}$,
$\beta_{1t} + \beta_{2t} + \beta_{3t} = \beta_{mt}$, $\quad \beta_{13} + \beta_{23} + \beta_{33} = \beta_{m3}$,

and whose ML parameter estimates ($i = 1, 2$) are displayed in Table 8.4.1 (3) with their standard errors in parentheses (see also Table 8.4.3) – cannot be rejected at the 0.05 significance level.

A8.4.8   The *null hypothesis* of joint homogeneity and summability of average demand – which is formalized by the three homogeneity- and summability-constrained equations of the DTLDS form, the ML parameter estimates of which are displayed in Table 8.4.2 (1) with their standard errors in parentheses (see also Table 8.4.3) – cannot be rejected at the 0.05 significance level.

A8.4.9   Given homogeneity and summability, the *null hypothesis* of symmetry of average demand – which is formalized by the symmetry-constrained DTLDS, that is, by the homogeneity- and summability-constrained three equations of the DTLDS with the additional symmetry constraints,

$$\beta_{12} = \beta_{21},$$
$$\beta_{31} = \beta_{m1} - \beta_{11} - \beta_{21}, \quad \beta_{32} = \beta_{m2} - \beta_{12} - \beta_{22},$$
$$\beta_{13} = \beta_{m1} - \beta_{11} - \beta_{21}, \quad \beta_{23} = \beta_{m2} - \beta_{12} - \beta_{22},$$

whose ML parameter estimates are displayed in Table 8.4.2 (2) with their standard errors in parentheses (see also Table 8.4.3) – cannot be rejected at the 0.05 significance level.

A8.4.10 Given homogeneity and summability, the *null hypotheses* of non-negativity and of monotonicity of aggregate demand – which are formalized by the non-negativity- and the monotonicity-constrained DTLDS, that is, by the homogeneity- and summability-constrained three equations of the DTLDS with, respectively, the additional non-negativity constraints,

$$\alpha_1 \leq 0, \ \alpha_2 \leq 0, \ \alpha_3 = -1 - \alpha_1 - \alpha_2 \leq 0,$$

and the monotonicity constraints,

$$\delta_1 = -s_{11} \geq 0$$
$$\delta_2 = -s_{22} - \lambda_{21}^2 \cdot \delta_1 \geq 0$$
$$\lambda_{21} = -(1/2\delta_1)(s_{12} + s_{21})$$
$$\lambda_{31} = -(1/2\delta_1)(s_{13} + s_{31})$$
$$\lambda_{32} = -(1/2\delta_2)(s_{23} + s_{32}) - (\delta_1/\delta_2)\lambda_{21} \cdot \lambda_{31},$$

the ML parameter estimates of which are displayed in Table 8.4.2 (1) with their standard errors in parentheses (see also Table 8.4.3) – can neither of them be rejected at the 0.05 significance level.

A8.4.11 The three-equation DTLDS in integrability-constrained form satisfies the following tests:

(1) Test of goodness of fit, as given (for example) by the 'measure of information inaccuracy'

$$I(\mathbf{w}_t, \ \hat{\mathbf{w}}_t) = \sum_i \mathbf{w}_{it} \log(\mathbf{w}_{it}/\hat{\mathbf{w}}_{it})$$

at a pre-set value.

(2) Regarding the residuals, the tests of

Table 8.4.3   Test statistics (TS) for the DTLDS

Hypothesis	Degrees of freedom	TS
Homogeneity	4	1.67
Summability	5	1.37
Homogeneity and summability	8	1.39
Given homogeneity and summability		
Symmetry	3	1.75
Non-negativity		
$-\alpha_1 \geq 0$	1	133.8
$-\alpha_2 \geq 0$	1	582.6
$-1 + \alpha_1 + \alpha_2 \geq 0$	1	61.0
Monotonicity		
$\delta_1 \geq 0$	1	-0.38
$\delta_2 \geq 0$	1	0.42

Source: adapted from Table 2 in Conrad and Jorgenson (1979, p. 164).

> (2.1) zero means
> (2.2) heteroscedasticity
> (2.3) autocorrelation
> (2.4) non-normality.

A8.4.1 to A8.4.11 are the axioms of the three-equation 24-observation DTLDS or 'DTLDS FRG 1950–73'. From these axioms A8.4.1 to A8.4.3 should be regarded as the structural axioms (compare with Definition 8.2.1). Observe that an empirical model of the theory is unique, up to isomorphism. This means that whereas the primal model of the 'DTLDS FRG 1950–73' is unique, isomorphic empirical structures which satisfy the axioms of the theory are also models of the theory – for example, empirical structures obtained by projections may also qualify as potential models of the theory. This idea is completed in the following:

Remark 8.4.1   An empirical structure isomorphic to that determined in Definition 8.4.1, A8.4.1 to A8.4.3, is a model of the 'DTLDS FRG 1950–73' if and only if it satisfies the axioms A8.4.4 to A8.4.11.

It goes without saying that the definition does not and cannot exclude non-empirical (isomorphic) structures as potential (formal) models of the theory but it does exclude them as intended (empirical) models.

The following question may be in order here: is it possible to speak of theorems of a level-four theory, that is, of a theory whose satisfying relational structure is a model of data? The answer is a firm yes. Although the results of the analysis performed on empirical systems are usually not referred to as 'theorems' in the applied econometric literature, it is clear that any statement derived by the rules of inference from the axioms of the theory – in particular, in our example, any derived proposition regarding properties of the equations system 'DTLDS FRG 1950–73' or its components – has the logical form of a theorem. Hence the axioms of the theory together with – more importantly – the derived sentences of the theory constitute in a formally rigorous sense the set of theorems of the theory of level four. To illustrate this briefly, let us go back to the notions of explicit groupwise separability and explicit additivity for ITLUF as defined in 8.2. We begin by readapting our framework to the special case of dimension $l = 3$.

Theorem 8.4.1   An indirect utility function **v** generating the DTLDS **d** of A8.4.5 can be represented by the indirect translog utility function (ITLUF) $\ln \mathbf{v} = \ln \mathbf{f}(\mathbf{p}_1/\mathbf{m}, \ \mathbf{p}_2/\mathbf{m}, \ \mathbf{p}_3/\mathbf{m}, \ \mathbf{t})$.

Theorem 8.4.2   A local second-order approximation to the ITLUF **v** of the three-equation DTLDS is the quadratic function in the ratios $\mathbf{p}_i/\mathbf{m}, \ i = 1, 2, 3, \ \ln \mathbf{v} = \alpha_o + \Sigma_i \ln(\mathbf{p}_i/\mathbf{m}) + (1/2)\Sigma_i\Sigma_j\beta_{ij} \ln(\mathbf{p}_i/\mathbf{m}) \cdot \ln(\mathbf{p}_j/\mathbf{m}) + (1/2)\beta_{tt}\mathbf{t}^2$.

Definition 8.4.2   The three-commodity ITLUF **v** is said to be *groupwise separable* in $\mathbf{p}_1/\mathbf{m}$ and $\mathbf{p}_2/\mathbf{m}$ from $\mathbf{p}_3/\mathbf{m}$ if it can be written in the form $\ln \mathbf{v} = \mathbf{f}[\ln \mathbf{v}_{12}(\mathbf{p}_1/\mathbf{m}, \ \mathbf{p}_2/\mathbf{m}, \ \mathbf{t}), \ \mathbf{p}_3/\mathbf{m}, \ \mathbf{t}]$ and it is said to be *explicitly groupwise separable* in $\mathbf{p}_1/\mathbf{m}$ and $\mathbf{p}_2/\mathbf{m}$ from $\mathbf{p}_3/\mathbf{m}$ if it can be written in the form $\ln \mathbf{v} = \ln \mathbf{v}_{12}(\mathbf{p}_1/\mathbf{m}, \ \mathbf{p}_2/\mathbf{m}, \ \mathbf{t}) + \ln \mathbf{v}_3(\mathbf{p}_3/\mathbf{m}, \ \mathbf{t})$.

Definition 8.4.3   The three-commodity ITLUF **v** is said to be *explicitly additive* if it can be written in the form $\ln \mathbf{v} = \ln \mathbf{v}_1(\mathbf{p}_1/\mathbf{m}, \ \mathbf{t}) + \ln \mathbf{v}_2(\mathbf{p}_2/\mathbf{m}, \ \mathbf{t}) + \ln \mathbf{v}_3(\mathbf{p}_3/\mathbf{m}, \ \mathbf{t})$.

Theorem 8.4.3   The translog approximation to an explicitly additive ITLUF is explicitly additive.

Theorem 8.4.4   If **v** is an ITLUF group separable in $\mathbf{p}_1/\mathbf{m}$ and $\mathbf{p}_2/\mathbf{m}$ from $\mathbf{p}_3/\mathbf{m}$, then its parameters satisfy the restrictions $\beta_{13} = \rho_3\alpha_1$ and $\beta_{23} = \rho_3\alpha_2$ where $\rho_3 = [\partial^2\mathbf{v}/\partial \ln \mathbf{v}_{12}\partial \ln(\mathbf{p}_3/\mathbf{m})]/(\partial \ln \mathbf{v}_{12})$ at the point of approximation; if **v** is explicitly groupwise separable, then the additional restriction $\rho_3 = 0$ is satisfied.

Theorem 8.4.5   Given the three-commodity DTLDS **d**, a necessary and sufficient condition for the ITLUF **v** to be explicitly additive is that **v** be explicitly groupwise separable in any two pairs of commodities from the third.

The last theorem implies that if the ITLUF satisfies all the restrictions for explicit groupwise separability for any two pairs of commodities with respect to the third – a total of three combinations, namely {1, 2} from 3, {1, 3} from 2, and {2, 3} from 1 – it is also explicitly additive or, in other words, the parameter restrictions for explicit additivity and those for explicit groupwise separability are identical.

To test the restrictions on the parameters of the ITLUF, one uses again the likelihood ratio $\lambda = \max L_\omega / \max L_\Omega$. According to Theorem 8.2.8, under the null hypothesis $-2 \ln \lambda = n(\ln |S_\omega| - \ln |S_\Omega|)$ is distributed asymptotically as χ^2 with a number of degrees of freedom equal to the number of restrictions to be tested. Table 8.4.4 shows the critical values of χ^2 and Table 8.4.5 displays the results of the test for the restrictions.

It is possible to relate some of the latter theorems on properties of the indirect utility functions and on the associated restricted estimation to the results of the tests in a few propositions.

Proposition 8.4.1   The tests on the basis of the restriction of Theorem 8.4.4 impose the acceptance of the hypothesis of explicit groupwise separability of the ITLUF **v** generating the 'DTLDS FRG 1950–73', for all pairs of two commodities from the third commodity.

Proposition 8.4.2   Proposition 8.4.1 and Theorem 8.4.5 impose the acceptance of the hypothesis of explicit additivity of the ITLUF **v** generating the 'DTLDS FRG 1950–73'.

Proposition 8.4.3   On the basis of Theorem 8.4.5, the additivity-restricted ML-estimated 'DTLDS FRG 1950–73' consists of the following three scalar demand functions (standard errors of estimates are given in parentheses):

$$w_1 = \frac{\begin{matrix} -0.148 - 0.196 \ln(p_1/m) - 0.012t \\ (0.001) \quad (0.021) \qquad\qquad (0.001) \end{matrix}}{\begin{matrix} -1 - 0.196 \ln(p_1/m) + 0.430 \ln(p_2/m) - 0.044 \ln(p_3/m) + 0.023t \\ (0.021) \qquad\qquad (0.223) \qquad\qquad (0.001) \qquad\qquad (0.004) \end{matrix}}$$

Table 8.4.4   Critical values of χ^2 divided by degrees of freedom

Degrees of freedom	0.10	0.05	0.01	0.005	0.001	0.0005
1	2.71	3.84	6.64	7.88	10.83	12.12
2	2.30	3.00	4.61	5.30	6.91	7.60

Source: Table 1 in Conrad and Jorgenson (1978, p. 23).

Table 8.4.5   Results of the test for restrictions

Hypothesis	Degrees of freedom	Critical value	Test statistic
Groupwise separability	Given summability and symmetry		
{1,2} from 3	1	10.32	0.61
{1,3} from 2	1	10.32	1.00
{2,3} from 1	1	10.32	0.48
Explicit groupwise separability	Given groupwise separability		
{1,2} from 3	1	10.32	0.55
{1,3} from 2	1	10.32	0.12
{2,3} from 1	1	10.32	0.24

Source: adapted from Table 2 in Conrad and Jorgenson (1978, p. 23).

$$w_2 = \frac{\begin{matrix} -0.803 - 0.430 \ln(p_2/m) & -0.038t \\ (0.001) \quad (0.223) & (0.006) \end{matrix}}{-1 - 0.196 \ln(p_1/m) - 0.430 \ln(p_2/m) - 0.044 \ln(p_3/m) + 0.023t}$$

$$w_3 = \frac{\begin{matrix} -0.049 - 0.044 \ln(p_3/m) & -0.003t \\ (0.0006) \ (0.001) & (0.0007) \end{matrix}}{-1 - 0.196 \ln(p_1/m) + 0.430 \ln(p_2/m) - 0.044 \ln(p_3/m) + 0.023t}.$$

We now bring to an end the sketch of the level-four theory by gathering together and reflecting on some of the results. Let us begin with the first aspect by listing its cognitive targets and by relating them to testing procedures. As we have stated in other parts of this study, it does not serve any useful purpose to distinguish at this level between the theory L_4 and its core of empirical claims $C(L_4)$. We may, more appropriately, identify the two concepts.

Proceeding this time from the most concrete level towards the more abstract ones, we may recognize that a first cognitive target of the theory has been to explain the very specific 1950–73 Federal Republic of Germany data on consumption. Within the chosen general framework (the DTLDS), the system that best explained these data has been the one we have called the 'DTLDS FRG 1950–73', the data-specific, concrete (data-conform) theory that postulates explicit additivity of the generating indirect translog utility function. As an extension of this target, it is clear that the estimated system may be used as a tool for projections. As stated in Chapter 6, projections are very important both in their cognitive and in their testing functions.

Following this, it has been a cognitive target to test the suitability of the direct translog demand theory – mathematical functional form and stochastic specification – as an explanation of empirical data and as a vehicle for the testing of the main propositions of the level-two theory. The success of the 'DTLDS FRG 1950–73' on both fronts has provided an instance of confirmation for the direct translog demand theory of level three as, first, a plausible explanation of empirical data on demand and, second, an effective parametric representation of fundamental properties of demand functions derived within the framework of the general theory of transitive consumer demand of level two. Notice that, in particular, the 'DTLDS FRG 1950–73' satisfies (in some cases, trivially) the five conditions for integrability. Moreover, intermediate results leading to the final system had already confirmed that the corresponding restrictions were appropriate.

A further cognitive target is closely related to the second aspect mentioned in the preceding paragraph, but is more general in scope. It goes beyond the direct translog demand theory to constitute one indirect test of the validity of a fundamental proposition of the general-class theory of level two, namely integrability, that is of the compatibility of the data with the hypothesis of constrained utility maximization.

Finally, and still less directly, we may recognize a last cognitive target which relates to the tests of some of the 'preceptive' theoretical characterizations of the foundations or general theory of level one. These include the most general theoretical characterizations – homogeneity, summability, compatibility with the hypothesis of constrained preference satisfaction – as well as the special theoretical characterizations – for instance, the special cases of representability of preferences, transitivity, additivity, and constrained utility maximization.

Of course, and partly facilitated by the construction of the examples, we may conclude here that the special case of a nested inclusion relation $C(L_1) \subseteq C(L_2) \subseteq C(L_3) \subseteq L_4$ is satisfied.

Returning one more time to the language of the level-four theory, it would seem justifiable to single out and emphasize the following empirical claims of L_4: (1) the 1950–73 FRG data on consumer demand are consistent with the three consumer demand equations which summarize the 'DTLDS FRG 1950–73'; (2) these three demand equations are integrable and thus consistent with the existence of a generating indirect translog utility function; and (3) plausibly, the generating indirect translog utility function belongs to the explicitly additive class of indirect utility functions.

8.5 INTER-LEVEL THEORETICAL LINKS

It is time to summarize the results of our investigation on the proposed four-level hierarchic scheme, and to draw some conclusions regarding the characterization of an 'empirical economic theory' or 'empirical economic-theoretical proposition' for the case of a representational system.

Suppose we confine ourselves to some special branch of economic analysis. At the bottom of the hierarchy, as we have had the opportunity to notice, we find a foundations, basic or general theory and a class of mathematical models with the characteristics described in 7.2. Next, at the lower intermediate level, we may find a couple of general-class theories, each of which is a distinct theoretical construct intended to cover a very wide class of still rather abstract mathematical structures. Then, at the upper intermediate level, we meet a collection of special-class theories each of which provides an alternative testable, parametric formulation for (usually some selected set of) propositions of one general-class theory. Each of these distinct special-class theories also determines an appropriate testing and/or estimation procedure; and, for each of these third-level theories, we identify an associated class of models, each model consisting of an idealization of a class of economic data. Finally, at the top, and related to a particular theory of the upper intermediate level, we find one or several data-specific theories each with its own primal 'model of data' (original observed empirical model).

Returning to our four examples of Chapters 7 and 8, immediately above the theory of consumer choice in R^l sketched in 7.2 we have, at level two, the stochastic theory of transitive consumer demand which we briefly described – alternatively, at this level, we might have focused on the more general but less complete theory of non-transitive consumer demand. One further step up, at level three, we have the direct translog demand system (DTLDS). However, we might also find at this level several other possible econometric formulations. Instances of such theories (and models) are the 'linear expenditure system' (Stone, 1954), the 'addilog system' (Houthakker, 1960), the 'indirect transcendental logarithmic demand system' (Christensen, Jorgenson and Lau, 1975), the 'Rotterdam demand system' (Barten, 1964; Theil, 1965) or the 'almost ideal demand system' (Deaton and Muellbauer, 1980). Like the DTLDS, each of these constitutes a theory in its own right whose links to L_2 and to L_1 could have been described in similar ways. For each of these theories we finally find at level four an observed structure, the primal model, corresponding to a particular economy and time interval – in our case, the primal model corresponding to the 'DTLDS FRG 1950–73' – and each defining a possible class of isomorphic empirical models, some of which may well have been determined via projections.

Let us examine further the relation of meaning between a theory L_1 or L_2, on the one hand, and a model S_4, on the other. We first observe that a particular proposition of L_1 or L_2 – for completeness, let us choose as our example the case of a property of demand, like homogeneity, which is reflected in propositions at both the levels of L_1 (Theorem 7.2.7) and L_2 (Theorem 7.4.8) – will in general lead to a different specification in each distinct special-class theory; compare, for example, the requirement $\Sigma_i \pi_{ij} = 0$, for the Rotterdam demand system, with the conditions of Theorems 8.2.1 and 8.2.7 for the DTLDS. Next, we observe that it is that special parametric specification, in the particular formulation of the concrete (data-conform) theory – for the case of the 'DTLDS FRG 1950–73' example refer to A8.4.6 of Definition 8.4.1 – that is immediately and directly confronted with data at level four. We now conclude that, on the contrary, the propositions of levels one and two are only mediately and indirectly contrasted with the data, a circumstance that is not without methodological consequences and that is not always well understood.

From the above description it seems to follow that while the acceptance or the rejection of the hypothesis of homogeneity of demand at level four in the context of an otherwise statistically strong level-four theory – strong in the sense of having successfully passed the relevant statistical tests of goodness of fit – would strengthen or seriously question, respectively, the homogeneity hypothesis of the abstract theory at levels one and two, positive or negative test results associated with a statistically poor theory of level four would have little or no bearing on the propositions of the level-one and level-two theories. In this sense, intuitively, whereas a statistically strong theory at level four always has (positive or negative) empirical consequences for the theory of levels one and two, a statistically weak theory of level four is of little or no consequence for the theories of level one and two – for instance, the functional specification corresponding to the chosen level-four theory may not be the appropriate one for the given data.

For the last time, let us recast and summarize our views on the main question, namely, that of the sense in which a basic, foundations or general theory and a general-class theory can be said to be empirical. The answer, as we have seen, is by no means a simple one. As we have had the opportunity to gather from our examples from consumer choice and demand analysis – see also the discussion by Suppes (1962) – theories at the different levels refer to set-theoretical structures of different logical types. Hence these structures and models, although connected to each other across levels in some essential ways, cannot in general be directly compared to one another. For instance, in our examples, we found non-observables at levels one (the preference correspondence) and two (the utility function), observables with strongly specified functional forms at level three (the DTLDS), and only data regarding purchases, prices, and expenditure at level four. We have also mentioned that sets with the cardinality of the continuum as well as continuously differentiable functions are typical occurrences at the lower levels of the scheme, while the discrete and finite character of the data are typical generic requirements and features at levels three and four, respectively.

The differences between the set-theoretical structures of levels one and two, on the one hand, and level four, on the other, are most important to the answer to the above question. Not too often does an empirical or observed structure qualify, in a rigorous logical sense, as a model of a whole abstract economic theory of the general-class type – let alone the foundations type. As a rule, the empirical structure which is a model of the related level-four theory will qualify as a model of only that selected set of statements of the level-one and level-two theories which we have called their core of empirical claims, or shorter, the empirical cores $C(L_1)$ and $C(L_2)$, respectively. This was the sense of Definition 6.1.1. This conclusion, in our view, is also in line with the actual practice in science – in economics and elsewhere. Seldom does the researcher confront the task of testing for empirical validity each and every one of the sentences of a theory. On the contrary, the theoretical system is made to produce a long list of propositions from which only a selected set is subject to empirical verification, the remainder playing only an auxiliary role, always contributing even if only partially to a tentative explanation of the economic phenomenon.

8.6 NOTES AND REMARKS

Volume III of the *Handbook of Econometrics* (Griliches and Intriligator, 1986) contains several articles relevant to the discussion of the current chapter, in particular the articles by Deaton (1986) on 'Demand Analysis' and by Jorgenson (1986) on 'Econometric Methods for Modelling Producer Behavior'. In relation to the current and the next chapter the reader would certainly find of interest the book by Epstein (1987).

Two basic theoretical works on the transcendental logarithmic system are the article by Christensen, Jorgenson and Lau (1975) and the chapter by Jorgenson, Lau and Stoker (1982). The illustrations for levels three and four of our scheme have been constructed on the basis of an article on the conditions for integrability of demand by Jorgenson and Lau (1979) and its application to German data by Conrad and Jorgenson (1979). The latter was completed with some empirical results on the structure of consumer preferences for the FRG, also by Conrad and Jorgenson (1978).

To conclude our references to individual consumer choice and demand theory, let us comment briefly on testing the integrability of systems of demand functions. From the preceding discussion, the reader may be left with the idea that all is simple and straightforward with regard to testing integrability. However, nothing would be further from the truth. There is a growing literature on the successes and failures of testing homogeneity and symmetry and on the possible causes of the failures. For interesting accounts of the experience regarding the Rotterdam demand system the reader is referred to Theil (1975, 1976, 1980), Laitinen (1978), Theil, Suhm and Meisner (1981), and Theil and Clements (1987). Regarding the use of estimated systems of equations as projection tools, we shall not add anything new at this point but, instead, refer the reader to what was said in 6.5. In Chapter 9 we shall have something more to say on this point in the context of phenomenological theories.

As an alternative illustration of the top two levels of our four-level scheme, one could also have chosen appropriate examples from the theories of production, for example Jorgenson (1986) for level three and Conrad and Jorgenson (1977) for level four.

It is our view that neither the notion of 'partial truth' as discussed, for instance, in Bunge (1967a, 1967b) nor the concept of 'approximation' as developed by Balzer, Moulines and Sneed (1987) – see also in the latter context Rolleri (1983) – is inconsistent with the model-theoretic characterization of empirical theories as given here and, in particular, with the notion of empirical model. One needs to keep clearly separate, of course, the set-theoretical entity 'empirical model of the theory' from the notion 'mediate referent of the theory' and distinguish accordingly between the relation theory to data, on the one hand, and theory to mediate referent, on the other.

Finally, we observe that as promised in 6.2.2 and 6.4 we have continued to assume in this chapter that for a level-four theory the equality $L_4 = C(L_4)$ is satisfied.

9 Phenomenological Theories and Theoretical Systems (I): Generic and Data-Specific Theory

A phenomenological theory is a hypothetico-deductive system which only includes phenomenological hypotheses; and phenomenological hypotheses are, according to Bunge (1967b),

> those which, whether they contain observational concepts or are rather abstract (that is, epistemological uplift) constructions, they do not meddle with the inner working of systems but only with their outward behavior. All input–output relations in thermodynamics, electrical engineering and economics are phenomenological to the extent that they do not refer to processes whereby inputs are converted into outputs.

From an epistemological point of view, as was previously pointed out, phenomenological theories are closer to phenomena epistemologically less deep than their representational counterparts.

In this chapter we shall discuss and illustrate with two different but typical examples the case of two-level phenomenological theoretical systems.

In Chapters 7 and 8 we described the ways representational theoretical systems receive empirical meaning in economics. In particular, we focused on the process by which the more abstract and general theories receive empirical meaning from the more concrete and data-specific members of the hierarchic semantic system. Formally, this analytic framework is still adequate to explain the case of a 'phenomenological theoretical system', a scheme that in the discussion to follow will consist, at most, of two levels. This reduction in the number of levels is a methodological reflection of the epistemological condition of being 'closer to phenomena', that is, of 'lesser theoretical depth', a condition that should not be confused with data-specificity. As we have seen in 8.4, a data-specific DTLDS theory is a representational theory which – even when axiomatized at the level of the observable demand functions – points to the unobservable 'constrained utility maximization' as the hypothesized interpretative underlying mechanism.

Our current semantic framework is thus reduced to two levels. At the lower level, we find a general phenomenological theory which, to avoid confusion with the general theories of the representational kind discussed in the two preceding chapters, we have decided to refer to as the 'generic theory'. At the upper level, in contact with actual data, we find 'data-specific' phenomenological theories.

9.1 GENERIC THEORY: LANGUAGE AND MODELS

At level one of the two-level hierarchy we find a testable theory, that is, an economic theory which incorporates, alongside sets of testable economic propositions, the relevant norms that govern measurement, estimation and testing procedures as well as the general conditions which determine the admissibility of the data. Whether stochastic or not, it certainly consists in an econometric language – see Klein (1989) – which has, formally if not epistemologically, very many common traits with a level-three language of a representational theoretical system. A generic theory – in particular the system of equations which summarizes its system of hypotheses – is often referred to as a 'prototype model'. To maintain our terminological consistency we may use the expressions 'prototype model' and 'theory of the prototype model' to refer to a satisfying relational structure and to the corresponding linguistic entity, respectively.

A structure of a level-one phenomenological system, denoted by S_1, is in all thinkable respects similar to a structure S_3 of a representational system since it must satisfy, here too, conditions which reflect basic features of actual data; and as was the case with L_3, the structural axioms of the generic theory L_1 do not point at any actual set of empirical data but, distantly, to collections of potential empirical structures.

A very common case of a level-one phenomenological system is that summarized by an econometric *system of equations in structural form*

$$\mathbf{A}\mathbf{y}_t + \mathbf{B}\mathbf{x}_t = \epsilon_t$$

where $\mathbf{y}_t$ is a vector of endogenous variables, $\mathbf{x}_t$ is a vector of predetermined (exogenous and/or lagged endogenous) variables, ϵ_t is a vector of random disturbances satisfying precise stochastic specifications and **A** and **B** are matrices of parameters to be estimated – more on this in Chapter 10. 'Each equation of this system corresponds to one of the basic laws which define the "model". The determination of these laws is the final objective of econometric research' – Malinvaud (1980).

To bring the analogy to a conclusion, here too it will not be the generic theory that is to be confronted with the structure of data of level two, but, rather, the adapted entity designated as the concrete (data-conform) theory.

9.2 FIRST EXAMPLE OF A GENERIC THEORY: LINEAR INPUT–OUTPUT ANALYSIS

Two good candidates to serve as illustrations for the case of generic phenomenological theories are input–output analysis of open economies, an economy-wide extended linear theory of production, and input–output analysis of closed economies, a linear general equilibrium or exchange theory. From these two theories we choose to focus on the former as it has more readily led to empirical applications, that is, to the formulation of level-two, data-specific theories.

As is well known, input–output analysis goes back to Leontief (1941). The current illustration of the analysis of an *open Leontief economy* or *open input–output system* is based on Gale (1960), Lancaster (1968), Stone (1984), and Weale (1984).

A simple picture of an economy is given by a system of n inter-related linear activities or industries each producing a single homogeneous output (or commodity). If x_i represents the total output of the ith activity and if x_{ij} denotes the fraction of this total used by the jth industry then one can write (for $i, j = 1, 2, \ldots, n$)

$$y_i = x_i - \Sigma_j x_{ij}$$

where y_i is the fraction of x_i that satisfies final demand for the ith commodity. Table 9.2.1 summarizes the transactions, in money values, that take place in such an economy. Using vector and matrix notation, $\mathbf{X} = [x_{ij}]$ is an n-square matrix of inter-industry flows, $\mathbf{y} = (y_1, \ldots, y_n)'$ is a column n-vector of final outputs or final demands, $\mathbf{x} = (x_1, \ldots, x_n)'$ is a column n-vector of total outputs and $\mathbf{z} = (z_1, \ldots, z_n)$ is a row n-vector of primary inputs (since they are measured here in money values, we may regard z_j as primary inputs cost for or value added to

Table 9.2.1 An input–output matrix

	Production: industries	*Final output*	*Totals*
Production: industries	**X**	**y**	**x**
Primary inputs	**z**	0	**μ**
Total	$\mathbf{x}^{-1}$	**μ**	

the jth sector). The scalar μ represents the money value of total final output (or final demand) and the total cost of primary inputs.

If we let **i** denote the column identity n-vector – that is $\mathbf{i} = (1, 1, \ldots, 1)'$ – we easily see that

$$\mathbf{x} = \mathbf{Xi} + \mathbf{y}.$$

Furthermore, letting $\underline{\mathbf{x}}^{-1}$ stand for the inverse of a diagonal matrix diag(**x**), we obtain the $n \times n$ input–output coefficients matrix $\mathbf{A} = [\mathbf{a}_{ij}]$ by setting

$$\mathbf{A} = \mathbf{X}\underline{\mathbf{x}}^{-1}.$$

The economy can now be summarized by the *quantity equation*

$$\mathbf{x} = \mathbf{Ax} + \mathbf{y} = (\mathbf{I} - \mathbf{A})^{-1}\mathbf{y}$$

where **I** is the $n \times n$ identity matrix.

There is a *price equation*, a dual formulation to the above quantity equation. From

$$\mathbf{x} = \mathbf{Xi} + \mathbf{y}$$

one can calculate the vector of primary input coefficients as

$$\mathbf{b} = \underline{\mathbf{x}}^{-1}\mathbf{z}.$$

If $\mathbf{p} = (\mathbf{p}_1, \ldots, \mathbf{p}_n)'$ is a column n-vector of output prices and **w** a column n-vector of prices of value-added per unit of output, it follows that

$$\mathbf{p}' = \mathbf{p}'\mathbf{A} + \underline{\mathbf{w}}\mathbf{b}$$

or, equivalently,

$$p' = \underline{w}b(I - A)^{-1}$$

where $\underline{w}$ is a diagonalization of w.

The complete equilibrium conditions for the open input–output system can be gathered now by means of the three vector equations

$$x = (I - A)^{-1}y \tag{1}$$

$$x'p = \mu = bw \tag{2}$$

$$p' = \underline{w}b(I - A)^{-1}. \tag{3}$$

There are different ways to endow an open input–output system with a stochastic mechanism – see for instance Gerking (1976), Divay and Meunier (1982), and Jackson and West (1989). However, for the sake of simplicity and brevity, especially to avoid being too repetitious regarding technical issues already illustrated in previous examples, we shall follow here a more traditional approach in the field which does not treat input–output systems as stochastic systems. This notwithstanding, a few references on stochastic input–output systems are given in the section on 'Notes and remarks' (9.7). In this section we refer to this generic version of the theory simply as the *non-stochastic open input–output system*, to be denoted by the acronym NSOIOS. In a very intuitive sense we are dealing here with a theory of a 'prototype model'.

Before continuing the main discussion, it will be convenient to agree on a few terminological and notational matters. In the remainder of the chapter, a vector x will be said to be positive, denoted $x >> 0$, if for all j, $x_j > 0$; it will be said to be semi-positive, denoted $x_j > 0$, if for all j, $x_j \geq 0$ and for at least one j, $x_j > 0$; and it will be said to be non-negative, denoted $x \geq 0$, if for all j, $x_j \geq 0$. Furthermore, a matrix A will be said to be semi-positive if all its rows and all its columns are semi-positive vectors. Finally, a semi-positive square matrix A will be said to be *decomposable* if there exists a permutation matrix P such that A can be written

$$PAP^T = \begin{pmatrix} A_1 & A_2 \\ A_3 & A_4 \end{pmatrix}$$

where A_1 and A_4 are square matrices (not necessarily of the same order) on the diagonal and A_3 is a (not necessarily square) matrix with only zero elements. When such a permutation matrix does not exist, **A** will be said to be an *indecomposable* matrix.

We next define the models of the generic non-stochastic open input–output system (NSOIOS). As in Chapters 7 and 8, we identify the level of structure and language using the appropriate subscript – the numeral '1' in this section and the numeral '2' in the following one.

Definition 9.2.1 The structure $S_1 = \langle \mathbf{X}_1, \mathbf{x}_1, \mathbf{y}_1, \mathbf{A}_1, \mathbf{z}_1, \mathbf{b}_1, \mathbf{p}_1, \mathbf{w}_1, \boldsymbol{\mu}_1 \rangle$ is a *model of the NSOIOS* if and only if it satisfies the following assumptions:

A9.2.1 $\mathbf{X}_1$ is the set of all $n \times n$ real semi-positive matrices of the form $[\mathbf{x}_{ij}]$ where the element $\mathbf{x}_{ij}$ represents the total quantity of commodities transferred from industry i to industry j, $i, j = 1, 2, \ldots, n$, during the period.

A9.2.2 $\mathbf{x}_1$ is the set of all $n \times 1$ real vectors of the form $(\mathbf{x}_j)$ where the element $\mathbf{x}_j$ represents total output of industry j, $j = 1, 2, \ldots, n$, during the period.

A9.2.3 $\mathbf{y}_1$ is the set of all $n \times 1$ non-negative real vectors of the form $(\mathbf{y}_j)$ where the element $\mathbf{y}_j$ represents total final demand for the output of industry j, $j = 1, 2, \ldots, n$, during the period.

A9.2.4 $\mathbf{A}_1$ is the set of all $n \times n$ semi-positive real matrices $[\mathbf{a}_{ij}]$ where the element $\mathbf{a}_{ij}$ represents the (i, j) input–output coefficient defined by $\mathbf{a}_{ij} = \mathbf{x}_{ij}/\mathbf{x}_j + \epsilon_{ij}$, where ϵ_{ij} is a measurement error with expected value $E\epsilon_{ij} = 0$.

A9.2.5 $\mathbf{z}_1$ is the set of all $1 \times n$ real vectors of the form $(\mathbf{z}_j)$ where the element $\mathbf{z}_j$ represents the quantity of primary inputs used by industry j, $j = 1, 2, \ldots, n$, during the period.

A9.2.6 $\mathbf{b}_1$ is the set of all $n \times 1$ real semi-positive vectors $(\mathbf{b}_j)$ where the element $\mathbf{b}_j$ represents the primary input–output coefficient in industry j defined by $\mathbf{b}_j = \mathbf{z}_j/\mathbf{x}_j$, $j = 1, 2, \ldots, n$, during the period.

A9.2.7 $\mathbf{p}_1$ is the set of all $n \times 1$ real vectors $(\mathbf{p}_j)$ where the element $\mathbf{p}_j$ represents the unit price of the output of industry j, $j = 1, 2, \ldots, n$, during the period.

A9.2.8 $\mathbf{w}_1$ is the set of all $n \times 1$ real semi-positive vectors $(\mathbf{w}_j)$ where the element $\mathbf{w}_j$ represents the price of value-added per unit of output in industry j, $j = 1, 2, \ldots, n$, during the period.

A9.2.9 μ_1 is the set of all positive real numbers μ representing total cost of primary inputs (total value added) during the period, that is, $x'p = \mu = bw$.

A9.2.10 Balance equations:

$$x - Ax = (I - A)x = y \qquad (1)$$

$$zi = \mu \qquad (2)$$

$$p' = p'A + \underline{w}b = \underline{w}b(I - A)^{-1} \qquad (3)$$

A9.2.11 Given (1) the actual vector of final demand y, (2) the projected value of total output $x^o = (x_1^o, \ldots, x_n^o)$, (3) the projected value of total intermediate demand $h^o = (h_1^o, \ldots, h_n^o) = Ax^o$, (4) the projected value of $\ldots\ldots$, and the tolerance limits $\lambda_x, \lambda_h, \ldots\ldots, x^o, h^o, \ldots\ldots$ satisfy the (Theil's) root mean square error (RMSE) tests $[\Sigma_j(x_j^o - x_j)^2/\Sigma_j x_j^2]^{1/2} < \lambda_x$, $[\Sigma_j(h_j^o - h_j)^2/\Sigma_j h_j^2]^{1/2} < \lambda_h$, $\ldots$, respectively.

Assumptions A9.2.1 to A9.2.9 are self-explanatory. In A9.2.10, three straightforward linear functional relations over the domains provide the 'phenomenological' description of the potential data – notice that only variables of the same epistemological level are involved in such description. Finally, to complete the list of axioms, we include tests of the predictive performance of the heart of the system – Equations (1) and (2) of A9.2.10 – in A9.2.11. We shall focus on the substance of the latter axiom when we discuss an analog requirement at the level of a data-specific theory (see Definition 9.5.1, Remark 9.5.1 and ensuing comment).

A central issue of open input–output analysis concerns the feasibility of the system to satisfy any final demand. The question may then be formulated as follows: given the vector of final demands $y \geq 0$, does $(I - A)x = y$ have a non-negative solution? The following concept is important in the sequel.

Definition 9.2.2 The system $x - Ax$ is said to be *productive* if there exists a non-negative vector x^* such that $x^* > Ax^*$. The matrix A is said to be productive when the system $x - Ax$ is productive.

Let us now sample a few propositions. The following result states conditions for the matrix **A** to be productive.

Theorem 9.2.1 The following statements are equivalent:

(1) the matrix **A** is productive;
(2) each principal minor of **A** is positive;
(3) the largest characteristic value of **A** is less than 1.

We have now a first substantive result on feasibility.

Theorem 9.2.2 If the matrix **A** is productive then the system $(\mathbf{I} - \mathbf{A})\mathbf{x} = \mathbf{y}$ has a unique non-negative solution for any final demand vector $\mathbf{y} \geq 0$.

We also have a parallel substantive result involving prices. Let us write $\underline{\mathbf{w}}\mathbf{b} = \mathbf{z}$.

Theorem 9.2.3 If the matrix **A** is productive then there exists a unique non-negative price vector **p** such that $\mathbf{p}' - \mathbf{p}'\mathbf{A} = \mathbf{z}$ for any value-added vector $\mathbf{z} \geq 0$.

The following proposition contains essential technical conditions for the solution of $(\mathbf{I} - \mathbf{A})\mathbf{x} = \mathbf{y}$ referred to the inverse of $(\mathbf{I} - \mathbf{A})$.

Theorem 9.2.4 If **A** is semi-positive indecomposable then the sum $\mathbf{I} + \mathbf{A} + \mathbf{A}^2 + \mathbf{A}^3 + \ldots$ converges.

We conclude our brief discussion of the NSOIOS at the generic-theory level with the following important result.

Theorem 9.2.5 If **A** is semi-positive indecomposable then $\mathbf{x} = (\mathbf{I} - \mathbf{A})^{-1}\mathbf{y} = (\mathbf{I} + \mathbf{A} + \mathbf{A}^2 + \mathbf{A}^3 + \ldots)\mathbf{y}$.

The transit from the level of the generic theory to the level of the data – that is the level of the prototype structure to the level of a specific empirical structure – is made here, too, by specializing the theory to the nature of the data, that is by formulating a concrete (data-conform) theory.

9.3   SECOND EXAMPLE OF A GENERIC THEORY: A THEORY OF CYCLICAL GROWTH

The second example of a generic phenomenological theory is a dynamic time-continuous system constructed by A. R. Bergstrom to study the joint generation of economic cycles and growth. This macroeconomic theory, interesting as it is from the economic-theoretical viewpoint, has the added attraction that it constitutes a pioneering incursion in the field of the econometric estimation of time-continuous systems. It is amenable to rigorous formal analysis – for example, in the area of stability – and it is applicable to the study of empirical economies – in 9.6 we shall meet an application of the system to data on the United Kingdom. Furthermore, the mathematical configuration of the theory is flexible enough to incorporate alternative policy rules – monetary, fiscal, and exchange rate regimes – thus providing a suitable framework for the study of some problems of theoretical as well as empirical economic policy. For the current presentation we have consulted Bergstrom (1966, 1967, 1978, 1984a, 1984b), and Bergstrom and Wymer (1976).

The primitives of the theories are the variables consumption (**C**), real income or output (**Y**), stock of fixed capital (**K**), real exports (**X**), real imports (**I**), inventories (**S**), employment (**L**), stock of money (**M**), interest rate (**r**), price level (**p**), wage rate (**w**) and time (**t**). Also explained is the determination of the variables **k** and **m**, the proportional rate of increase of the fixed capital stock and of the money stock, respectively. All these variables are related through a system of thirteen differential equations – the symbol D is used here to denote the differential time operator d/dt – two of which are of the second order, several are non-linear and eleven are stochastic.

As with the other examples of this study, our aim is an illustrative one and the exposition is thus incomplete, very condensed and radically simplified, only pointing at those issues relevant to our specific methodological objectives.

A relational structure for this theory – we shall refer to it from now on as the Bergstrom theory of cyclical growth (BTCG) – consists of the thirteen domains of the primitive variables, a sample space of random disturbances and the thirteen relations relating these domains. On this basis, a definition of a model of the theory easily follows.

Definition 9.3.1   The structure $S_1 = \langle C_1, K_1, Y_1, S_1, E_1, I_1, L_1, p_1, w_1, M_1, r_1, (E_1, v_1), D \rangle$ is a *model of BTCG* if and only if it satisfies the following assumptions:

A9.3.1 C_1 is the set of all finite sequences $\{C(t): t_1 \leq t \leq T\}$ of positive real numbers where $C(t)$ represents aggregate real consumption at time t.

A9.3.2 K_1 is the set of all finite sequences $\{K(t): t_1 \leq t \leq T\}$ of positive real numbers where $K(t)$ represents aggregate real fixed capital at t.

A9.3.3 Y_1 is the set of all finite sequences $\{Y(t): t_1 \leq t \leq T\}$ of positive real numbers where $Y(t)$ represents real aggregate net income or output at t.

A9.3.4 S_1 is the set of all finite sequences $\{S(t): t_1 \leq t \leq T\}$ of positive real numbers where $S(t)$ represents real aggregate stocks or inventories at t.

A9.3.5 X_1 is the set of all finite sequences $\{X(t): t_1 \leq t \leq T\}$ of positive real numbers where $X(t)$ represents real aggregate exports at t.

A9.3.6 I_1 is the set of all finite sequences $\{I(t): t_1 \leq t \leq T\}$ of positive real numbers where $I(t)$ represents real aggregate imports at t.

A9.3.7 L_1 is the set of all finite sequences $\{L(t): t_1 \leq t \leq T\}$ of positive real numbers where $L(t)$ represents total employment at t.

A9.3.8 p_1 is the set of all finite sequences $\{p(t): t_1 \leq t \leq T\}$ of positive real numbers where p_t represents the price level at t.

A9.3.9 w_1 is the set of all finite sequences $\{w(t): t_1 \leq t \leq T\}$ of positive real numbers where w_t represents the real wage rate at t.

A9.3.10 M_1 is the set of all finite sequences $\{M(t): t_1 \leq t \leq T\}$ of positive real numbers where $M(t)$ represents the real volume of money at t.

A9.3.11 r_1 is the set of all finite sequences $\{r(t): t_1 \leq t \leq T\}$ of real numbers where $r(t)$ represents the real interest rate at t.

A9.3.12 D stands for the non-linear system of stochastic differential equations of up to the second order, where t is the real line, D stands for d/dt, $0 < \alpha_1 < 1$, $\alpha_4 > -1$, $0 < \alpha_6 < 1$, and all other parameters are positive with the possible exception of λ_3:

Proportional-change-in-consumption function

$$DC/C = \gamma_1 \log(\alpha_1 Y/C) + \epsilon_1(t), \tag{1}$$

Proportional-change-in-employment function

$$DL/L = \gamma_2 \log\{\alpha_2 \exp(-\lambda_1 t)[Y^{-\alpha_4} - \alpha_3 K^{-\alpha_4}]/L\} + \epsilon_2(t), \tag{2}$$

Change in rate of proportional change of fixed capital

$$Dk = \gamma_3\{\gamma_4[\alpha_3(Y/K)^{1-\alpha_4} - r + Dp/p] + \alpha_5 - k\} + \epsilon_3(t), \tag{3}$$

Output adjustment function

$$DY = \gamma_5[(1 - \alpha_6)(C + DK + X) - Y] + \gamma_6[\alpha_7(C + DK + X) - S] + \epsilon_4(t), \tag{4}$$

Change-in-import function

$$DI = \gamma_7[\alpha_6(C + DK + X) - I] + \gamma_8[\alpha_7(C + DK + X) - S] + \epsilon_5(t), \tag{5}$$

Proportional-change-in-export function

$$DX/X = \gamma_9 \log\{[\alpha_8 p^{-\alpha_9} \exp(\lambda_2 t)]/X\} + \epsilon_6(t), \tag{6}$$

Mark-up proportional price adjustment equation

$$Dp/p = \gamma_{10} \log\{\alpha_{10}\alpha_2 w \exp(-\lambda_1 t)[1 - \alpha_3(Y/K)^{\alpha_4}]^{-(1+\alpha_4)/\alpha_4}/p\} + \epsilon_7(t), \tag{7}$$

Proportional wage-rate adjustment equation

$$Dw/w = \gamma_{11} \log\{\alpha_2 \exp(-\lambda_1 t)[Y^{-\alpha_4} - \alpha_{33} K^{-\alpha_4}]^{-1/\alpha_4}/\alpha_{11} \exp(\lambda_3 t)\} + \epsilon_8(t), \tag{8}$$

Proportional interest rate (that is, money market) adjustment equation

$$Dr/r = \gamma_{12} \log[\alpha_{12} p Y^{\alpha_{13}} r^{\alpha_{14}}] + \epsilon_9(t), \tag{9}$$

Policy relation linking the change in the money supply and the balance of payments

$$\mathbf{Dm} = \gamma_{13} \log(\mathbf{X}/\alpha_{15}\mathbf{I}) + \gamma_{14} \log[\alpha_{16} \exp(\lambda_3 \mathbf{t})/\mathbf{L}] +$$

$$\gamma_{15}\mathbf{D} \log(\mathbf{X}/\alpha_{15}\mathbf{I}) + \gamma_{16}\mathbf{D} \log[\alpha_{16} \exp(\lambda_3 \mathbf{t})/\mathbf{L}] + \epsilon_{10}(\mathbf{t}), \quad (10)$$

Change in stocks equation

$$\mathbf{DS} = \mathbf{Y} + \mathbf{I} - \mathbf{C} - \mathbf{DK} - \mathbf{X}, \tag{11}$$

Proportional rate of change of fixed capital stock

$$\mathbf{DK}/\mathbf{K} = \mathbf{k}, \tag{12}$$

Proportional rate of change of the stock of money

$$\mathbf{DM}/\mathbf{M} = \mathbf{m}. \tag{13}$$

A9.3.13 $\mathbf{E}_3$ is the space of random disturbances $\epsilon_i(\mathbf{t})$, white noise, distributed according to a distribution ν_1 such that

(i) $E(\int_{t_1}^{t_2}\epsilon_i(\mathbf{t})) = 0$ $(i = 1, 2, \ldots, n)$,

(ii) $E(\int_{t_1}^{t_2}\epsilon_i(\mathbf{t})\int_{t_1}^{t_2}\epsilon_j(\mathbf{t})) = s_{ij}$ $(i, j = 1, 2, \ldots, n)$, and

(iii) $E(\int_{t_1}^{t_2}\epsilon_i(\mathbf{t})\int_{t_3}^{t_4}\epsilon_j(\mathbf{t})) = 0$ $(i, j = 1, 2, \ldots, n)$,

for $\mathbf{t}_1 > \mathbf{t}_2 > \mathbf{t}_3 > \mathbf{t}_4$.

A9.3.14   The equations system $\mathbf{D}$ of A9.3.12 is identified.

It is immediate that Assumptions A9.3.1 to A9.3.11 determine the set of admissible data (structural axioms) while Assumptions A9.3.13 and A9.3.14 characterize the stochastic properties of the dynamic system described in A9.3.12 together with the identifiability requirement.

Focusing next on the axiomatic nucleus of the theory, we first note that the system summarized in A9.3.12 is a synthesis of Keynesian and neoclassical propositions given in a dynamic form. At least one of these propositions, namely Equation (10), is of a policy nature and as such could have been left blank in the current presentation or could have been filled, according to specific requirements, with alternative consistent statements. We now comment briefly on the scalar components of the differential system **D**.

Equation (1), a scalar differential equation, is a Keynesian consumption relation involving a time-lag; similarly, time-lags are included in Equations (2) to (10), nine scalar differential equations, describing, in that order, the behaviour of employment, of the change in the proportional rate of increase in fixed capital, of the rate of increase in output, of the rate of increase in imports, of the proportional rate of change in the demand for exports, of the imperfectly competitive price adjustment mechanism, of the wage rate adjustment mechanism, of the interest rate (or money market) adjustment mechanism, and of the influence of the balance of payments on the money supply; the parameters γ appearing in all these time-lags involving relations represent thus 'speeds of response'. The remaining equations are definitional.

Let us now give a few examples of derived statements of the theory. We begin with a proposition of major economic-theoretical importance as it refers to the existence of a particular solution of the system. For the sake of brevity, we confine ourselves here to an abridged version of an existence theorem – for the complete version and, in particular, for the definitions of the variables with asterisks see Bergstrom and Wymer (1976).

Theorem 9.3.1   The deterministic part of the differential equations system of A9.3.12 (1) to (13) in Definition 9.3.1 has the particular solution:

$$
\begin{aligned}
C &= C^* \exp[(\lambda_1 + \lambda_3)t], \\
L &= L^* \exp(\lambda_3 t), \\
k &= \lambda_1 + \lambda_3 = k^*, \\
Y &= Y^* \exp[(\lambda_1 + \lambda_3)t], \\
I &= I^* \exp[(\lambda_1 + \lambda_3)t], \\
X &= X^* \exp[(\lambda_1 + \lambda_3)t], \\
p &= p^* \exp\{[(\lambda_2 - \lambda_1 - \lambda_3)/\alpha_9]t\}, \\
w &= w^* \exp\{[(\lambda_2 - \lambda_1 - \lambda_3)/\alpha_9 + \lambda_1]t\}, \\
r &= r^*, \\
m &= (\lambda_2 - \lambda_1 - \lambda_3)/\alpha_9 + \alpha_{13}(\lambda_1 + \lambda_3) = m^*, \\
S &= S^* \exp[(\lambda_1 + \lambda_3)t], \\
K &= K^* \exp[(\lambda_1 + \lambda_3)t], \\
M &= M^* \exp\{[(\lambda_2 - \lambda_1 - \lambda_3)/\alpha_9 + \alpha_{13}(\lambda_1 + \lambda_3)]t\}.
\end{aligned}
$$

In a way, this is the point of departure of the analysis of the dynamic properties of the system, in particular of the conditions for local asymptotic stability. However, given our limited purpose, we skip this fundamental part of the theory and focus instead on some econometric issues. Here, again, we simplify the actual issue and content ourselves with a broad sketch of the problems involved.

The differential equations system of A9.3.12 can be written as

$$Dx(t) = f[x(t), t, \alpha, \gamma, \lambda] + \epsilon(t) \qquad (1)$$

where $x(t) = [x_1(t), \ldots, x_{13}(t)]'$, $\alpha = [\alpha_1, \ldots, \alpha_{16}]'$, $\gamma = [\gamma_1, \ldots, \gamma_{16}]'$, $\lambda = [\lambda_1, \lambda_2, \lambda_3]'$ and $\epsilon(t) = [\epsilon_1(t), \ldots, \epsilon_{10}(t), 0, 0, 0]'$, and where $x_1 = \log C$, $x_2 = \log L$, $x_3 = k$, $x_4 = \log Y$, $x_5 = \log I$, $x_6 = \log X$, $x_7 = \log p$, $x_8 = \log w$, $x_9 = \log r$, $x_{10} = m$, $x_{11} = \log S$, $x_{12} = \log K$, and $x_{13} = \log M$.

Estimates of the parameters of the non-linear system (1) can be obtained as estimates of an appropriate linear approximation of that system. This we state next – see Bergstrom (1966, 1984b) and Bergstrom and Wymer (1976).

Theorem 9.3.2 A linearization of (1) around the sample means of the variables can be obtained as the differential equation

$$Dx(t) = A(\underline{x}, \alpha, \gamma, \lambda)x(t) + b(\underline{x}, \alpha, \gamma, \lambda) + c(\underline{x}, \alpha, \gamma, \lambda)t + \epsilon(t) \quad (2)$$

where (a) $\underline{x}$ is the sample mean of $x(t)$; (b) the elements of the matrix A and the vectors b and c are known functions of $\underline{x}$, α, γ and λ and obtained by a Taylor series expansion of f around x; and (c) $\epsilon(t)$ is assumed to be a white noise vector such that for $t_1 < t_2 < t_3 < t_4$, (i) $E\{\int_{t_1}^{t_2}\epsilon(t)dt\} = 0$, (ii) $E\{\int_{t_1}^{t_2}\epsilon(t)dt\int_{t_3}^{t_4}\epsilon(t)dt\} = 0$, and (iii) $E\{\int_{t_1}^{t_2}\epsilon(t)dt\int_{t_2}^{t_1}\epsilon(t)dt\} = (t_2 - t_1)\Sigma$, where Σ is a positive semi-definite matrix.

For the next step, estimation, we need a discrete approximation of the continuous linear system (2). This is the content of the following proposition – see Bergstrom (1966) and Bergstrom and Wymer (1976).

Theorem 9.3.3 A sample $x(1), \ldots, x(T)$ generated by system (2) satisfies the following

$$\{x(t) + A^{-1}(b + A^{-1}c + dt)\}$$
$$= e^A\{x(t - 1) + A^{-1}[b + A^{-1}c + d(t - 1)]\} + \epsilon(t) \qquad (3)$$

in which the elements of **A**, **b** and **c** are functions of $\underline{x}$, $\boldsymbol{\alpha}$, $\boldsymbol{\gamma}$ and $\boldsymbol{\lambda}$.

In particular, we have this result – Bergstrom and Wymer (1976):

Corollary 9.3.1   From system (3) in Theorem 9.3.3 it follows that

$$\left\{\int_{t-1}^{t}\mathbf{x}(\tau)d\tau + \mathbf{A}^{-1}[\mathbf{b} + \mathbf{A}^{-1}\mathbf{c} + \mathbf{d}(t - 1/2)]\right\}$$

$$= e^{A}\left\{\int_{t-1}^{t-2}\mathbf{x}(\tau)d\tau + \mathbf{A}^{-1}[\mathbf{b} + \mathbf{A}^{-1}\mathbf{c} + \mathbf{d}(t - 3/2)]\right\}$$

$$+ \int_{t-1}^{t}\int_{\tau-1}^{\tau}e^{A(\tau-\theta)}\epsilon(\theta)d\theta\ d\tau. \tag{4}$$

Finally, we reach this result – see Bergstrom (1966), Bergstrom and Wymer (1976):

Theorem 9.3.4   Quasi-maximum likelihood estimates of the unknown parameters of system (1) together with their *t*-values can be obtained from the quasi-maximum likelihood estimates of the parameters of system (4) by replacing in (4) the data-vector $\int_{t-1}^{t}\mathbf{x}(\tau)d\tau$ by the moving averages vector $\mathbf{y}(\tau)$ and then minimizing the determinant of the covariance matrix of the residuals with respect to the parameter vectors $\boldsymbol{\alpha}$ and $\boldsymbol{\lambda}$.

This completes our small sample of results of the level-one BTCG.

9.4   DATA-SPECIFIC THEORY: LANGUAGE AND MODEL

From a formal point of view, all that has been said in 8.3 regarding the language of a data-specific representational theory still applies to the case of a data-specific phenomenological theory. Indeed, the difference between the kinds of theory is of an epistemological rather than of a formal nature. Representational explanations are, simply, epistemologically deeper. Formally, the language of a data-specific phenomenological theory is that of arithmetic and applied statistics, in unison with reference structure and cognitive objectives.

It is clear that only an empirical structure can qualify as an intended model of the concrete (data-conform) version of a phenomenological theory at level two. Moreover, once again, as at any other level, the determination of the requirements that define an empirical structure as a model of the level-two phenomenological theory is a function of the appropriate theory.

Finally, regarding the relations between theory and mediate referent and between empirical model and mediate referent – as well as the role of 'approximation theory' and the notion of 'partial truth' – we still stand by what we said in 8.3. In this context, we refer once again to Bunge (1967b) and Balzer, Moulines and Sneed (1987).

9.5 FIRST EXAMPLE OF A DATA-SPECIFIC THEORY: AN APPLIED INPUT–OUTPUT SYSTEM

As an example of a data-specific phenomenological theory we have chosen a radically simplified input–output representation of the economy of the Netherlands corresponding to the years 1948–61 – Tilanus (1968). The system consists of four sectors or industries (agriculture, manufacturing, construction and services, which are given the identifying numbers 1, 2, 3 and 4, respectively), a row to deal with value added and columns to represent the components of final demand (see Table 9.5.1). Because we have chosen here a non-stochastic framework to parallel the generic theory of 9.2, the treatment in this section lacks the statistical–econometric flavour of 8.4.

As usual, we begin by identifying the models of the theory.

Definition 9.5.1 The empirical structure $S_2 = \langle \mathbf{X}_2, \mathbf{x}_2, \mathbf{y}_2, \mathbf{z}_2 \rangle$ is the *primal model of the four-industry NSOIOS for the Netherlands 1948* if and only if $\langle \mathbf{X}_1, \mathbf{x}_1, \mathbf{y}_1, \mathbf{A}_1, \mathbf{z}_1, \mathbf{b}_1, \mathbf{p}_1, \mathbf{w}_1, \boldsymbol{\mu}_1 \rangle$ is a model of the NSOIOS and the following conditions are satisfied:

A9.5.1 $\mathbf{X}_2$ is a possible empirical realization of $\mathbf{X}_1$ (in this specific case the 4×4 semi-positive matrix of real numbers $\mathbf{X} = [\mathbf{x}_{ij}]$ shown below, where the element $\mathbf{x}_{ij}$ represents the total quantity of commodities transferred from industry i to industry j, $i, j = 1, 2, 3, 4$, in the Netherlands during the year 1948) (*source*: Tilanus, 1968):

$$\begin{pmatrix} 2.7 & 0.1 & 0.0 & 0.4 \\ 0.6 & 2.6 & 0.9 & 0.8 \\ 0.0 & 0.1 & 0.3 & 0.0 \\ 0.3 & 0.7 & 0.3 & 1.2 \end{pmatrix}.$$

A9.5.2 $\mathbf{x}_2$ is a possible empirical realization of $\mathbf{x}_1$ (in this specific case the 4×1 vector of real numbers $\mathbf{x} = (\mathbf{x}_j)$ shown below, where the element $\mathbf{x}_j$ represents the total quantity

Table 9.5.1   An input–output system for the Netherlands, 1948

	Industries: 1	2	3	4	Sub-total	Final demand: Export	Consumption	Investment	Sub-total	Total
Production:										
1. Agriculture	2.7	0.1	0.0	0.4	3.2	1.2	3.1	0.0	4.3	7.5
2. Manufacture	0.6	2.6	0.9	0.8	4.9	2.0	2.3	0.8	5.1	10.0
3. Construction	0.0	0.1	0.3	0.0	0.4	0.0	0.9	1.7	2.6	3.0
4. Services	0.3	0.7	0.3	1.2	2.5	1.8	3.7	0.0	5.5	8.0
Sub-total	3.6	3.5	1.5	2.4	11.0	5.0	10.0	2.5	17.5	28.5
Imports	1.2	2.3	0.3	0.8	4.6	0.0	0.6	0.8	1.4	6.0
Value-added	2.7	4.2	1.2	4.8	12.9	0.0	2.1	0.0	2.1	15.0
Sub-total	3.9	6.5	1.5	5.6	17.5	0.0	2.7	0.8	3.5	21.0
Total	7.5	10.0	3.0	8.0	28.5	5.0	12.7	3.3	21.0	49.5

Source: Tilanus (1968, p. 5). The figures are in billions of current guilders.

of commodities produced by industry j, $j = 1, 2, 3, 4$, in the Netherlands during the year 1948) (*source*: idem):

$$\mathbf{x} = (7.5 \quad 10.0 \quad 3.0 \quad 8.0)'.$$

A9.5.3 $\mathbf{y}_2$ is a possible empirical realization of $\mathbf{y}_1$ (in this specific case the 4×1 non-negative vector of real numbers $\mathbf{y} = (\mathbf{y}_j)$ shown below where the element $\mathbf{y}_j$ represents total final demand for the output of industry j, $j = 1, 2, 3, 4$, in the Netherlands during the year 1948) (*source*: idem):

$$\mathbf{y} = (4.3 \quad 5.1 \quad 2.6 \quad 5.5)'.$$

A9.5.4 $\mathbf{z}_2$ is a possible empirical realization of $\mathbf{z}_1$ (in this specific case the 1×4 non-negative vector of real numbers $\mathbf{z} = (\mathbf{z}_j)\}$ shown below where the element $\mathbf{z}_j$ represents the primary input used by industry j, $j = 1, 2, 3, 4$, and by final demand in the Netherlands during the year 1948) (*source*: idem):

$$\mathbf{z} = (2.7 \quad 4.2 \quad 1.2 \quad 4.8).$$

A9.5.5   The NSOIOS, as formalized by the equations

$$x - Ax = (I - A)x = y \qquad (1)$$

$$zi = \mu \qquad (2)$$

$$p' = p'A + \underline{w}b = \underline{w}b(I - A)^{-1} \qquad (3)$$

is satisfied, where A below is the computed 4×4 semi-positive input-coefficient matrix

$$\begin{pmatrix} 0.36 & 0.01 & 0.00 & 0.05 \\ 0.08 & 0.26 & 0.30 & 0.10 \\ 0.00 & 0.01 & 0.10 & 0.00 \\ 0.04 & 0.07 & 0.10 & 0.15 \end{pmatrix}$$

and b below is the given value-added coefficients row vector

$$b = (0.36 \quad 0.42 \quad 0.40 \quad 0.60).$$

A9.5.6   Given the actual final demand vector y, the actual output vector x, ... and the intermediate demand vector h, the projected output vector x^o, ... and the projected intermediate demand vector h^o do satisfy the (Theil's) root mean square error (RMSE) tests at the prescribed levels of tolerance.

A9.5.1 to A9.5.5 are the axioms of the 'four-sector NSOIOS for the Netherlands 1948' or 'NSOIOS NL 1948', from which A9.5.1 to A9.5.4 constitute the subset of structural axioms. A9.5.5 summarizes the crucial hypotheses of open input–output analysis, relativized by the preceding five axioms to a data-conform version of the theory. A9.5.6 adapts the tests already introduced in the generic theory of level one.

The sequence of axioms included in Definition 9.5.1 is rather limited and thus merely illustrative. This is particularly true regarding testing procedures since it is obvious that, even in a non-stochastic context, one may want to subject the theory to a more conclusive list of tests. One possible way to approach this issue is to 'extend' the content of Definition 9.5.1 by determining the empirical structures isomorphic to the primal model – essentially the products of projection exercises – that are also admissible as intended models of the theory. This is done next.

Remark 9.5.1 An empirical structure isomorphic to that determined in Definition 9.5.1, A9.5.1 to A9.5.5, is a model of the 'NSOIOS NL 1948' if it also satisfies axiom A9.5.6.

Whereas Definition 9.5.1 focuses on an empirical structure, the primal model, which within the tolerance limits for errors of rounding and approximation satisfies the axioms by construction, Remark 9.5.1 extends the class of prospective models to those which are principally the result of projection exercises. This circumstance in no way trivializes the role of the former definition. While Definition 9.5.1, on the one hand, reminds us that the data-specific theory is dependent on a particular structure of data (that is, the matrix $\mathbf{A}$ has been computed from such data), Remark 9.5.1, on the other hand, determines a wider class of prospective uses and thus of prospective models of the theory while establishing, at the same time, a minimum test criterion in the current non-stochastic framework. Intuitively, if an actual final demand vector $\mathbf{y}$ is given – for instance, the values for 1960 instead of the original values of 1948 – it is required that the projected vectors $\mathbf{x}^o$, $\mathbf{h}^o$ and so on satisfy the prescribed test. Observe, however, that it would also be legitimate to take as final demand a forecast vector $\mathbf{y} \bullet$ – instead of the 'actual' (contemporarily unknown) final demand $\mathbf{y}$ – provided it will satisfy a tolerance bound by itself – for instance $[\Sigma_j (y_j \bullet - y_j)^2 / \Sigma_j y_j]^{1/2}$ $< \lambda_y$ – while, naturally, the projected vectors satisfy the prescribed tests.

It is in this sense that to project successfully may be understood as predicting accurately – that is, within the tolerance limits determined by the axioms of the theory – the values of some isomorphic empirical models for the theory. If in our input–output system of Remark 9.5.1 we choose any arbitrary – in the sense of 'non-empirical' – final demand vector $\mathbf{y}$, it is clear that equation $\mathbf{x} - \mathbf{Ax} = (\mathbf{I} - \mathbf{A})\mathbf{x} = \mathbf{y}$, or more specifically, the derived form $\mathbf{x} = (\mathbf{I} - \mathbf{A})^{-1}\mathbf{y}$, will give us the corresponding values of say $\mathbf{x}$ or $\mathbf{h}$. The numerical values of $\mathbf{x}$ or $\mathbf{h}$, together with the consistent values of all remaining variables, accessible by means of Remark 9.5.1, clearly generate a numerical model of our 'four-sector NSOIOS NL 1948'; however, this model is not an (intendedly) empirical one.

In scientific forecasting, instead, we would compare the actual $\mathbf{x}$ or $\mathbf{h}$ generated by the economy for the actual $\mathbf{y}$ (or satisfactory forecast $\mathbf{y} \bullet$) to the predicted $\mathbf{x}^o$ or $\mathbf{h}^o$, computed by the predicting device for the same $\mathbf{y}$ or $\mathbf{y} \bullet$. We collect such examples in the following two empirical remarks.

Empirical remark 9.5.1 The values in year 1960 for the economy of the Netherlands of actual final demand, predicted total output and actual total output were, respectively, $\mathbf{y}$ = (11.30, 18.00, 6.00, 17.60), $\mathbf{x}^o$ = (20.13, 32.75, 7.03, 25.18) and $\mathbf{x}$ = (19.90, 31.50, 8.00, 24.00), respectively. Hence Theil's RMSE [$(\mathbf{x}^o, \mathbf{x})/\mathbf{y}$] = 0.04 < 0.05 and the relevant condition of Remark 9.5.1 is satisfied.

Similarly,

Empirical remark 9.5.2 The values in year 1960 for the economy of the Netherlands of actual final demand, predicted total intermediate demand and actual total intermediate demand were, respectively, $\mathbf{y}$ = (11.30, 18.00, 6.00, 17.60), $\mathbf{h}^o$ = (8.83, 14.75, 1.03, 7.58) and $\mathbf{h}$ = (8.60, 13.5, 2.0, 6.4), respectively. Hence Theil's RMSE [$(\mathbf{h}^o, \mathbf{h})/\mathbf{y}$] = 0.11 < 0.15 and the relevant condition of Remark 9.5.1 is satisfied.

We close the discussion with a numerical result on equilibrium prices.

Proposition 9.5.1 Assume that the same wage rate $\mathbf{w}$ = 1 prevails in each industry. Then the price equation $\mathbf{p}' = \mathbf{p}'A + \underline{\mathbf{w}}\mathbf{b} = \underline{\mathbf{w}}\underline{\mathbf{b}}(I - A)^{-1}$ of A9.5.5 (3) has the solution $\mathbf{p}' = (\mathbf{p}_1, \mathbf{p}_2, \mathbf{p}_3, \mathbf{p}_4)$ = (0.27, 0.25, 0.24, 0.24) with normalization rule $\Sigma_j \mathbf{p}_j = 1.0$.

9.6 SECOND EXAMPLE OF A DATA-SPECIFIC THEORY: AN APPLIED THEORY OF CYCLICAL GROWTH

The differential equations system which summarizes the BTCG is certainly general enough to serve as the basis for empirical systems of equations used in the description of a whole class of empirical macroeconomies. Not surprisingly, Bergstrom refers repeatedly to the system as a 'prototype model' (for instance, Bergstrom, 1967, 1976, 1984a) and we think that it is an appropriate example to illustrate the case of a generic phenomenological theory.

However, our current interest is in illustrating the second level, the data-specific theory, of a two-level phenomenological system. As it happens, the BTCG has been used for studies of the UK economy and, in particular, it has been fitted to quarterly data covering the period 1955–66. Observe that whereas each of the domains of the structure S_1 may consist of a continuum of values – for example the non-negative or the positive real line – possible realizations in S_2 can only consist of sequences of discrete data, in this particular example quarterly observations. From the econometric point of view, on the other hand, the novelty rests upon the fact that the parameters of a time-continuous system (a system of differential equations) are estimated by means of discrete sets of data – see Bergstrom (1966, 1984b) and Bergstrom and Wymer (1976).

We shall now designate our level-two theory as the 'BTCG UK 1955–66' and go on to define its primal model of data.

Definition 9.6.1   The empirical structure $S_2 = \langle C_2, K_2, Y_2, S_2, X_2, I_2, L_2, p_2, w_2, M_2, r_2, D \rangle$ is the *primal model of BTCG UK 1955–66* if and only if $\langle C_1, K_1, Y_1, S_1, X_1, I_1, L_1, p_1, w_1, M_1, r_1, (E_1, v_1), D \rangle$ is a model of BTCG and the following conditions are satisfied:

A9.6.1 C_2 is a possible empirical realization of C_1 (in this specific case, the sequence (C_t: $t = 1, 2, \ldots, 48$) of quarterly observations of real aggregate consumption in the UK during the period 1955–66. *Source*: Appendix 1 in Bergstrom and Wymer, 1976).

A9.6.2 K_2 is a possible empirical realization of K_1 (in this specific case, the sequence (K_t: $t = 1, 2, \ldots, 48$) of quarterly observations of real aggregate fixed capital in the UK during the period 1955–66. *Source: idem*).

A9.6.3 Y_2 is a possible empirical realization of Y_1 (in this specific case, the sequence (Y_t: $t = 1, 2, \ldots, 48$) of quarterly observations of real aggregate income in the UK during the period 1955–66. *Source: idem*).

A9.6.4 S_2 is a possible empirical realization of S_1 (in this specific case, the sequence (S_t: $t = 1, 2, \ldots, 48$) of quarterly observations of real aggregate inventories in the UK during the period 1955–66. *Source: idem*).

A9.6.5 X_2 is a possible empirical realization of X_1 (in this specific case, the sequence (X_t: $t = 1, 2, \ldots, 48$) of quarterly observations of real aggregate exports of the UK during the period 1955–66. *Source: idem*).

A9.6.6 I_2 is a possible empirical realization of I_1 (in this specific case, the sequence (I_t: $t = 1, 2, \ldots, 48$) of quarterly observations of real aggregate imports in the UK during the period 1955–66. *Source: idem*).

A9.6.7 L_2 is a possible empirical realization of L_1 (in this specific case, the sequence (L_t: $t = 1, 2, \ldots, 48$) of quarterly observations of total employment in the UK during the period 1955–66. *Source*: *idem*).

A9.6.8 p_2 is a possible empirical realization of p_1 (in this specific case, the sequence (p_t: $t = 1, 2, \ldots, 48$) of quarterly observations of the price level in the UK during the period 1955–66. *Source*: *idem*).

A9.6.9 w_2 is a possible empirical realization of w_1 (in this specific case, the sequence (w_t: $t = 1, 2, \ldots, 48$) of quarterly observations of the real wage rate in the UK during the period 1955–66. *Source*: *idem*).

A9.6.10 M_2 is a possible empirical realization of M_1 (in this specific case, the sequence (M_t: $t = 1, 2, \ldots, 48$) of quarterly observations of the real volume of money in the UK during the period 1955–66. *Source*: *idem*).

A9.6.11 r_2 is a possible empirical realization of r_1 (in this specific case, the sequence (r_t: $t = 1, 2, \ldots, 48$) of quarterly observations of the real interest rate in the UK during the period 1955–66. *Source*: *idem*).

A9.6.12   **D**, the *maintained hypothesis*, is the system of simultaneous stochastic differential equations:

Proportional-change-in-consumption function

$$DC/C = g_1 \log(a_1 Y/C) + e_1(t), \qquad (1)$$

Proportional-change-in-employment function

$$DL/L = g_2 \log\{a_2 \exp(-l_1 t)[Y^{-a_4} - a_3 K^{-a_4}]/L\} + e_2(t), \qquad (2)$$

Change in proportional rate of change in fixed capital

$$Dk = g_3\{g_4[a_3(Y/K)^{1-a_4} - r + Dp/p] + a_5 - k\} + e_3(t), \qquad (3)$$

Output adjustment function

$$DY = g_5[(1 - a_6)(C + DK + X) - Y] + g_6[a_7(C + DK + X) - S] + e_4(t), \qquad (4)$$

Change-in-import function

$$DI = g_7[a_6(C + DK + X) - I]$$
$$+ g_8[a_7(C + DK + X) - S] + e_5(t), \qquad (5)$$

Proportional-change-in-export function

$$DX/X = g_9 \log\{[a_8 p^{-a_9} \exp(l_2 t)] / X\} + e_6(t), \quad (6)$$

Mark-up proportional price adjustment equation

$$Dp/p = g_{10} \log\{a_{10} a_2 w \exp(-l_1 t)[1 - a_3(Y/K)^{a_4}]^{-(1+a_4)/a_4}/p\}$$
$$+ e_7(t), \qquad (7)$$

Proportional wage-rate adjustment equation

$$Dw/w = g_{11} \log\{a_2 \exp(-l_1 t)[Y^{-a_4} - a_{33} K^{-a_4}]^{-1/a_4} a_{11} \exp(l_3 t)\}$$
$$+ e_8(t), \qquad (8)$$

Proportional interest rate (that is, money market) adjustment equation

$$Dr/r = g_{12} \log[a_{12} p Y^{a_{13}} r^{a_{14}}] + e_9(t), \qquad (9)$$

Policy relation linking the changes in the proportional rate of change of the money supply and the balance of payments

$$Dm = g_{13} \log(X/a_{15}I) + g_{14} \log[a_{16} \exp(l_3 t)/L] + g_{15} D \log(X/a_{15}I)$$
$$+ g_{16} D \log[a_{16} \exp(l_3 t)/L] + e_{10}(t), \qquad (10)$$

Change in stocks equation

$$DS = Y + I - C - DK - X, \qquad (11)$$

Proportional rate of change of fixed capital stock

$$DK/K = k, \qquad (12)$$

Proportional rate of change of the stock of money

$$DM/M = m, \qquad (13)$$

Table 9.6.1   Estimates a_i, g_i and l_i of the parameters α_{ij}, γ_i and λ_i and t-values

i	g_i	t	a_i	t	l_i	t
1	0.2454	5.71	0.9206	215.18	0.0058	17.29
2	0.0990	4.08	0.0037	108.04	0.0113	13.49
3	0.0886	3.36	1.2180	24.07	0.0008	0.85
4	1.1492	3.87	1.0000*			
5	0.6437	5.25	0.0042	1.52		
6	0.0000*		0.1632	75.46		
7	0.3486	3.51	1.5263	66.15		
8	0.0448	7.72	1365.1909	62.11		
9	0.2926	4.18	1.0000*			
10	0.1312	3.40	1.0000*			
11	0.1047	2.85	22.1379	34.57		
12	0.1990	1.33	0.0537	0.62		
13	0.0422	2.69	1.0000*			
14	0.0000*		0.8289	2.08		
15	0.1562	4.68	1.0000*			
16	0.0000*					

* indicates a coefficient which is *a priori* restricted.

Source: Bergstrom (1978, pp. 90–1) and Table 1 in Bergstrom and Wymer (1976).

where the estimates e_{it} – or $e_i(t)$ – of the random disturbances $\epsilon_i(t)$, namely the residuals, satisfy the condition (i) $E(\int_{t1}^{t2} e_{it}) = 0$ ($i = 1, 2, \ldots, n$), (ii) $E(\int_{t1}^{t2} e_{it} \int_{t1}^{t2} e_{jt}) = s_{ij}$ ($i, j = 1, 2, \ldots, n$), and (iii) $E(\int_{t1}^{t2} e_{it} \int_{t3}^{t4} e_{jt}) = 0$, ($i, j = 1, 2, \ldots, n$), for $\mathbf{t_1} > \mathbf{t_2} > \mathbf{t_3} > \mathbf{t_4}$; and where the quasi-maximum likelihood estimates a_i, g_i and l_i of the parameters α_i, γ_i and λ_i, respectively (displayed in Table 9.6.1 with their **t**-values in parentheses) have been obtained by the procedure described in Theorem 9.3.4.

The following existence result constitutes an important analytic piece of BTCG UK 1955–66 and is given here as an example of a theorem formulated at the level of a data-specific theory – see Bergstrom (1978, p. 94). It is the applied version of the general Theorem 9.3.1 of the generic theory BTCG. This will complete our discussion of the current example of a level-two phenomenological theory.

Theorem 9.6.1   The differential equation system of A9.6.12 has a particular solution:

$$C(t) = (5427.1)e^{(0.0066)t}$$
$$L(t) = (24.3)e^{(0.0008)t}$$
$$k(t) = 0.0066$$
$$Y(t) = (6055.8)e^{(0.0066)t}$$
$$I(t) = (1320.2)e^{(0.0066)t}$$
$$X(t) = (1320.2)e^{(0.0066)t}$$
$$p(t) = (1.0112)e^{(0.0047)t}$$
$$w(t) = (237.0)e^{(0.0105)t}$$
$$r(t) = 0.0088$$
$$m(t) = 0.0113$$
$$S(t) = (9976.3)e^{(0.0066)t}$$
$$K(t) = (85829.6)e^{(0.0066)t}$$
$$M(t) = (16571.4)e^{(0.0113)t}.$$

9.7   NOTES AND REMARKS

According to Lange (1959), the origins of input–output analysis are probably related to the work of W. Leontief and associates in the Soviet Union. Interestingly enough, the input–output systems, in particular the 'closed' one, have been alternatively interpreted as an aggregate and linearized Walrasian general equilibrium system – see for instance Chenery and Clark (1959) – or a disaggregate and extended Marxian reproduction scheme – cf. Lange (1959). Even if the two interpretations were not true from the vantage point of the historical roots of input–output theory, the two are fully compatible from a modern theoretical perspective.

For the origins of input–output analysis in the West see Leontief (1941 and 1953). A very good introduction to the subject, especially applications, is the book by Chenery and Clark (1959). For a formal development of input–output theory and its place within the more general theory of linear economic models, the reader is referred to Dorfman, Samuelson and Solow (1958), Gale (1960) and Morishima (1964).

From its origins and until relatively recently the input–output approach to economics was essentially non-stochastic in nature. From the new efforts to reformulate input–output systems as stochastic systems the reader will find relevant information in Jackson and West (1989); the book containing their article has an interesting introduction by Klein (1989) about the relations between input–output analysis and econometrics; a comparison between the non-stochastic and the stochastic approach is to be found in Divay and Meunier (1982).

According to Gerking (1976), one may formulate input–output as an econometric system on the following foundation. From 9.2, one rewrites Equation (1) as

$$x = Ax + y + \epsilon,$$

where ϵ is an $n \times 1$ vector of random disturbance, and then estimates A using time series on x and y. Alternatively, using cross-section data on samples of firms for each industry and using r to denote the rth firm in an industry, one may define

$$x_{ij}(r) = a_{ij}x_j(r) + \epsilon_{ij}(r) \quad i, j = 1, 2, \ldots, n$$

where the random element ϵ_{ij} is assumed to be identically and independently distributed for all r.

Input–output analysis is one of the branches of economics that has most frequently been used in applied research. However, when it comes to choosing an example to illustrate the case of a data-specific theory in 9.5, it soon becomes apparent that most actual empirical systems are rather awkward as they are too disaggregated, that is, they include too many sectors for our limited methodological objectives. Although the work of Tilanus (1968) is no exception to the rule, the book has for us the advantage that it includes in its first chapter – for expository purposes – the 'small' and very aggregative system that we have selected as an example.

As stated in 9.1, level-one phenomenological theories are frequently summarized in econometric *structural systems of equations* of the form

$$Ay_t + Bx_t = \epsilon_t,$$

where y_t is a vector of endogenous variables, x_t is a vector of predetermined (exogenous and/or lagged endogenous) variables, ϵ_t is a vector of random disturbances and A and B are matrices of parameters to be estimated. Historically important instances of such systems are macroeconometric theories which incorporate general Keynesian (Keynes, 1936) or neoclassical hypotheses or syntheses of these two approaches. Within this rather wide class of theories, the system we have called the Bergstrom theory of cyclical growth (BTCG) deserves a special place on account of its innovative methodological features.

The 'generic' Bergstrom cyclical growth theory is explained in detail in Bergstrom (1967, 1978, 1984a) and Bergstrom and Wymer (1976);

this material also includes examples of an empirical application of this theory, that is, of a 'data-specific' Bergstrom theory of cyclical growth. For the very interesting and pioneering work in the development of the econometric bridge between 'generic' and 'data-specific' time-continuous systems the reader is referred to Bergstrom (1966), the several articles in Bergstrom (1976) – especially the aforementioned article by Bergstrom and Wymer (1976) – and Bergstrom (1984b). For the latter subject, Gandolfo (1981) should also be consulted.

10 Phenomenological Theories and Theoretical Systems (II): Data-Contingent Theory

The phenomenological theoretical systems described in Chapter 9 consist of two levels, namely, the generic theory L_1, comprehensive and abstract even if morphologically simple, and the data-specific theory L_2, the formal language that accounts for a concrete empirical structure. As a bridge between L_1 and L_2 we encounter the concrete (data-conform) theory, simply a specialized and redesigned version of the generic theory to meet the requirements of a given structure of data.

A data-contingent phenomenological theory, on the other hand, is a theory that from the outset has been conceived to apply to a well-defined empirical structure – for example, time series for 38 macroeconomic variables of the US economy for the period 1929–52 – the famous Klein–Goldberger 'model' (Klein and Goldberger, 1955, and Goldberger, 1959). Its point of departure is not a full-fledged, formal, generic theory but rather an instance of what we have characterized in preceding discussions as a concrete (data-conform) theory. An important difference to point out, however, is that whereas in the two-level framework the concrete (data-conform) theory is formally founded upon and consists of a specialization of a pre-existent generic theory, the data-contingent theory, in its mathematical expression, is an arrangement of originally independent hypotheses often belonging to different disciplines (within and without economics) and assembled together with an *a priori* well-determined empirical structure in view – thus the label data-contingent theory.

10.1 DATA-CONTINGENT THEORY: LANGUAGE AND MODEL

Typical cases of the theories we have in mind here are the so-called econometric 'models' of regional, national and international economies. However, before continuing the main discussion, a terminological clarification may be in order.

In the remainder of this chapter, we shall once again place the word model – and derived expressions, like modelling – within quotation marks when the expression is used in a sense other than the logical one. 'Model' may thus denote a theory or a system of equations representing the assumed relations which constitute a particular economic system; and 'modelling' is the activity of constructing such a 'model'. Econometricians use the expression 'model' when they refer to the algebraic equation system before estimation and reserve the word 'structure' for the estimated, numerical system of equations. Here too, this econometrician's sense of 'structure' differs not only from the logical sense of (relational) structure as we have been using it throughout this study, but also from a second econometrician's concept of structure present in the expression 'system of equations *in structural form*' as opposed to the expression 'system of equations *in reduced form*' or 'system of equations in *non-structural form*'.

As known from Chapter 9, a structural form may be written

$$\mathbf{A}\mathbf{y}_t + \mathbf{B}\mathbf{x}_t = \epsilon_t$$

where $\mathbf{y}_t$ is a vector of endogenous variables, $\mathbf{x}_t$ is a vector of predetermined (exogenous and/or lagged endogenous) variables, ϵ_t is a vector of random disturbances and $\mathbf{A}$ and $\mathbf{B}$ are matrices of the appropriate dimensions. On the other hand, the reduced form may be written

$$\mathbf{y}_t + \mathbf{C}\mathbf{x}_t = \mu_t$$

where the vector of endogenous variables $\mathbf{y}_t$ is expressed as a function of the vector of predetermined (exogenous and/or lagged endogenous) variables $\mathbf{x}_t$ and the vector of random disturbances μ_t. Here the new matrix $\mathbf{C}$ is equal to $\mathbf{A}^{-1}\mathbf{B}$ and the vector μ_t to $\mathbf{A}^{-1}\epsilon_t$. Since, under the appropriate conditions, both the structural form and the reduced form may be estimated, it is usual to refer to these two approaches as the *structural 'modelling' approach* and the *reduced form* or, also, the *non-structural 'modelling' approach*, respectively. We use this terminology in what follows.

To focus our discussion, let our language be a macroeconometric 'model' of a national economy. Traditionally, in the *structural 'modelling' approach*, the language would consist of a blend of some existing theoretical propositions – usually from the field of macroeconomics and statistics – often with some claims of a more *ad hoc* nature. In Goldberger's (1959, p. 1) words, (the) construction of an econometric 'model' [our quotation marks] involves an interweaving of economic theory, empirical techniques and empirical investigation. Hypotheses are drawn from many fields of economic theory and fitted together to form a self-contained system of simultaneous relationships. A priori information and preliminary empirical observations are employed in this formulation phase. Formal methods of statistical inference are applied to the body of observed data in the estimation stage. The result is a 'model' [our quotation marks] which characterizes, quantitatively, the structure of the economic system.

In more recent econometric 'modelling', in the *non-structural 'modelling' approach* – see for instance Sims (1980a, 1980b) and the critical article by Cooley and LeRoy (1985) – the language is completely borrowed or almost so from a branch of mathematical statistics (for example, time-series analysis), without or almost without reference to any economic-theoretical background, and is then shaped so as to apply to a given structure of data. 'The exclusive purpose of non-structural "modelling" [our quotation marks] is to capture the probabilistic characteristics of the data under examination and to answer questions that can be resolved with that information' – Cooley and LeRoy (1985).

The structural axioms of such phenomenological theories directly point to a structure the domain of which is made up of very specific statistical data. The uniqueness – up to isomorphism – of the intended model is manifest. In the case of the structural 'modelling' approach, the main aim of the exercise is to provide a macroeconomic theoretical explanation of the working of a particular economic system during a particular period of time. Additionally, the 'model' may serve as a projection device. On the other hand, '[b]ecause non-structural "modelling" [our quotation marks] is concerned exclusively with characterizing the data, it makes sense to define two non-structural "models" [our quotation marks] as observationally equivalent if and only if they generate the same probability distribution for the observed variables' – Cooley and LeRoy (1985).

In the following two sections we move on to examine two specimens of theories, each corresponding to one of the types just described. However, before doing so, it may be convenient to emphasize once again the 'non-essential' and mainly didactic issue of the number of levels of a theoretical system. In principle, the comparison of a two-level system with a single-level one suggests the following difference. Whereas a level-two theory – structural or non-structural – checks a generic, level-one theory – for instance, Keynesian or time-series business cycle theory, respectively – *vis-à-vis* a structure of data, a single-level system is a more *ad hoc* construction which only points to and is justified by a specific data structure. However, no matter how appealing this explanation may be 'in principle', the fact is that most theories that we may regard as single-level systems do include in their formalizations pieces borrowed from 'general theories' – economic and/or statistical – while level-two theories, in their concrete (data-conform) versions, often need to concede to the rough reality of the data at the expense of the purity of the 'general theory'. The fact that we are dealing here mainly with differences of degree should not be forgotten.

10.2   EXAMPLE ONE: A MACROECONOMETRIC STRUCTURAL EQUATION SYSTEM

There are many econometric systems which could have served well here as illustrations of the structural estimation approach. The one we shall focus on has been chosen because it is representative of a style of research in the field, because of its quality, and because it is smaller than many of its potential competing candidates; it is a study on the macrodynamics of the American economy for the period 1902–52 carried out by Morishima and Saito (1972). As is the case with the other example given in this chapter, the axiomatic formulation is ours.

The subject of analysis is a log-linearized macroeconomic 'model' of the Keynesian type constructed to mirror the American economy of the period 1902–52 (excluding 1941–5) at a very high level of aggregation. The system explains nine endogenous variables – Y (net national income), C (consumption), D (depreciations), K (capital stock), N (employment), p (price level), w (wage rate), r (corporate bond yield) and h (hours worked per person) – as functions of six exogenous variables – I (gross investment), B (balance of trade), M (money), L (labour), t (time) and u (a dummy variable) and eight lagged endogenous variables – C_{t-1}, L_{t-1}, M_{t-1}, K_{t-1}, w_{t-1}, h_{t-1}, p_{t-1} and p_{t-2}; it consists of two definitional equations (identities) and seven stochastic equations and it was estimated by the method of two-stage least squares (TSLS).

The main objectives of the two authors' research were to compute and study the behaviour of some multipliers, discuss a few policy-theoretical issues, and analyse some short- and long-run dynamic properties of the estimated 'model'. In what follows we shall call it the

'Morishima–Saito dynamic system for the USA 1902–52' (or the MSDSUSA, for short) and refer to Morishima and Saito (1972).

Although, all in all, the MSDSUSA may be said to belong to the Keynesian type of macrosystems, the theoretical foundations of its structural equations combine Keynesian notions (consumption and demand for money), neoclassical concepts (a Cobb–Douglas production function) as well as empirical generalizations (wage determination), each adapted to the task at hand, namely, to describe the dynamic behaviour of the American economy for a specific period of time. Hence, the statistical evaluation part of the exercise did not consist in testing Keynesian or neoclassical macrotheory – although it involved testing some Keynesian and some neoclassical sectoral hypotheses – but rather in evaluating an eclectic construct with a certain overall Keynesian flavour and built to describe the American economy of 1902–52. We define next the primal model of the theory.

Definition 10.2.1 The empirical structure $S = \langle Y, C, K, M, D, I, B, L, N, h, p, w, r\rangle$ is the *primal model of the nine-equation Morishima–Saito dynamic system for the USA 1902–52 (MSDSUSA)* if and only if the following conditions are satisfied:

A10.2.1   **Y** is the sequence (Y_t: $t = 1900, \ldots, 1940, 1946, \ldots,$ 1952) of observations of national income (billions of 1929 dollars) in the USA for the period 1900–52. *Source*: Morishima and Saito (1972).

A10.2.2   **C** is the sequence (C_t: $t = 1900, \ldots, 1940, 1946, \ldots,$ 1952) of observations of aggregate consumption (billions of 1929 dollars) in the USA for the period 1900–52. *Source: idem.*

A10.2.3   **K** is the sequence (K_t: $t = 1900, \ldots, 1940, 1946, \ldots,$ 1952) of observations of end-of-year capital stock (in billions of 1929 dollars) in the USA for the period 1900–52. *Source: idem.*

A10.2.4   **M** is the sequence (M_t: $t = 1900, \ldots, 1940, 1946, \ldots,$ 1952) of observations of cash balances (billions of current dollars) in the USA for the period 1900–52. *Source: idem.*

A10.2.5   **D** is the sequence (D_t: $t = 1901, \ldots, 1940, 1946, \ldots,$ 1952) of observations of capital consumption allowances (in billions of 1929 dollars) in the USA for the period 1901–52. *Source: idem.*

A10.2.6   **I** is the sequence ($\mathbf{I}_t$: $t = 1901, \ldots, 1940, 1946, \ldots,$ 1952) of gross aggregate investment (billions of 1929 dollars) the terms of which are computed by the formula $\mathbf{I}_t = \mathbf{K}_t - \mathbf{K}_{t-1} + \mathbf{D}_t$. *Source*: *idem*.

A10.2.7   **B** is the sequence ($\mathbf{B}_t$: $t = 1901, \ldots, 1940, 1946, \ldots,$ 1952) of trade balance (in billions of 1929 dollars) the terms of which are computed by the formula $\mathbf{B}_t = \mathbf{Y}_t - \mathbf{C}_t - \mathbf{I}_t + \mathbf{D}_t$. *Source*: *idem*.

A10.2.8   **L** is the sequence ($\mathbf{L}_t$: $t = 1900, \ldots, 1940, 1946, \ldots,$ 1952) of observations of population fifteen years of age and over (millions of persons) in the USA for the period 1900-52. *Source*: *idem*.

A10.2.9   **N** is the sequence ($\mathbf{N}_t$: $t = 1900, \ldots, 1940, 1946, \ldots,$ 1952) of observations of persons engaged (millions of persons) in the USA for the period 1900–52. *Source*: *idem*.

A10.2.10   **h** is the sequence ($\mathbf{h}_t$: $t = 1900, \ldots, 1940, 1946, \ldots,$ 1952) of observations of hours worked per person per year (thousands of hours) in the USA for the period 1900–52. *Source*: *idem*.

A10.2.11   **p** is the sequence ($\mathbf{p}_t$: $t = 1900, \ldots, 1940, 1946, \ldots,$ 1952) of observations of the price level (1929 base: 1) in the USA for the period 1900–52. *Source*: *idem*.

A10.2.12   **r** is the sequence ($\mathbf{r}_t$: $t = 1900, \ldots, 1940, 1946, \ldots,$ 1952) of observations of the corporate bond yield (per cent per annum) in the USA for the period 1900–52. *Source*: *idem*.

A10.2.13   **w** is the sequence ($\mathbf{w}_t$: $t = 1900, \ldots, 1940, 1946, \ldots,$ 1952) of observations of the wage rate (thousands of current dollars) in the USA for the period 1900–52. *Source*: *idem*.

A10.2.14   The *maintained hypothesis* is formalized by the two identities:

Net national product or national income:

$$\mathbf{Y}_t = \mathbf{C}_t + \mathbf{I}_t - \mathbf{D}_t + \mathbf{B}_t \tag{a}$$

Capital formation:

$$\mathbf{K}_t = \mathbf{K}_{t-1} + \mathbf{I}_t - \mathbf{D}_t \tag{b}$$

together with the seven stochastic equations:

Consumption function:

$$\log(C_t/L_t) = \alpha_{11} \log(Y_t/L_t) + \alpha_{12} \log(M_t/p_tL_t)$$
$$+ \alpha_{13} \log(C_{t-1}/L_{t-1}) + \alpha_{10} + e_{1t} \quad (1)$$

Liquidity preference function:

$$\log(M_t/p_t) = \alpha_{21}[\beta_{21} \log Y_t + \beta_{22} \log(M_{t-1}/p_t) + \beta_{20}]$$
$$+ \alpha_{22} \log r_t + \alpha_{23}u + \alpha_{20} + e_{2t} \quad (2)$$

Production function:

$$\log Y_t = \beta_{31} \log h_tN_t + \beta_{32} \log K_{t-1} + \alpha_{31}t + \alpha_{32}u$$
$$+ \alpha_{30} + e_{3t} \quad (3)$$

Relative share equation:

$$\log(w_tN_t/p_tY_t) = \alpha_{41} + e_{4t} \quad (4)$$

Wage determination equation:

$$\log(w_t/h_t) = \alpha_{51} \log(w_{t-1}/h_{t-1})$$
$$+ \alpha_{52}[(1/5)\log(p/p_{t-1}) + (4/5)\log(p_{-1}/p_{t-2})]$$
$$+ \alpha_{53} \log(N_t/0.57L_t) + \alpha_{50} + e_{5t} \quad (5)$$

Hours worked equation:

$$\log h_t = \alpha_{61} \log(w_{t-1}/p_{t-1}h_{t-1}) + \alpha_{61} \log(N_t/0.57L_t)$$
$$+ \alpha_{60} + e_{6t} \quad (6)$$

Depreciation equation:

$$\log D_t = \alpha_{71} \log K_{t-1} + \alpha_{70} + e_{7t} \quad (7)$$

(where **u** is a dummy variable (0 before 1941; 1 after 1946), and **t** is time in years (1927: 0) and where the random disturbances e_{it} are distributed with $E(e_{it}) = 0$, $E(e_{is} e_{jt}) = \sigma_{ij}$ if $s = t$ and $E(e_{is} e_{jt}) = 0$, if $s \neq t$; and whose two-stage least squares parameter estimates $\underline{\alpha}_{ij}$ of α_{ij} – together with the *a priori* given values of $\underline{\beta}_{ij}$ of β_{ij} – are displayed in Table 10.2.1 with their t-values in parentheses).

A10.2.15 The seven stochastic equations satisfy the following tests at the prescribed levels of significance – see Table 10.2.1:
(1) test of goodness of fit (R^2 adjusted for degrees of freedom);
(2) regarding the residuals, the tests of
(2.1) zero means
(2.2) heteroscedasticity
(2.3) autocorrelation (δ^2/S^2).

Assumptions A10.2.1 to A10.2.13 constitute the structural axioms: they point to a particular structure of data. Assumption A10.2.14 lays down the formal system of hypotheses. Observe that it makes sense to speak here of a one-level or single-level theoretical system because it is within this single level that the theory is built up. Clearly enough, we may refer collectively to all those diverse theoretical, empirical and methodological approaches which support the different pieces of the actual theory as its *foundations*, being aware, however, that such foundations taken together do not amount to a theory in its own right – in the sense of a theory of the preceding level within a hierarchic system – but rather to a collection of multifarious inspirational notions. Theory, in the one-level system, thus amounts to concrete (data-conform) theory.

For a thorough discussion of the economic meaning and theoretical background of the hypotheses which make up the structural system described in A10.2.14 the reader is referred to Morishima and Saito (1972). The same work contains a description of the estimation and other statistical aspects here summarized in A10.2.15.

We would like to conclude our brief presentation of the MSDSUSA with a reference to a few results on some of its properties, given here in the form of theorems. In particular, we focus our attention on the derivation of the impact-multipliers of the MSDSUSA.

We begin by finding the reduced form of the system of A10.2.14 formed by Equations (a) and (1) to (7). To do this we first replace identity (a) by its log-linear approximation – see Morishima and Saito (1972) – (a') $(C^*/Y^*)\log C_t + [(I^* + B^*)/Y^*]\log(I_t + B_t) - \log Y_t -$

Table 10.2.1   Estimates of parameters α_{ij} t-values, and given values β_{ij}

								R^2	δ^2/S^2
Equation (1):	α_{11} 0.349 (6.5)	α_{12} 0.160 (4.1)	α_{13} 0.460 (5.8)	α_{10} 0.007				0.98	2.19
Equation (2):	α_{21} 1.190 (34.2)	α_{22} −0.202 (2.3)	α_{23} −0.048 (2.2)	α_{20} −0.650	β_{21} 0.586	β_{22} 0.414	β_{20} 0.295	0.98	1.11
Equation (3):	α_{31} 0.006 (15.4)	α_{32} 0.052 (3.1)	α_{30} −0.243	β_{31} 0.824	β_{32} 0.176			0.93	0.73
Equation (4):	α_{11} −0.084 (3.1)								
Equation (5):	α_{51} 1.006 (52.4)	α_{52} 0.456 (2.1)	α_{53} 0.188 (1.1)	α_{50} 0.017				0.99	1.98
Equation (6):	α_{61} −0.282 (17.4)	α_{62} 0.343 (6.1)	α_{60} 0.324					0.91	1.09
Equation (7):	α_{11} 1.593 (18.8)	α_{11} −2.817						0.89	0.14

Source: Morishima and Saito (1972).

$(D^*/Y^*)\log D_t = (C^*/Y^*)\log C^* + [(I^* + B^*)/Y^*]\log(I^* + B^*) - \log Y^*$
$- (D^*/Y^*)\log D^*$, where starred symbols denote the sample means of the respective variables. Then we arrange the variables Y_t, C_t, D_t, N_t, p_t, w_t, r_t and h_t as the column vector X_t and the variables M_t, $(I + B)_t$, L_t, M_{t-1}, L_{t-1}, C_{t-1}, K_{t-1}, p_{t-1}, p_{t-2}, w_{t-1} and h_{t-1} as the column vector Z_t. The system (a′) and Equations (1) to (7) can now be written as

$$A \log X_t + B \log Z_t + ct + du + m = 0$$

where A and B are matrices of structural coefficients and c, d and m are column vectors of the coefficients of trend, dummy and the constant terms, respectively.

Theorem 10.2.1   The reduced form of the system of A10.2.14 using the approximation (a′) for (a) is given by $\log X_t = F \log Z_t + gt + hu + i$ or $X_t = \log^{-1}(F \log Z_t + gt + hu + i)$, where $F = -A^{-1}B$, $g = -A^{-1}c$, $h = -A^{-1}d$ and $i = -A^{-1}m$.

From the reduced form of the system of A10.2.14 given by Theorem 10.2.1 the following results easily follow.

Theorem 10.2.2   The MSDSUSA with the log-linearization (a') for (a) and the values of C^*, Y^*, I^*, B^* and D^* fixed at the sample means of the respective variables has the following impact multipliers:

$$\partial Y / \partial (I + B) = 1.352, \qquad \partial N / \partial (I + B) = 0.705,$$

$$\partial Y / \partial (M/p) = 0.292, \qquad \partial p Y / \partial M = 0.380,$$

$$\partial N / \partial (M/p) = 0.156.$$

This completes our description of the MSDSUSA.

10.3   EXAMPLE TWO: A MACROECONOMETRIC VECTOR AUTOREGRESSIVE SYSTEM

Under certain circumstances and for primarily technical–statistical and mathematical reasons, econometricians prefer to estimate, test and work with the reduced form of a system of equations rather than the structural system which originated it. In particular, they will use the estimated reduced form to generate projections. This procedure is conceptually straightforward in so far as one begins with a given system in structural form, that is, one embodying all relevant *economic-theoretical restrictions*, then derives from it the corresponding reduced-form system to perform the desired statistical operations and finally, with the results thus obtained, one returns if necessary to the original structural system.

There is an alternative way, however, in which the reduced-form or, perhaps more properly stated, the non-structural approach to econometric research is used. In general terms, the method consists in formulating from the outset a system of equations which has all the external *appearances* of a reduced-form system although it does not presuppose or does not need to presuppose any pre-existent structural system. There are several variants of this approach, the most remarkable common future of which is the design of equations systems with the shallowest possible economic-theoretical foundations, relying, instead, on pure statistical constructs originating in time-series analysis. One version of this 'atheoretical' approach to macroeconometrics – for a critique see Cooley and LeRoy (1985) – are the so-called vector autoregressive processes (VAR) which we describe and illustrate next.

We have chosen as an example a study by Hsiao (1979) on the relations between quarterly data on money and on national income in the Canadian economy between 1955 and 1977. The article publishing the results has the distinct advantages of being technically highly competent while at the same time expressing very well a tenor which is characteristic among the enthusiasts of the approach. In relation to the latter, the author explains that he is 'interested in fitting vector autoregressions as opposed to fitting econometric "models" based on supposed a priori knowledge or economic theory because on many occasions there are competing theories of economic activity' and, pointing to the sources of the chosen approach, he reminds the reader that '[t]o avoid infecting the "model" by spurious a priori constraints, Sims (. . .) suggested an alternative strategy for empirical "model" building by treating all variables as joint dependent and fitting an unconstrained vector autoregression' – see Hsiao (1979) and Sims (1980a). The latter will be denoted here by

$$\mathbf{z}_t = \sum_{l \in A} \Psi_l \mathbf{z}_{t-l} + \mathbf{w}_t$$

where $\mathbf{z}_t$ is an $r \times 1$ vector of random variables, $\mathbf{w}_t$ is an $r \times 1$ vector of white-noise innovation terms, and $A = \{1, 2, \ldots, M\}$.

In the part of Hsiao's (1979) system we are reconstructing here, the vector $\mathbf{z}_t$ consists of two components: $\mathbf{x}_t$, denoting M1, 'narrow money' (demand deposits plus bank notes and coins) and $\mathbf{y}_t$, denoting GNP (gross national product). The novelty of Hsiao's (1979) method consisted in admitting autoregressive processes of different order in each of the two equations, excluding lagged terms with non-significant coefficients and thus reducing the number of parameters to be estimated. To succeed with the latter goal, the basic strategy of Sims (1980a) was completed with a decision rule making use of Akaike's (1969) final prediction error (FPE) criterion and Granger's (1969) definitions of 'causality' and of 'feedback'.

The FPE criterion is a technical concept that will not be discussed here in any detail although it will be used and referred to in the context of our exposition. It is applied to each equation to determine the order of lags in Ψ_{ij} and it is defined as the asymptotic mean squared error of the variable, say $\mathbf{y}_t$,

$$\text{FPE}(\mathbf{y}_t) = E(\mathbf{y}_t - \underline{\mathbf{y}}_t)^2,$$

where $\underline{y}_t$ is the predictor of y_t – refer to Hsiao (1979) and Akaike (1969).

To make the exposition self-contained, we give next the definitions of Granger causality and Granger feedback. To do this we first introduce the sets $X^*_t = \{x_s: s < t\}$ and $Y^*_t = \{y_s: s < t\}$ and use $\sigma^2(y_t | B)$ to denote the mean squared error of the minimum mean squared prediction error of y_t given the information set B – see Hsiao (1979).

Definition 10.3.1   If $\sigma^2(y_t | Y^*, X^*) < \sigma^2(y_t | Y^*)$, we say that x Granger causes y, denoted by $x \Rightarrow y$.

Definition 10.3.2   If $\sigma^2(y_t | Y^*, X^*) < \sigma^2(y_t | Y^*)$ and $\sigma^2(x_t | Y^*, X^*) < \sigma^2(y_t | X^*)$ we say that a feedback between x and y is present, denoted $x \Leftrightarrow y$.

The bivariate autoregressive system can be written

$$y_t = \psi_{11}(L)y_t + \psi_{12}(L)x_t + u_t$$

$$x_t = \psi_{21}(L)y_t + \psi_{22}(L)x_t + v_t$$

where L is the lag operator, $Ly_t = y_{t-1}$. Application of the relevant tests – see details in Hsiao (1979) – led to an equation for GNP including six lagged values of itself and eight lagged values of M1 and an equation for M1 including nine lagged values of itself and four lagged values of GNP as the optimal choice. The values of the variables are subjected to a prefiltering procedure to remove the trend that consists in taking the second difference of their logarithm. The latter eliminates the longer common movements of the series. Finally, a test of Granger causality confirms the hypothesis of a feedback between GNP and M1. We define next the primal model of the theory where, for reasons of brevity, we only refer to a few of the key tests involved.

Definition 10.3.3   The empirical structure $S = \langle Y, X, y, x \rangle$ is the *primal model of the quarterly data vector autoregressive system GNP-M1 of the Canadian economy 1955I–77IV (VARCAN 1955–77)* if and only if the following conditions are satisfied:

A10.3.1   **Y** is the sequence $(y_t: t = 1955I, \ldots, 1977IV)$ of quarterly observations of nominal GNP for the Canadian economy as reported by Statistics Canada in 'National Income and Expenditure Accounts' (Cat. No. 13–001, CANSIM No. D40252). Our immediate source: Appendix of Hsiao (1979).

A10.3.2　**X** is the sequence $(\mathbf{x}_t: t = 1955\text{I}, \ldots, 1977\text{IV})$ of seasonally adjusted quarterly observations of nominal M1 stock as reported in the Bank of Canada Review, 'Currency and Demand Deposits' (CANSIM B1609). Our immediate source: Appendix of Hsiao (1979).

A10.3.3　The *maintained hypothesis* is formalized by the bivariate autoregressive system

$$\begin{pmatrix}(1 - L)^2 \log \mathbf{y}\\(1 - L)^2 \log \mathbf{x}\end{pmatrix} = \begin{pmatrix}\psi_{11}^6(L) & \psi_{12}^8(L)\\\psi_{21}^4(L) & \psi_{22}^9(L)\end{pmatrix}\begin{pmatrix}(1 - L)\log \mathbf{y}\\(1 - L)\log \mathbf{x}\end{pmatrix} + \begin{pmatrix}\mathbf{a}\\\mathbf{b}\end{pmatrix} + \mathbf{v}\begin{pmatrix}\mathbf{u}\\\mathbf{v}\end{pmatrix}$$

where the vector $\mathbf{z} = (\mathbf{y}, \mathbf{x})$ is a stationary time series, the components u and v of $\mathbf{w} = (\mathbf{u}, \mathbf{v})$ are white-noise innovations with zero mean and constant covariance matrix

$$E\mathbf{w}'\mathbf{w} = \boldsymbol{\delta}_{s,t}\boldsymbol{\Omega}$$

and whose ordinary least squares parameter estimates are displayed in Table 10.3.1 with their t-values in brackets.

A10.3.4　The vector autoregressive system satisfies the likelihood ratio test against the higher-order autoregressive process and the likelihood ratio test against the lower-order autoregressive process – see Table 10.3.2.

From the four assumptions listed above A10.3.1 and A10.3.2 are the structural axioms while A10.3.4 in conjunction with A10.3.3 sets the standards of statistical admissibility. The axiom proper A10.3.3 also exposes the little there is of substantive theory, namely an autoregressive process describing a feedback circuit involving GNP and M1. The extreme simplicity of the description may suggest a superficial and yet 'generic' theory. This conclusion is, however, misleading. Extreme descriptive simplicity – $\mathbf{y}_t = \mathbf{f}(\mathbf{y}_{t-1}, \ldots, \mathbf{y}_{t-m}, \mathbf{x}_{t-1}, \ldots, \mathbf{x}_{t-r}, \mathbf{u}_t)$ and $\mathbf{x}_t = \mathbf{g}(\mathbf{y}_{t-1}, \ldots, \mathbf{y}_{t-n}, \mathbf{x}_{t-1}, \ldots, \mathbf{x}_{t-s}, \mathbf{v}_t)$ – creates only an appearance of generality – for example, a claim to the effect that, 'in any economy, there is a feedback between GNP and M1'. First, the latter claim, despite its scanty substantive content, is inconsistent with some explanations of the interactions between the monetary sector and the real sector

Table 10.3.1   Autoregressive estimates of GNP and M1 and *t*-values

Coefficient on lag of	Dependent variable	GNP	M1
GNP	(–1)	–0.683	0.239
		(–6.334)	(1.831)
	(–2)	–0.554	–0.065
		(–4.202)	(–0.410)
	(–3)	–0.435	–0.300
		(–3.086)	(–1.928)
	(–4)	–0.446	–0.387
		(–3.120)	(–3.050)
	(–5)	–0.155	
		(–1.146)	
	(–6)	–0.283	
		(–2.642)	
	(–7)		
	(–8)		
M1	(–1)	0.078	–0.693
		(0.878)	(6.645)
	(–2)	0.185	–0.655
		(1.760)	(–5.453)
	(–3)	0.119	–0.368
		(1.083)	(–2.681)
	(–4)	0.210	–0.705
		(2.136)	(–5.485)
	(–5)	0.315	–0.584
		(3.229)	(–4.294)
	(–6)	0.071	–0.376
		(0.688)	(–2.867)
	(–7)	0.116	–0.260
		(1.257)	(–2.100)
	(–8)	0.192	–0.284
		(2.182)	(–2.328)
	(–9)		–0.284
			(–2.687)
Standard error of the regression		0.10	0.013

Source: Table 3 of Hsiao (1979, p. 557).

of an economy. Second, what a stricter interpretation of Hsiao's (1979) result leads to is not a 'generic' claim but rather a statement to the effect that 'in the Canadian economy, between 1955I and 1977IV, there was serious evidence of a feedback involving GNP and M1 through a bivariate autoregressive process of order ($m = 6$, $n = 4$, $r = 8$, $s = 9$)'.

Table 10.3.2 Likelihood ratio test of the system of A10.3.3 against an alternative (AL) autoregressive process of higher and lower order

Maximum order fitted for	*Higher order*				*Lower order*		
	AL1	AL2	AL3	AL4	AL1	AL2	AL3
Ψ_{11}	9	6	7	8	6	6	6
Ψ_{12}	9	9	8	8	6	0	8
Ψ_{21}	9	5	4	4	2	4	0
Ψ_{22}	9	10	10	11	9	9	9
Degrees of freedom	9	3	2	4	4	8	4
Likelihood ratio statistics	9.27	1.48	1.44	1.44	12.67*	12.94**	14.39**

* significant at 5% level
** significant at 1% level.

Source: adapted from Tables 5 and 6 of Hsiao (1979, p. 558).

A careful reading of Hsiao's (1979) report seems to emphasize the *data-contingent* nature of the formal theory inasmuch as the specific characteristics of the data are attributed to a particular policy behaviour of the Canadian central bank during the period in question.

It is clear that, in an epistemological sense, non-structural theories of the VAR type are as shallow as theories can possibly be. Indeed, their theoretical contents are confined to the description of the input–output type of relations between the current value of a vector variable and the lagged values of its own and possibly of other variables, and to the suggestion of directions of causation. Evaluated in the context of the successive stages of longer-run research programmes, they would seem to correspond more closely to the initial, exploratory products of scientific inquiry than to the mature results of the more advanced stages of theory building. This is in accordance with the quoted view of Cooley and LeRoy (1985) regarding what they consider to be 'the exclusive purpose of non-structural "modelling"' (our quotation marks), namely, the probabilistic characterization of a given empirical structure. However, despite such features, these extreme forms of phenomenological description are theories in a formal sense and must be dealt with as such.

The article which has served as the basis for this discussion does not contain any explicit theorem and none will be stated in this section.

Of course, this is not to be taken to mean that formal theorems – for instance, adding to the characterization of the autoregressive system – could not be derived in the context of this theory.

10.4 NOTES AND REMARKS

Econometricians use the word 'model' in a way that is very close to the logical sense for the case of concrete (data-conform) theories, namely to denote the set of equations that formalize the hypotheses before estimation; however, they usually do not make explicit reference to the domains of the structures as components of those same models. For a comparison of terminologies and concepts, see Suppes (1960).

Four excellent books on econometrics which emphasize different aspects of the method are Amemiya (1985), Judge *et al.* (1985a) – at a higher technical level, Judge *et al.* (1985b) – and Malinvaud (1980). An important technical reference is, again, the *Handbook of Econometrics* edited by Griliches and Intriligator (1983, 1984, 1986). In his history of econometrics, Epstein (1987) devotes several chapters to the development of the structural approach – often called, with reference to its historical origins, the 'Cowles Commission approach'. Space is also devoted there to the discussion of the non-structural line of research, in particular vector autoregressions.

In the 'Notes and remarks' section of Chapter 9 we pointed out the close links between Keynesian macroeconomics (Keynes, 1936) and some Keynesian–neoclassical syntheses, on the one hand, and structural macroeconometric systems, on the other. There, we tried to accentuate the distinction between the generic theory – the 'prototype model' (Bergstrom, 1984a) or, logically more strictly, the theory of the prototype model – and the data-specific theory. Here, of course, our interest has been directed towards theories having a unique intended/empirical structure as target. Further examples of this type of theories can be found in Morishima *et al.* (1972).

The proposal 'to estimate "macromodels" as unrestricted reduced forms by treating all variables as endogenous . . .', where 'unrestricted' is to be understood as 'without restriction based on supposed *a priori* knowledge', is to be found in Sims (1980a). Technical aspects of VAR systems are discussed in Judge *et al.* (1985a). For the notion of Granger causality see Granger (1969, 1989). Some examples of research on the relation between money and output in the USA during specific periods are Sims (1972, 1980a, 1980b), and Litterman and Weiss (1985). An interesting application of VAR systems to test the presence of common stochastic trends (cointegration) in business cycles is to be found in King *et al.* (1991); also in the field of applied business cycle analysis, see Blanchard and Quah (1989). Finally, we refer once again to the detailed methodological critique of the non-structural approach contained in the article by Cooley and LeRoy (1985).

In the 'Notes and remarks' section of Chapter 5 we briefly mentioned the effects of the 'rational expectations revolution' on macroeconomic theories. Here we need mention its parallel effects upon the econometric methodology following the *Lucas critique*. For an examination of the various aspects relating macroeconomics, policy, rational expectations and econometrics the reader is referred to Lucas and Sargent (1981).

Part IV   Non-Intendedly Empirical Economic Theories

11 Methodology of Non-Experimental Economic Research (I): On the Foundations of Non-Intendedly Empirical Theories

Even if the ultimate cognitive goal of theoretical physics is to explain physical reality, one may claim that the body of theoretical physics comprises a wide network of interrelated individual physical theories some of which do not have as their immediate goals the explanation of empirical physical structures. As we pointed out in 5.2, the theory of perfect gas contributes, indirectly and in concert with other theories, to our understanding of actual gases even if what this theory immediately explains is the perfect gas model, and such a model is not an empirical structure. In isolation, in a very direct way, the theory of perfect gas cannot be said to be an 'empirical theory' in the sense discussed in Part III.

Moreover, if it is true that non-empirical theories do occur in physics, although sparingly, economics typifies the case of a discipline with empirical goals whose theoretical body consists of a network of theories a substantial number of which are not empirical. We have already referred to the case of some normative or prescriptive theories. In this and the next chapter we focus instead on those theories which have all the appearances of explanatory empirical theories but which cannot be characterized as empirical economic theories in the sense of Part III, not because their cores of empirical claims lack empirical models, but rather because they lack such cores, that is, because they were built without explicit *intendedly* empirical models in mind. We first encountered these theories in the context of the taxonomy developed in Part II.

We shall claim in this and the next chapter that the prominent place non-intendedly empirical theories occupy in economics is a direct methodological consequence of the discipline's predominantly non-experimental nature. It is the aim of this chapter to contribute to the clarification of this issue. Later on, in Chapter 12, we refer to a sample of such theories to illustrate their nature and cognitive function.

In readings on the methodology of science, especially but not only in those with a principal focus on the problems of the physical sciences – see, for instance, Morgenthaler (1961) – one often finds a description of the *scientific method* as an approach which consists of a sequence of procedures involving the following steps: (1) close observation of the phenomenon; (2) construction of a theory which explains the observations; (3) prediction of observables from the theory using deduction; (4) performance of *experiments* to test the validity of the theory.

In principle, there is nothing wrong with such an account. However, a closer look at the actual practice of scientific research in general, and economic research in particular, might well suggest that it is too simplistic in two important respects: first, in relation to its description of the relation theory–data in at least the case of more general theories – see Part III of this study – and, second, for its omission of any reference to the methodological consequences of the cases when step (4) is not available.

Relating step (4) of the above account to one of the characteristics of economics and to two of the emerging methodological consequences, we would like to stress the following three facts. First, as long as the expressions 'experiment' and 'experimental method' are given their classical, restrictive meaning – more on this point in the following pages – economics has been, at least until the present, overwhelmingly non-experimental. Methodological consequences of this feature of economics have been, second, the very existence of econometrics as a non-experimental method of empirical research and, third, the development of a very extensive simulation research methodology. This last point is the main subject of the following discussion.

11.1 ECONOMIC EXPERIMENT, EXPERIMENT SIMULATION AND SIMULATION EXPERIMENT

To have a suitable benchmark at our disposal, we examine first the classical meaning of the expression 'scientific experiment'. Stemming from the natural sciences and adopted by the philosophy of science, it is the one we shall strictly adhere to in this study. Next, we compare this meaning with other uses and meanings given to the expression in recent economic literature. Prominent among these diverging uses and meanings are those appearing in the writings of the scholars of the *experimental economics school*, which we shall examine in this context.

What is the meaning given to *scientific experiment* in the natural sciences? The German encyclopaedia *Grosse Brockhaus*, Vol. 3, p. 733, 16th edition, 1953, characterizes an experiment as 'any natural event which is purposely performed under conditions which are transparent to the extent that, depending on outcome, it becomes possible to draw conclusions (by induction) regarding the regularity (*Gesetzmässigkeit*) underlying the development of the event in question' – our translation from German.

Two points of the above characterization deserve to be highlighted, namely, the special importance given to the transparency of the conditions under which the event is performed, and the proposition that the 'drawn conclusions' refer to the law governing the event itself, that is, the object of the experiment.

In the section of the *Encyclopaedia Britannica* devoted to philosophy of science – specifically, *Macropaedia*, Vol. 16, p. 382, 15th edition, 1977 – one finds a very detailed characterization. On the relation between fact and theory one reads:

On the one hand the facts in question may be discovered by using observational methods – that is, by recording them as and when they occur naturally, without employing any special contrivances affecting their occurrence. This situation is, of course, the normal case in astronomy, in which the object of study cannot be influenced or controlled. Alternatively, they may be discovered by using experimental methods – that is, by devising special equipment or apparatus with the help of which those processes or phenomena are caused to occur on demand and under specially controlled conditions. In this case, the scientist can attack scientific problems – to use Kant's vivid metaphor – by 'putting Nature to the question', as in much of physics and fundamental biology.

Once again, let us focus on the two points deemed fundamental in the given characterization. First, there is the set of 'specially controlled conditions' which surround the occurrence of the event; second, there is the proposition that what the experimenter does is to 'cause to occur on demand' the investigated processes or phenomena. This latter aspect is emphasized with the reference to Kant.

Summarizing the fundamental aspects of the two characterizations, what a scientist does when performing an experiment is to *cause to produce on demand*, under *controlled, transparent conditions*, the *event*, *process* or *phenomenon* which is, *in itself*, the object of the investigation. In slightly different words, an experiment renders on demand, under controlled conditions, the occurrence of one or more instances of a class of well-defined processes or phenomena. A much more detailed but similar view may be found in Bunge (1967b, chapter 14). From this viewpoint, it follows immediately that the *experimental method* is the method that uses scientific experiments as the obvious research procedure.

How do the words *experiment* and *experimental method* appear within or, at least in association with, economics? We believe they occur in at least six different uses and with six different meanings.

To begin with, possibly in a more prescriptive than explanatory context, and especially at the microeconomic level, there is a first meaning of the word 'experiment' which, if not frequent in practice, would point to procedures that are, in principle, imaginable. We are thinking here of the possibility of employing experiments to evaluate and to decide between alternative policies for small, relatively autonomous subsystems like a team or a firm – for example, in the area of organization theory. This concept of experiment, as stated above of rather infrequent occurrence in economics, is possibly closest to the classical meaning discussed above.

In a more metaphorical sense, 'experiment' is sometimes used to denote an actual economic–historical experience – 'an experiment of nature' – or to express an evaluation with respect to a factual situation – 'the government is "experimenting" with the people with its economic policies'.

Finally, and most importantly, we need to refer here to the meanings given to the word 'experiment' by those scholars who refer to themselves as 'experimentalists', as the practitioners of *experimental economics*. A perusal of recent publications – Smith (1990, 1991), Davies and Holt (1993), Kagel and Roth (1995) – immediately shows the wide range of their research focuses – public goods, externalities, coordination and equilibrium, bargaining, industrial organization, assets markets, asymmetric information, auctions, games, and individual decision making. The most common approaches and the corresponding meanings assigned to the word 'experiment' can be gathered, however, in three broad categories.

The first and second categories are referred to in the following quotation of a distinguished representative of the *experimental economics school* when, in one of its articles, he announces that '[I]t is the premise of this paper that the study of the decision behavior of suitably motivated individuals and groups in laboratory or other socially isolated settings such as hospitals ... has important and significant application to the development and verification of theories of the economic system at large' – Smith (1976).

The first category mentioned by Smith (1976) is, so far as applications are concerned, the most common one. It includes a very large and heterogeneous class of exercises performed in laboratories and consisting of a diversity of games, for instance, and very often hypothetical decision-making games, played by fictitious decision makers (frequently economics or business college students) mostly involving, though sometimes not, some form of economic rewards – so far as we are aware, 'profits' but not 'losses' – to motivate the players' interest and to introduce an additional element of 'realism'.

It should be clear that no matter how well designed the realization conditions and the controls for these laboratory events, what we are facing in all these instances are not experiments in the rigorous sense previously discussed, but games – in the broadest not only in the game-theoretical sense of the word – aimed at *simulating experiments*. Smith (1991) himself reminds us of his earlier 'idea that an experiment might be described as a "simulation"', for instance when he refers – properly – to 'management decision games and games designed to simulate oligopolistic market phenomena' – Smith (1962).

The second case mentioned by Smith (1976) points to studies carried out within 'socially isolated settings such as hospitals', and refers to the so-called *token economies*, small-scale socioeconomic systems that are developed, under controlled conditions, among institutionalized individuals – for example 'psychiatric patients, mental retardates, juvenile delinquents, and convicts' – see Kagel (1972).

A question immediately arises: do exercises with token economies qualify as experiments in the strict sense we have adhered to? In our view, the answer depends on the aim of the exercise. If this aim were, as seldom if ever seems to be the case, the testing of propositions suggested to obtain in similar small-scale socioeconomic settings – that is, in hospitals, prisons or psychiatric institutions – the token-economy exercises would clearly have the status of experiments. Instead, token-economy exercises have only the status of experiment simulations when they are auxiliary tools for the investigation of those other systems which are the customary objects of microeconomic and macroeconomic research, that is, consumers, firms, and national and international economic systems. As Kagel (1972) himself has recognized, 'the generality of experimental results in the token economy may be limited by differences between institutionalized and noninstitutionalized populations with respect to economic behavior'. There may exist substantial differences, indeed, between the very specific set of economic relations binding the members of a small and very particular economic subsystem of a hospital, prison or psychiatric institution and those involving the agents of a national or international economy.

The third and final category includes laboratory events where the role of economic agents is played neither by fictitious players in hypothetical economic situations nor by the inhabitants of token economies, but by animals. For instance, rats were used to test aspects of the neoclassical theory of consumption by Kagel *et al.* (1975) and choice under uncertainty by Battalio *et al.* (1985). Here again, the strict application of the chosen experimental criterion characterizes these exercises as experiment simulations.

There is, however, a second-level use of the word 'experiment' that is justified. In the examples of the preceding paragraph, for instance, the laboratory hypothetical decision game and the rat-behaviour experience are two *analogues* of an economic decision process under uncertainty. On the one hand, probing in the laboratory with one of the former amounts to *simulating* experiments with the latter (thus, *experiment simulations*). On the other hand, probing in the laboratory with one of the former also means *experimenting* with one of the analogues (hence, *simulation experiment*). Expressing the event in all its extension, we may say, 'experimenting with the simulation of an experiment'.

11.2 ECONOMICS AND THE SCOPE OF THE EXPERIMENTAL METHOD

The first – and less common – use of the expression 'economic experiment' mentioned in the preceding section coincides with its standard meaning in science. This is a convenient place to summarize and comment on our conclusions regarding the remaining five uses of 'experiment' in the economic literature and on a few related issues.

The first conclusion claims that neither the so-called 'experiments of nature' nor the unpleasant economic-policy experiences mentioned earlier can be considered experiments in more than a metaphorical sense. These are straightforward issues which do not necessitate further consideration.

The second conclusion states that if we use the classical yardstick for the characterization of a scientific experiment, most laboratory practices of the *experimental economics school* do not qualify as such but as experiment simulations, that is, empirical procedures performed *in lieu* of actual experiments – compare this view with Bunge (1967b, Vol. II, p. 266). Indeed, such procedures do not aim at 'causing to occur on demand' instances of the process or phenomenon which is the subject of the analysis but, instead, of another process or phenomenon which substitutes for and, it is hoped, satisfactorily imitates the former one. Moreover, if we reach for help to the second-level terminology referred to above, the correct vocabulary would relate to experiments with the analogues or simulation experiments.

The second conclusion can be further illustrated with two examples. Suppose that parallel to (1) an economic theory of choice under uncertainty we construct (2) a theory of choice under uncertainty for a simulation laboratory game involving students, and (3) a theory of choice under uncertainty for a simulation laboratory experience involving rats. While the laboratory exercises with the students and the laboratory experiences with the rats may be rightly called experiments in regard to (2), the theory of the students' game and (3) the theory of the rats' choice, respectively, they do not constitute experiments for (1) the economic theory of choice under uncertainty – clearly, such choices have not been 'caused to occur on demand' in the laboratory, but merely simulated by the hypothetical choices of the students and the behaviour of the rats. Furthermore, this time from a model-theoretic perspective, even if the empirical structures generated in the laboratory with the students' game and the rats' experience qualified as empirical models of the respective laboratory theories, they would not qualify as possible empirical interpretations, let alone models, of the economic theory of choice under uncertainty.

From what has been discussed so far, a third conclusion easily follows. Although there exists the possibility of a limited use of the (in the strict sense) experimental method in economics – and experiments should be performed whenever possible – the fact remains that due to ethical considerations and to practical limitations, economics remains to date an overwhelmingly non-experimental discipline.

The third conclusion which has followed the argument of this section does not state anything that has not already been said in the context of the history of methodological discourse in economics. And in this connection, it may be timely to sound a warning to the effect that nothing that is being said here should be construed as criticism, at least in general, of the objectives and of the laboratory procedures of the *experimental school of economics*.

The ingenuity of the approaches and the richness of procedures of contemporary *experimental economics* have been competently documented in the handbook by Kagel and Roth (1995) and the work by Davies and Holt (1993), and will not be further discussed in any detail in this book. Let us simply recognize that they should make a remarkable contribution to the economics research methodology. However, having said this, let us add that it is to be regretted that this most interesting arsenal of empirical research tools should have been so inappropriately labelled, namely, as *experimental economics.*

From the viewpoint of the mediate economic theories that *experimental economics* aims to relate to – as opposed to its laboratory counterparts, hypothetical games, token economies or animal-behaviour settings – its content is made up not of experimental situations in the strict sense but rather, as explained above, of laboratory simulation-of-experiment situations. And this mislabelling is unfortunate for two reasons.

First, it appears paradoxical – albeit an obvious consequence of the naming subterfuge – that the very reason for the existence as well as the particular features of current *experimental economics* is the predominantly non-experimental nature of economics research. Second, and this is not a quibble, the mislabelling regrettably hides the very important epistemological and methodological differences between techniques founded upon classical experimentation, on the one hand, and those based on procedures geared at simulating – not producing – experimental situations, on the other.

In all those situations – not very frequent, indeed – in which experiments, in the classical sense, may be performed in economics, we shall refer in the remainder of this study to 'economic experiments'. However, when referring to the typical empirical research procedures of the *experimental economics school* we shall use 'laboratory simulation of experiments' or 'laboratory experiment simulations'.

The current discussion – including our reference to *experimental economics* – suggests the crucial importance that simulation methods have acquired in economic research. Since, in our view, several different research approach categories may be profitably interpreted as distinct simulation operation classes – such an interpretation is developed in the remainder of this book – it may seem opportune at this point to introduce and elaborate on the important notion of simulation in science.

The *Encyclopaedia Britannica Micropaedia* (1977, p. 222) gives us the following characterization:

Simulation: in social science and education a research and teaching technique designed to reproduce under test conditions various phenomena likely to occur under real conditions. It is similar to role playing, or game playing, in which the actors (be they human beings, computers or mathematical components) are initially given specified rules, relationships, operating 'tools' and other variables and are left to interact.

Key phrases in this description are 'to reproduce' – as opposed to 'to produce' – 'role playing' and 'game playing'.

So far as the possible 'actors' of simulations are concerned, the description just quoted is quite comprehensive. The case of 'human beings' as actors – we may also add, animals – is clearly the one so well documented by Kagel and Roth (1995) or Davies and Holt (1993) and which we have called *laboratory experiment simulations*. The case in which the 'actors' are played by 'mathematical components' will be the subject of the following section and will occupy the centre of the discussion in the final chapter. In that latter context we use the expression *analytic simulation of experiments*. Finally, we have left the important case when the 'actors' are played by a 'computer'. With this case we deal next.

According to Adelman (1968), in the *International Encyclopaedia of the Social Sciences*, Vols. 13/14, p. 268, '"[s]imulation" of an economic system means the performance of experiments upon an analogue of the economic system and the drawing of inferences concerning the properties of the economic system from the behavior of its analogue. The analogue is an idealization of a generally more complex real system, the essential properties of which are retained in the analogue.'

The analogue of the 'real system', once again, may consist of a laboratory system of living subjects – human or animal – a mathematical system, or a computable structure stored in a computer. Exercises performed in the latter situation are often referred to as *simulation experiments*. The expression is correct in so far as the operations consist of experiments performed on an analogue (simulations) of the 'real system' and they imply *causing the simulations* to occur on demand and under specially controlled conditions – compare this with our comments on the second-level use of the word 'experiment', in the last paragraph of 11.1.

It is now time to summarize our results on the extension of the use of the experimental method in economics and to draw a few methodological consequences. We have examined in some detail several meanings with which the expressions 'experiment' and 'experimental method' occur in the economic literature and have concluded that the classical scientific notions – those that have been common currency in the natural sciences for centuries – should preserve their traditional designations in any scientific–methodological discourse. Not that other methodological approaches should not be allowed, but simply that they should be distinguished in content as well as in name.

With the strict concept of scientific experiment at hand, we have asked ourselves the question about the actual scope of the experimental method in economics. A careful examination of existing economic literature easily shows that its scope is certainly rather narrow.

In principle and without focusing on the technical aspects of any particular laboratory experience, we have recognized the past and the potential contribution to economic knowledge of the laboratory experiment simulations such as those described in Smith (1990, 1991), Davies and Holt (1993) or Kagel and Roth (1995). However, methodological soundness requires that the recognition, in principle, of the legitimacy of both strict experiments and simulation of experiments as possible testing procedures be completed by a normative methodological framework that classifies the laboratory results obtained by means of the one and of the other approach in two distinct categories. Such categories should unambiguously acknowledge their distinct ontological, epistemological and methodological import.

11.3 METHODOLOGICAL FOUNDATIONS OF NON-INTENDEDLY EMPIRICAL THEORIES

The focus of this chapter has been, thus far, the overwhelmingly non-experimental nature of economic science. At the level of empirical research, this has led to consequences and responses, two of which are worthwhile mentioning again here.

Historically, a fundamental methodological response to this trait of economics has been the development of econometrics, a special branch of mathematical statistics as well as an assortment of sophisticated non-experimental empirical methods. Since much has been written about econometrics in this context – for a cross-section of topics relating to the nature of econometrics, see Wold (1969a, 1969b), Mosbaek and Wold (1970a, 1970b), Epstein (1987), and Stigum (1990) – we shall abstain here from further comments on the subject.

A more recent methodological response to the non-experimental nature of economics is represented by the ever-expanding application of simulation methods in economic research. Such applications take very different directions, in particular, three prominent ones. The first has been labelled – paradoxically, in our view – *experimental economics*; the second direction is usually referred to as 'computer simulation'; and the third is called in this book 'analytic simulation of experiments'.

In relation to the simulation approaches collectively named *experimental economics* we have already made extensive comments. So far as computer simulations in economics are concerned, we note that they are used in at least two wide areas, namely, in the numerical solution and analysis of empirical economic structures – see, for instance, Wang, Klein and Rao (1995) – and in computation-intensive assisted studies of otherwise analytically intractable or, at least, difficult problems of mathematical economics and statistics – see, for instance, Taylor and Uhlig (1990) and Nagar (1960).

From the meanings given the word 'simulation' so far in this chapter, two have the common feature of being a procedure applied *in lieu* of an experiment – that is, a procedure by means of which some of the expected or postulated characteristics of an experiment are imitated. Simulation in the first sense has human beings as 'actors' and the technical emphasis of our description lies in the experiment-simulation aim of the operation. Simulation in the second sense has computers as 'actors' and the technical emphasis of our description lies in the simulation-experiment side of the exercise.

Yet a third possible sense for 'simulation' was left open in the *Encyclopaedia Britannica*'s (1977) description, namely, the case when the 'actors' in the simulation are mathematical components. And it is this third sense that gives content to the class of procedures called here *analytic simulation of experiments* which constitutes, we claim, the fundamental function of non-intendedly empirical theories in economics.

The third sense of 'simulation' is no less legitimate than the others, even if it happens to occur at the theoretical level. In contrast to the notion of empirical theory or, perhaps more properly, of intendedly empirical theory, we recall the notion of non-intendedly empirical theory as described in Part II; and parallel to the concepts of computer simulation of experiment and, especially, of laboratory (that is, empirical) simulation of experiment we introduce the idea of analytic (that is, theoretical) simulation of experiment.

The approaches and procedures encapsulated in this concept, which will occupy our attention throughout the remainder of this study, are in our view a consequence of and methodological response to the predominantly non-experimental nature of economics; they just happen to take place at the theoretical level and, frequently, far removed from any empirical context. In a way, as we shall see, the recuperation of this particular notion of simulation of experiment is tantamount to a revalorization, albeit at a formally rigorous level, of the role of *Gedanken Experimente* (thought experiments) as tools of scientific research. However, it is essential to emphasize that linguistic precision also commits us here to prefer the expression 'analytic simulation of experiment' over 'analytic experiment' or 'thought experiment', for these analytic operations are not experiments but procedures used *in lieu* of experiments.

11.4   NOTES AND REMARKS

An interesting exposition of methodological problems and of procedures which are involved in causal inference in the non-experimental sciences – including references to the econometric method – is to be found in Blalock (1964); regarding econometrics as a response to the non-experimental nature of most of economics, see Wold (1969a, 1969b).

Recent works which provide extensive coverage of *experimental economics*, including the discussion of methodological issues, are the *Handbook of Experimental Economics* edited by Kagel and Roth (1995) and the volume by Davies and Holt (1993).

An illustrative introduction to the type of approaches and games used by the scholars of the 'experimentalist' school is given in Smith (1990, 1991). The latter volume gathers some, by now classical, articles written by Professor Smith alone and in collaboration on subjects which cover a wide variety of areas including methodology, competitive market behaviour, induced value theory, the effect of institutions on market performance, auction markets, different topics in the economics of public goods, and natural monopolies; the former volume, edited by Professor Smith, contains articles by several authors – including the editor – covering such different subjects as oligopoly theory (Friedman, 1969), studies of income distribution performed via token economies (Battalio, Kagel and Reynolds, 1977), price controls and auction markets (Isaac and Plott, 1981) and several others.

Seminal papers for the laboratory experiment-simulation approach are Smith (1962 and 1964). The token-economy approach is described in a communication by Kagel (1972). I am thankful to Professor Melvin Cross for calling my attention to the article by Battalio *et al.* (1985), one in which work with laboratory animals is reported. Finally, for a more formalistic and methodological discussion, see the article by Smith (1982).

In Vol. 5, p. 825 of the *Brockhaus Enzyklopädie* – 17th edition (1968) of *Der Grosse Brockhaus* – an experiment is succinctly characterized as 'the artificial bringing about and modification of observational conditions for the acquisition of scientific data' – our translation from German. The word artificial (*künstlich*) is used here in obvious contrast to the concept 'spontaneous occurrence'.

A discussion of 'experiment' and 'experimental method', deeper than the one offered in this chapter, is to be found in Bunge (1967b).

Finally, the reader should be warned that the loose use of the word 'experiment' – that is, to denote a diversity of procedures at variance with the classic scientific meaning – not only occurs in economics but has proliferated also in other disciplines. The result is beginning to be an unfortunate need to use qualifiers – 'experiment in the sense of the natural sciences', 'experiment in the sense of biology', 'experiment in the sense of the social sciences', 'experiment in the sense of the behavioural sciences' – thus avoiding uncertainty at the price of linguistic heaviness.

12 Methodology of Non-Experimental Economic Research (II): Cognitive Functions of Non-Intendedly Empirical Theories

Economic theorists construct theories about economic phenomena and then contrast those theories with data, through the roundabout paths described in Part III. However, they face the handicap of being only seldom able to subject those theories to experimental control. Usually, economic processes cannot be 'caused to occur on demand' and variables, parameters, and structural settings cannot be manipulated 'under specially controlled conditions'. Hence the emergence of a methodology consisting in the simulation of experiments – which includes, in a prominent position, the *analytic simulation of experiments* – should not be surprising. In the latter case, procedures which are not viable at the actual experimental level are substituted, albeit only imperfectly and incompletely, by alternative operations performed at a rigorous analytic level.

12.1 NON-INTENDEDLY EMPIRICAL THEORIES AS ANALYTIC EXPERIMENT SIMULATIONS

The role of so-called *thought experiments* in scientific research has always been controversial. Nevertheless, thought experiments, or as we prefer to called them, *analytic simulations of experiments*, have played and continue to play their part in the process of theory building, even in the more developed spheres of science. In economics, where laboratory experiments in the strict sense are the exception rather than the rule, analytic experiment simulation becomes, by necessity, a method to be reckoned with. What should be stressed is that while

186

analytic simulation of experiments does have a place, even if sometimes only a modest one, in the process of theory building, that place is bound to acquire prominence when actual experimentation is not possible.

There are two traits of theoretical economics research which are, in our view, related methodological consequences of the limitations of the experimental method and which express themselves in matters of form and content. The first is the preference among contemporary theorists for the construction of formalized mathematical theories. The other is the conspicuous presence of theories which are, by any direct evidence, not intended as empirical theories.

From a formal point of view, axiomatic theories – in contrast to less rigorous ones – have the advantage of the lesser ambiguity of their languages and of the strong distinctness of their models; while their propositions are intelligible and well formulated their relational structures are clearly identifiable and transparent.

From an instrumental point of view, axiomatic theories are easier to alter analytically by means of the purposeful and systematic manipulation of their assumptions. As far as one can go analytically, and short of the actual experimental experience, the latter is a partial, imperfect but, nevertheless, legitimate substitute procedure for the controllable conditions of the laboratory.

From within – see for instance Kaldor (1972) – and from without – see for example Rosenberg (1989) – the economics profession, voices are regularly raised which either condemn this state of affairs in theoretical economics or, at least, express frustration with the supposed 'empirical irrelevance' of such theories.

Some of these normative views of how economic research, in general, and theoretical economics, in particular, should or should not proceed, seem to stem from a failure to understand the non-experimental constraints we have been referring to and to draw the necessary methodological consequences.

Of course, in economics as elsewhere, irrelevant theories are built. However, a particular non-empirical theory – as the theory of perfect gas in physics – is relevant or irrelevant not in isolation but in the context of other theories; moreover, its contribution to the understanding of the 'real world' may often be indirect, precisely through the contrasting description of some 'imaginary worlds'.

12.2 OBJECTIVES OF AND APPROACHES TO ANALYTIC EXPERIMENT SIMULATIONS

There is a *modus operandi* in economic-theoretical research which consists, broadly speaking, of the following two steps. In the first step, a class S of (mathematical) ideal structures is constructed with the aim that an $S \in S$ will in part mirror empirical and in part sketch non-empirical but logically possible economic systems. In the second step, a theory is developed to explain or to 'operate' – the latter even if only in a figurative sense – the structures in S.

In what follows, we list examples of research objectives and techniques which, in our view, fit well into the category of analytic experiment simulations. They are confined within the wide field of *general equilibrium analysis*. Of course, the examples could have been chosen from any other field of theoretical economics. However, theories of *general economic equilibrium* do benefit from some distinct features which tilt the choice in their favour. Historically, throughout the development of economic analysis until today, they have occupied a pre-eminent position at the centre of theoretical economics; systemically, they are interwoven into a web of theoretical components, and it is this network that comes, within economics, closest to the image of a unified, general theoretical framework; finally, especially so during the last half-century, their systematic, step-by-step unfolding – both as individual theories and as theoretical systems – provides eloquent examples of the investigative approach, which we call here the analytic simulation of experiments.

In this general context and by focusing on the actual investigation process, it is easy to identify a far-reaching research programme developed around a prominent *nucleus*, the Arrow–Debreu theoretical system (Arrow and Debreu, 1954), and consisting of a steady output of nucleus-founded and nucleus-inspired analytic activity, the aims of which include the development of new intendedly empirical theories, the construction of new non-intendedly empirical theories and the sharpening and development of alternatives to existing analytic approaches.

 · Although the list of objectives and of related analytic techniques which we shall refer to cannot be thorough, let alone exhaustive, it will facilitate the task of distinguishing some broad categories of operations tentatively identified with respect to some common, if only very general, trait. From this point of view, we differentiate analytic procedures which focus primarily on the relational structures of a theory or their internal properties from those primarily concerned with matters of language or research strategy, including in the latter category those probing into the adequacy of a specific mathematical tool or method.

Let us begin with a concise description of the original nucleus of the research programme.

12.3 THE NUCLEUS OF A RESEARCH PROGRAMME: ARROW–DEBREU THEORY AND MODELS

The publication of the article by Arrow and Debreu (1954) marked a milestone in the development of general equilibrium analysis. On the one hand, it signalled the culmination of a process of several decades aimed at proving the consistency of the theoretical systems built in the Walrasian tradition. On the other hand, it made available a new general analytic framework for the investigation of the working of economies while, at the same time, initiating a new formal style.

Whereas the proclaimed objective of the article was a rather limited if fundamental one, namely, to state 'very general conditions under which a competitive equilibrium will exist' (Arrow and Debreu, 1954), its effects went far beyond that objective, as they led to a new approach and established new standards of rigour for theoretical research. In its static–analytical framework and in addition to the already-mentioned equilibrium 'existence problem', the research focused principally on the relations between equilibrium and optimum (the 'optimality problem'), the number and local uniqueness of equilibria (the 'determinacy problem'), the computation of equilibria and the relations between equilibria, on the one hand, and other solution concepts, on the other.

An Arrow–Debreu economy consists of a finite number of units executing production plans and a finite number of units realizing consumption plans. Such production and consumption plans are always expressed as real, finite-component vectors of commodities.

A plan for the jth production unit is thus an l-vector $y_j = (y_{1j}, \ldots, y_{lj})$ in the Euclidean space R^l. A plan for the ith consumption unit is, analogously, an l-vector $x_i = (x_{1i}, \ldots, x_{li})$ in the Euclidean space R^l. A positive (respectively, negative) component of a production vector represents an output (respectively, input). A negative (respectively, positive) component of a consumption vector represents an output or provision of labour services (respectively, input or consumption proper).

The Euclidean space R^l is called the commodity space. The subset of production (consumption) plans in R^l which are *a priori* feasible for the jth production unit (respectively, ith consumption unit) is called the jth unit's production set (respectively, ith unit's consumption set) and denoted $\mathbf{Y}_j$ (respectively, $\mathbf{X}_i$). The ith consumer's taste is represented by a utility indicator function (or utility function), a real-valued, monotonic non-decreasing function $\mathbf{u}_i$ with domain $\mathbf{X}_i$.

The set $\mathbf{Y} = \Sigma_j \mathbf{Y}_j$ (respectively, $\mathbf{X} = \Sigma_i \mathbf{X}_i$) is the aggregate production (respectively, consumption) set. Defining aggregate supply by $\mathbf{y} = \Sigma_j \mathbf{y}_j$, aggregate demand by $\mathbf{x} = \Sigma_i \mathbf{x}_i$ and total resources by $\mathbf{w} = \Sigma_i \mathbf{w}_i$, one obtains excess demand as $\mathbf{x} - \mathbf{y} - \mathbf{w}$. A price system $\mathbf{p}$ is an l-vector $(\mathbf{p}_1, \ldots, \mathbf{p}_l)$, a member of the price set $\mathbf{P} \subset \mathbf{\Omega}$, where $\mathbf{\Omega}$ is the non-negative orthant of R^l.

Given a price system $\mathbf{p}^*$ each production unit $j \in J$ chooses a production plan $\mathbf{y}_j^*$ which maximizes its profit $\mathbf{p}^* \mathbf{y}_j$ within its production set $\mathbf{Y}_j$. Given a price system $\mathbf{p}^*$, each consumption unit $i \in I$ chooses a consumption plan $\mathbf{x}_i^*$ which maximizes its utility indicator function $\mathbf{u}_i(\mathbf{x}_i)$, subject to the budget constraint $\mathbf{p}^* \mathbf{x}_i \leq \mathbf{p}^* \mathbf{w}_i + \Sigma_j \alpha_{ij} \mathbf{p}^* \mathbf{y}_j^*$ within the consumption set $\mathbf{X}_i$. In the preceding inequality, $\mathbf{w}_i \in R^l$ and $\alpha_{ij} \in [0, 1]$ represent the initial endowment vector of the ith consumer and a contractual claim of the share of profit by the ith consumer on the jth firm, respectively.

A competitive economy is one in which each agent takes prices as given and these are independent of the agent's individual choice decisions. Evidence of the consistency of a competitive economy is the existence of a competitive or Walrasian solution for such a system. As stated above, the immediate objective of the article by Arrow and Debreu (1954) was to state general conditions for the existence of equilibrium.

The proof of the existence of a competitive equilibrium for an economic structure like the one described above was originally given by Arrow and Debreu (1954) using the game-theoretical concept of a Nash equilibrium (see Nash, 1950) in the context of an 'abstract economy' – a generalization of the notion of a game. The Arrow–Debreu conditions for the existence of an equilibrium are now formally taken up in the following definition of the models of the Arrow–Debreu theory. The current axiomatic formulation deviates slightly from the original and has been dictated by the illustrative ends of this chapter.

Definition 12.3.1   An *Arrow–Debreu model* or *economy* is a structure $\mathscr{E} = \langle R^l, R, \mathbf{P}, J, I, \langle \mathbf{Y}_j \rangle, \langle \mathbf{X}_i, \succcurlyeq_i, \mathbf{w}_i, \alpha_{ij} \rangle, \mathbf{x}_i^*, \mathbf{y}_j^* \rangle$ such that:

    A12.3.1 $J = \{1, 2, \ldots, n\} \subset N$;

    A12.3.2 $I = \{1, 2, \ldots, m\} \subset N$;

    A12.3.3 $\forall j \in J$: $\mathbf{Y}_j$ is a closed subset of R^l containing 0;

A12.3.4 $\forall j \in J$: $\mathbf{Y}_j$ is convex;

A12.3.5 $\mathbf{Y} \cap \Omega = \{0\}$;

A12.3.6 $\mathbf{Y} \cap (-\mathbf{Y}) = \{0\}$;

A12.3.7 $\forall i \in I$: $\mathbf{X}_i$ is a closed subset of R^l which is bounded from below by a vector $\boldsymbol{\xi}_i$;

A12.3.8 $\forall i \in I$: $\succcurlyeq_i$ is a preference relation on $\mathbf{X}_i$;

A12.3.9 $\forall i \in I$: $\mathbf{w}_i \in R^l$;

A12.3.10 $\forall i \in I$: $\mathbf{X}_i$ is convex;

A12.3.11 $\forall i \in I$: $\succcurlyeq_i$ is representable by a utility indicator function $\mathbf{u}_i$: $\mathbf{X}_i \to R$ such that:

    (a) for any $\mathbf{x}_i \in \mathbf{X}_i$, there is an $\mathbf{x}_i' \in \mathbf{X}_i$ such that $\mathbf{u}_i(\mathbf{x}_i') > \mathbf{u}_i(\mathbf{x}_i)$;

    (b) if $\mathbf{u}_i(\mathbf{x}_i) > \mathbf{u}_i(\mathbf{x}_i')$ and $\lambda \in [0, 1] \subset R$ then $\mathbf{u}_i[\lambda \mathbf{x}_i + (1 - \lambda)\mathbf{x}_i'] > \mathbf{u}_i(\mathbf{x}_i')$;

A12.3.12 $\forall i \in I$: for some $\mathbf{x}_i \in \mathbf{X}_i$, $\mathbf{x}_i << \mathbf{w}_i$;

A12.3.13 $\forall (i, j)$: $\boldsymbol{\alpha}_{ij} \geq 0$; $\forall j \in J$, $\Sigma_{i=1}^m \boldsymbol{\alpha}_{ij} = 1$;

A12.3.14 $\mathbf{P} = \{\mathbf{p}: \mathbf{p} \in R^l, \mathbf{p} \geq 0; \Sigma_{h=1}^l \mathbf{p}_h\}$;

A12.3.15 $\forall j \in J$: $\mathbf{y}_j^* = \max \mathbf{p}^* \mathbf{y}_j$ over $\mathbf{Y}_j$ for $\mathbf{p}^* \in \mathbf{P}$;

A12.3.16 $\forall i \in I$: $\mathbf{x}_i^* = \max \mathbf{u}_i(\mathbf{x}_i)$ over $\{\mathbf{x}_i \in \mathbf{X}_i: \mathbf{p}^* \mathbf{x}_i \leq \mathbf{p}^* \mathbf{w}_i + \Sigma_{j=1}^n \boldsymbol{\alpha}_{ij} \mathbf{p}^* \mathbf{y}_j^*$.

Let us first comment in some detail on the axioms of the set-theoretical predicate of Definition 12.3.1. Such a discussion should help us understand the nature and the objectives of the analytic experiment simulations to be dealt with in the remainder of the chapter.

First of all, let us agree that the *structural axioms* – the assumptions that determine the possible realization of the theory – are A12.3.1–A12.3.3, A12.3.7–A12.3.9, A12.3.13–A12.3.16.

While fixing the finite-dimensional space R^l as the commodity space, the first and the second triple of axioms give the profile of a finite number of firms (n) and of a finite number of consumers (m), respectively, in very general terms; the *closure* of $\mathbf{Y}_j$ ($\mathbf{X}_i$), a mathematical (that is, linguistic) requirement, only means that if vectors arbitrarily close to $\mathbf{y}_j$ ($\mathbf{x}_i$) belong to $\mathbf{Y}_j$ ($\mathbf{X}_i$) then $\mathbf{y}_j$ ($\mathbf{x}_i$) too belongs to $\mathbf{Y}_j$ ($\mathbf{X}_i$); $0 \in \mathbf{Y}_j$ establishes the 'possibility of inaction' for the firms; the lower bound for $\mathbf{X}_i$ amounts to imposing a lower limit for a consumer's consumption proper and an upper limit for the consumer's potential supply of labour; Assumption A12.3.8 introduces the preference scale of the consumer and, finally, Axiom A12.3.9 refers to the consumer's initial endowment and is self-explanatory. Whereas Assumption A12.3.13 characterizes a 'private-ownership economy', Assumption A12.3.14 characterizes the set of prices. Note that the latter assumption, in addition to introducing a price normalization rule, directly imposes the non-negativity of prices and the condition that not all be zero. Completing the list, A12.3.15 and A12.3.16 describe the 'laws of behaviour' of firms and consumers, respectively.

All remaining assumptions in Definition 12.3.1 will be regarded, in the sequel, as *axioms proper*. Assumption A12.3.4 (A12.3.10), the *convexity* of $\mathbf{Y}_j$ ($\mathbf{X}_i$), says that commodities are divisible, that if two production (consumption) plans are possible so are their respective convex combinations, and exclude increasing returns to scale in production as well as in the transformation of consumption proper into labour services. Assumptions A12.3.5 and A12.3.6 exclude, for the aggregate production sector, the possibility of 'free production' – an output without an input – and the possibility of a reversible production process – two production vectors such that the outputs of one exactly match the inputs of the other – respectively. Assumption A12.3.11 directly establishes the representability of $\geqslant_i$ by means of a real, continuous, non-satiated and quasi-concave function $\mathbf{u}_i$ – and thus, indirectly, the continuity, non-satiability and convexity (for any real number $\mathbf{r}$, the set $\{\mathbf{x}_i \colon \mathbf{x}_i \in \mathbf{X}_i, \mathbf{u}_i(\mathbf{x}_i) \geq \mathbf{r}\}$ is a convex set) of the preference relation. Finally, the very strong Assumption A12.3.12 places the initial endowment of a consumer in the interior of the consumption set – the consumer owns a positive amount of each commodity.

The definition of a competitive equilibrium for the economy $\mathscr{E}$ now follows.

Definition 12.3.2   A competitive or Walrasian equilibrium for the economy $\mathscr{E}$ is a state $(\mathbf{y}^*, \mathbf{x}^*, \mathbf{p}^*)$ of $\mathscr{E}$ where (1) each production unit $j \in J$ chooses a profit maximizer $\mathbf{y}_j^*$ in its production set $\mathbf{Y}_j$; (2) each consumption unit $i \in I$ chooses a utility maximizer $\mathbf{x}_i^*$ in its budget set $\{\mathbf{x}_i \in \mathbf{X}_i \colon \mathbf{p}^*\mathbf{x}_i \leq \mathbf{p}^*\mathbf{w}_i + \Sigma_j \mathbf{\alpha}_{ij}\mathbf{p}^*\mathbf{y}_j^*\}$; and (3) aggregate demand equals aggregate supply in each market, that is, aggregate excess demand $\mathbf{x}^* - \mathbf{y}^* - \mathbf{w} = 0$.

The following result is a central piece of the Arrow–Debreu theory.

Theorem 12.3.1   The private-ownership economy $\mathscr{E}$ of Definition 12.3.1 has a competitive or Walrasian equilibrium $(\mathbf{p}^*, \mathbf{x}^*, \mathbf{y}^*)$.

This completes the description of the Arrow–Debreu model and the sketch of its theory. In what follows, we show how the model – or, more properly, class of models – and its language have been and are the subjects of the kind of analytic operations which we call analytic simulations of experiments.

In the manner described at the end of 12.2, we shall refer, first, to operations consisting in the *definition of a new structure* through the alteration of an existing one or by a fundamentally new design; second, to the *modification of an internal property of a structure*; and, third, to operations aimed at *scrutinizing the linguistic and methodological aspects* of a theory.

This three-way distinction is only meant as an aid to our understanding of the issues by emphasizing the possible primary goal of an operation and separating it from its structural or linguistic consequences.

As we shall see, however, analytic operations of the structural kind (for example, change in structure or properties) usually necessitate analytic operations of a linguistic kind (change in structural or proper axioms) and linguistic operations (for instance, change in axioms) lead to the definition of new structures.

For the sake of clarity in the discussion, we need to keep in mind the distinctions we made in this study – see the end of 3.2 and beginning of 4.2 – in regard to three reference concepts, namely, the *immediate ideal referent* of a theory, intendedly or non-intendedly empirical – called an 'ideal' or 'mathematical economic structure'; the *immediate empirical referent* of a theory – defined as an 'empirical economic structure' in Definition 4.2.1; and the *mediate empirical referent* of a theory – a more or less fuzzy chunk of reality, referred to as a 'real-world economic system'.

A 'real-world economic system' – the mediate referent of a theory, an international, national, regional economy; a market; an economic agent, to mention a few – is usually a highly complex structure in itself. This complexity is augmented by the fact that economic systems are merely relatively autonomous subsystems of larger, encompassing, 'real-world systems'. It is the task of the economic theorist intellectually to extricate the economic subsystem from the conceptual whole it is interwoven with, to reconstruct it with the necessary details, and to draw a blueprint describing the channels which connect the former and the latter. In a few words, this task involves the definition of a set-theoretical predicate – the ideal immediate referent, a class of mathematical structures – and the construction of a theory appropriate to explain or 'operate' the relevant structures.

The choice of a particular class of relational structures as subjects of theoretical inquiry involves matters of content and of form. Among the matters of content, a pre-eminent place is usually occupied by the intellectual interest elicited in the researcher by the empirical mediate referent (real-world system) or the purely logical system (possible logical world) that the relational structure – that is, the immediate referent – is supposed, respectively, to mirror or to embody. Among the matters of form, two factors, both associated with the propriety of the definition of the set-theoretical predicate, suggest themselves, namely the researcher's need for sufficient transparency of structure and for an appropriate degree of conceptual rigour.

According to Nowak (1989), new ideal structures may be constructed by positive or negative potentialization, in the new ideal structure, of properties of known empirical structures, or by the incorporation into (respectively, elimination from) the new ideal structure of non-existing (respectively, existing) properties of known empirical structures.

12.4 FIRST KIND OF ANALYTIC EXPERIMENT SIMULATION: DEFINING AND REDEFINING A STRUCTURE

The first kind of experiment simulations we have in mind refer to operations performed on the structural axioms of a theory, namely, by characterizing the potential models of a new theory or modifying the class of the possible interpretations of a pre-existing one.

12.4.1 Characterizing competition: economies with 'many' agents

In general equilibrium analysis – see Arrow and Hahn (1971), Hildenbrand (1974), Mas-Colell (1985) – it is common practice to construct mathematical structures which include some characteristics that are *limit idealizations* of known or hypothesized features of empirical structures. Such objectives are usually pursued by means of constructing theories whose models are the results of more or less radical modifications introduced to the original Arrow–Debreu model. Efforts to characterize rigorously the limit notion of 'perfect competition' belong to this class of endeavour.

A competitive economy is one where each agent has a negligible capacity individually to influence social outcomes. The limit concept of a perfectly competitive economy, therefore, suggests itself as an economic structure with 'very many very small agents'. The natural framework of such a system is an economy with a continuum of agents – see Aumann (1964).

In one possible formalization of a perfectly competitive economy – see Hildenbrand (1974, 1982) – the finite set J of firms of the Arrow–Debreu model is dropped while the finite set I of consumers is replaced by $(A, \mathcal{B}, \mu)$, an *atomless measure space of agents*, where A is the set of agents, the class $\mathcal{B}$, usually a σ-algebra or a σ-field, is the collection of all possible coalitions of members of A, and μ is a probability measure. For any $E \in \mathcal{B}$, $\mu(E)$ represents the proportion of agents in A that are members of the coalition E. In particular, the measure of an individual agent $a \in A$ is $\mu(\{a\}) = 0$, emphasizes the agent's negligible nature. In the new setting, agent a is identified with the characteristics $X(a)$, $\geqslant(a)$ and $w(a)$, and a coalition E can be made to own a production set Y_E – a coalition production economy.

The core of a competitive economy

Given an economy of any size – understanding by 'size' its number of traders – agents may find it convenient to form trading coalitions to improve the utility of each of their members. An *Edgeworth* or *core allocation* is a settlement reached after all possible improving coalitions have been tried, and the set of all such allocations constitutes the *core of the economy*. Moreover, the size of the core depends on the extent to which improving coalitions can be formed and this extent, in turn, depends on the size of the economy. It is known that for an Arrow–Debreu economy, the set of Walrasian equilibrium allocations is properly contained in, that is, is strictly smaller than, the core.

Edgeworth's conjecture

It was Edgeworth's (1881) 'conjecture' that the core of an economy would shrink with increasing number of agents and that in the limit – when this number grew without bound and thus the relative 'weight' of each one became negligible – the core would consist only of the competitive solutions, that is, the Walrasian equilibrium allocations.

A rigorous criterion would thus characterize a perfectly competitive economy – a limit notion in the sense described above – as an 'economy where its core equals its set of competitive equilibrium allocations'. Key items for such characterization are the *core–equilibria equivalence theorems*, presented in several alternative mathematical frameworks and with different proofs. Celebrated approaches to core–equilibria equivalence have made use of sequences of 'expanding' finite economies (Debreu and Scarf, 1963), an economy with a continuum of traders

(Aumann, 1964), an economy where coalitions replace individual consumers as primitive elements of the structure (Vind, 1964, 1965), an economy where the class $\mathcal{B}$ of coalitions is a Boolean ring rather than the customary σ-algebra or σ-field (Armstrong and Richter, 1984), or using a 'non-standard economy' (Brown and Robinson, 1975; Anderson, 1978). For a detailed survey of most of the above development, see Hildenbrand (1982).

The rate of convergence of the core

In the context of the analytic exercises described in the preceding paragraph, one may mention the studies devoted to characterizing the 'distance' mediating properties of the 'limit economy' – and its characteristic objects – and properties of a 'large' but finite economy – and its corresponding objects – the latter being an arbitrarily high term of an appropriately expanding sequence of finite economies; see, for instance, Grodal (1975).

12.4.2 Economies with 'many' commodities

In the examples given thus far, the *commodity space* of the ideal economy has been the finite-dimensional linear space R^l. However, analysis did detect, relatively early – see, for example, Debreu (1954) and Bewley (1972) – several meaningful and well-defined economic phenomena which could not be adequately characterized in the finite-dimensional domain of an Arrow–Debreu structure. In particular, certain typical problems related to 'equilibrium under uncertainty', 'finance economics', 'intertemporal allocation' and 'equilibrium with commodity differentiation' seemed to occur 'naturally' in the context of a relational structure with the appropriate infinite-dimensional domain space – see Mas-Colell and Zame (1991).

The need to respond to these new questions has led a growing number of researchers to analytic experiment simulations involving a diversity of infinite-dimensional relational structures. As opposed to what happens in equilibrium analysis with a finite number of commodities, where R^l is the canonical space, there is no single infinite-dimensional space that would arise as the 'natural framework' for the variety of circumstances listed above. Even within each application category, technical considerations may determine the existence of more than one possible candidate space.

From a methodological viewpoint, although economies with infinitely many commodities are constructed to be subjected to new and specific queries – for example, in intertemporal analysis, concerning the inner recursiveness of the structures; see Mas-Colell and Zame (1991) – they are also put to the standard general questions of equilibrium existence, determinacy, core–equilibrium equivalence and so on. More on this follows in 12.4.3 and 12.6.

12.4.3 The determinacy of equilibria

An Arrow–Debreu economy is a complex structure and one would expect it to have a unique equilibrium only under rather strong additional assumptions – see conditions for global uniqueness in Arrow and Hahn (1971) and Mas-Colell, Whinston and Green (1995). What one might hope for, instead, is an Arrow–Debreu economy to have a multiplicity of locally unique equilibria.

An economy with a multiplicity of equilibria is said to be *locally determinate* if each of its equilibrium price vectors is locally unique. An equilibrium price vector is locally unique if there does not exist another normalized price vector arbitrarily close to it, that is, if it is unique in an open neighbourhood. A locally unique equilibrium – as opposed to an equilibrium point in a continuum of equilibria – is also referred to as a determinate equilibrium.

The 1970s saw very intensive research into the question of the determinacy of equilibria. First, variants of Arrow–Debreu economies were studied, including the special case of pure exchange economies; very strong results on local uniqueness were obtained (Debreu, 1970); these analytic simulations of experiments were then extended to 'large economies' like the systems described in 12.4.1; the strong results on local uniqueness persisted – see K. Hildenbrand (1974) and H. Dierker (1975).

By the middle of the 1980s the situation, so far as results are concerned, could be summarized as follows. For 'almost all' – in some rigorous sense – structures within the rather large class of ideal economies studied, equilibria were not only locally unique, they even occurred in finite, odd numbers. Economies with a continuum of equilibria were, indeed, most rare accidents.

However, a limit for the above results was shown in an article by Kehoe *et al.* (1989) where a 'large-square' economy – an economy with 'many' agents, in the sense of 12.4.1, and 'many' commodities, in the sense of 12.4.2 – was investigated. Specifically, the authors focused on a pure exchange economy where the commodity space H is a separable, infinite-dimensional Hilbert space, agents are indexed by the interval [0, 1], and a consumer is identified with an excess-demand function. In contrast to the previous conclusions, the new result states that for such a 'large-square' economy indeterminacy, the presence of a continuum of equilibria, is an inherent possibility.

12.4.4 Equilibrium with alternative agents' characteristics

Progress in equilibrium analysis was frequently made after 1954 by focusing on relational structures obtained from the original Arrow–Debreu model by modifications of the primitive objects of the structures representing the agents' characteristics. A few examples are given next. Once again, it must be noted that such structural alterations necessarily led to parallel changes in the linguistic features of theories, in particular in their structural axioms. We shall consider the latter aspect later on, in 12.6.

Preference relations and utility functions

In a few studies which closely followed in time the Arrow and Debreu (1954) article – including Debreu (1959 and 1962) – a consumer's taste is identified not directly with a utility indicator function but with a complete preordering – a reflexive, transitive and complete relation on the consumption set – satisfying global or local non-satiation, a continuity condition and a rather weak convexity property.

Non-transitive, non-total consumers

A consumer in an Arrow–Debreu economy is characterized by a utility function which presupposes a preference–indifference relation which, in addition to satisfying a continuity assumption, is reflexive, transitive and complete. Several studies which followed the article by Arrow and Debreu (1954) focused on consumers whose primitive characteristics directly included, instead of a utility function, a reflexive preference–indifference relation – Debreu (1959, 1962) – or an irreflexive preference relation – Hildenbrand (1974). In all cases, whether reflexive or irreflexive, these relations were transitive and complete or total. The study of consumers without transitive and complete or total tastes was led by Sonnenschein (1971) and carried a long step forward by Mas-Colell (1974), Gale and Mas-Colell (1975), Shafer and Sonnenschein (1975) and Kim and Richter (1986), signalling a remarkable breakthrough in general equilibrium analysis.

12.4.5 Imaginary economic systems: alternative organizational settings

There is a line of theoretical research with a very respectable tradition in economics, which focuses on the design and analysis of formal structures which are the blueprints of imaginary – as opposed to actual – organizational alternatives. These mathematical structures may incorporate properties and relations that represent, usually at a high level of abstraction, properties and relations of known empirical structures. However, more interestingly, these mathematical systems may purposely include (respectively, exclude) properties and relations lacking (respectively, having) analogous properties and relations of known empirical structures.

In a nutshell, the aims of a theory of this kind may include the description of mathematical laws of behaviour or rules of operation of some thinkable (logically possible) yet not empirical relational structure as well as learning about an empirical system by contrasting it to an imaginary one.

Although some of the theories and models in the category have only a distant relation to our current examples centred around the Arrow–Debreu theory and models, they do provide excellent illustrations of non-intendedly empirical theories and of the analytic simulation of experiments method. The reader is referred for concrete examples to organization theory (Marschak, 1986) and the theory of decentralized allocation mechanisms – Hurwicz (1973, 1986).

Among the theories directed at describing hypothetical laws of behaviour of and rules of operation on alternative decentralized allocation mechanisms, and this time within the context of general equilibrium analysis, one must refer to theories of market socialism and labour-managed economies. The subject has, of course, a rather extended history – think, for instance, of the pioneer works by Barone (1908) and Lange (1938) – but what we have in mind here are more recent investigations which may be seen as analytic simulation of experiments performed within an original Arrow–Debreu structure – Drèze (1976) refers explicitly to Debreu (1959); see also Drèze (1974) – or on one of its more recent descendants – Ichiishi (1977).

12.4.6 Imperfectly competitive economies

Although the literature devoted to imperfect competition is extensive, most of it corresponds to partial equilibrium analysis. The development of imperfect competition theories in a general equilibrium framework has been much more difficult, slower and, so far, less successful, than the development of theories of perfectly competitive economies.

Analytic experiment simulations in this field, one might expect, would aim at two distinct objectives. The first is to contribute to the construction of new explanatory non-intendedly empirical theories and thus to provide better insight into the working of imperfectly competitive structures; the second is to help in the transition from non-intended empirical theories of perfect and imperfect competition to the development of full-fledged empirical theories of imperfect competition.

Within the general equilibrium framework and closer to the examples of this chapter we shall refer to two different approaches.

The first approach involves theories of monopolistic competition with their main focus on the question of the existence of monopolistic–competitive equilibrium. Important examples are the work of Negishi (1961, 1972), where price-setting firms face subjective (that is, expected) demand functions and where the definition of monopolistic–competitive equilibrium includes the competitive solution as a special case; and the work of Arrow and Hahn (1971), in a structure where prices are set by firms with increasing returns to scale – see also the survey article by Bénassy (1991).

The second approach has been developed in the context of core analysis. It consists in the determination of whether or not core–equilibria equivalence is fulfilled in 'large' economies which include, alongside their 'many small traders', a sector of 'few large traders'. A 'large trader' is interpreted here, as the case may be, as a monopolist, duopolist, oligopolist or, simply, as an agent with a disproportionately large initial endowment.

One direction has been followed by Farrell (1970) and Jaskold-Gabszewicz (1977) with an increasing Debreu–Scarf sequence of a two-commodity, two-agent-types economy, where only the number of agents of one type replicates to infinity – the 'small traders' of the 'limit economy' – while the number of agents of the other type remains constant – the 'large traders' of the 'limit economy'. Another direction – 'mixed markets' – has been followed by Shitovitz (1973, 1974), where the continuum of 'small agents' (atomless sector) of an Aumann-type economy is augmented by a finite or countably infinite number of 'large traders' (atoms or individual agents with positive measure).

12.5 SECOND KIND OF ANALYTIC EXPERIMENT SIMULATION: MODIFYING AN INTERNAL STRUCTURAL PROPERTY

This section refers to operations which affect some secondary properties of a structure rather that those determined by the structural axioms. Many standard examples involve economies with different agents' characteristics.

12.5.1 Consumers without a 'survival warranty'

The consumers of the Arrow–Debreu model possess a very strong and enviable characteristic: they are able 'to survive' without trade. Debreu (1962) studied the existence of equilibrium for an economy where this 'survival warranty' was not directly imposed but where, instead, a structural condition ensured the compatibility of the consumption and production sectors. Some years later, Moore (1975) studied an economy where the survival condition had been totally removed and replaced by an 'irreducibility' requirement.

12.5.2 Externalities in consumption and production

In the Arrow–Debreu model externalities are excluded from both the consumption and the production sectors. In particular, individual consumption sets as well as consumers' preferences are independent of each other; the same situation prevails in the production sector regarding the production sets of individual firms.

McKenzie (1955) studied economic structures where individual utility functions are interdependent or dependent on prices and activity levels. Arrow and Hahn (1971) and Shafer and Sonnenschein (1975, 1976) included agents with interdependent feasible-choice sets.

12.5.3 Production without 'irreversible' activities

Contrary to the Arrow–Debreu model, McKenzie (1959, 1961) and Debreu (1962) studied economies where the aggregate production process need not be irreversible.

12.5.4 Production without 'free disposal'

In Arrow and Debreu (1954), the price vectors of the economy are confined by A12.3.10 to the simplex $P = \{p: p \in R^l, p \geq 0; \Sigma_{h=1}^{l} p_h = 1\}$. In Debreu (1959) – see also 2.7 in this book – prices are not confined to non-negative values but, instead, the economy or all firms may freely dispose of all commodities – in other words, the production sector possesses the ability of 'free disposal' $(-\Omega \subset \mathbf{Y})$. The result is similar but indirect in the sense that, as a consequence of 'free disposal', the relevant price systems are non-negative. More recent studies – see, for instance, Hart and Kuhn (1975) – focus on relational structures, the production sectors of which do not necessarily satisfy such a condition.

12.5.5 Non-convexities I: economies with indivisible commodities

The commodity space of the Arrow–Debreu model is the Euclidean R^l space. Consumption and production sets are convex. Commodities are thus infinitely divisible and can be the object of transactions provided they occur in finite quantities and satisfy the other feasibility conditions enumerated in Definition 12.3.1.

What can be expected, instead, when the economic structure includes indivisibilities, that is, when some commodities can only be traded in integer quantities? The issue has been the subject of several investigations. In particular, Dierker (1971), Broome (1972) and Mas-Colell (1977b) studied the problem in the context of a pure exchange economy – think of the model of Definition 12.3.2 with the production set $\mathbf{Y} = \{0\}$.

In Broome's (1972) article, the commodity space of the economy is a subset of R^l, defined by $\mathbf{F} = \{\mathbf{x} \in R^l: [\forall r \in (1, \ldots, n_d), \mathbf{x}_r$ is real] and $[\forall r \in (n_d + 1, \ldots, l), \mathbf{x}_r$ is an integer]$\}$ and it is required that at least one commodity should be divisible, that is $n_d \geq 1$. Nguyen (1976) could improve and extend some of Broome's (1972) results by studying a similar economic structure augmented with a production set $\mathbf{Y}$.

12.5.6 Non-convexities II: fixed costs and increasing returns to scale

In addition to the case of indivisible commodities, non-convexities in the production sector of an economy may occur when fixed costs or increasing returns to scale are present. To this one may add, in relation to the consumption sector, the case when preferences do not satisfy a convexity condition.

There exists a growing literature on the existence of (marginal pricing or average pricing) equilibria – for example, Mantel (1979), Beato and Mas-Colell (1985), Brown, Heller and Starr (1992); equilibrium and optimality – Dierker (1989), Quinzii (1991); the number and local uniqueness of equilibria – Kamiya (1988); and the computation of equilibria – Kamiya (1987).

12.6 THIRD KIND OF ANALYTIC EXPERIMENT
SIMULATION: PROBING LANGUAGE AND METHOD

Several theoretical improvements to equilibrium analysis were achieved after 1954 through the elimination or substitution of axioms of the original Arrow–Debreu theory. Especially when these changes affect structural axioms, the respective operations should be regarded as the linguistic counterparts to the alterations of structure described in 12.4.

Moreover, operations are often performed on the axioms proper of a theory. Indeed, there is a line of research which includes, in an idealized and succinct description, the following procedures. Given an abstract theory one establishes, in very general terms, the class S of its possible (ideal) realizations, as determined by the structural axioms; thereafter, and with due account to its axioms proper, one determines the subclass $M \subset S$ of models of the theory; finally, by systematic trying and probing – dispensing with or substituting – one or more axioms proper at a time, one modifies the original theory (strictly speaking, creates a new theory) and then determines a new class $N \subset S$ of models for the new theory. This method, carried on in an orderly fashion, allows for rigorous comparisons of models and theoretical propositions. In some sense, it is the closest to the experimental method that one might' hope to reach analytically. We may claim that what the theorist is doing in such circumstances amounts to checking the dependence of deductive results on initial assumptions.

Theories of mathematical economics often consist of intricate webs of propositions where it is difficult to determine, by direct examination, the status of every axiom. Alternative methods are then called for. As a note of caution, let us say that no reference is intended here to the full-fledged *logical reconstruction* of theories as attempted by the 'structuralist school' – see, for instance, Balzer (1982, 1985), Haslinger (1983), Hands (1985) – but rather to the methods used more or less routinely by the practitioner theorist to establish the ways in which and the extent to which a particular analytic result depends on a given assumption. This general procedure can adopt different forms. In what follows we give a short list of specific ends which are frequently pursued with this approach.

12.6.1 Probing the indispensableness of axioms

We begin by introducing a notion of 'essentialness' to be understood here in the sense of 'indispensability' or 'indispensableness'.

Definition 12.6.1   Let **t** be a proposition of a theory **L** having the axiom basis $\{A_i: i = 1, 2, \ldots, n\} = A$. One says that A_k is *essential* or *indispensable* for **t** if it is true that **t** follows from **A** – symbolically, $A \vdash t$ – and that **t** does not follow from $A \backslash \{A_k\}$ – symbolically $\neg\ (A \backslash \{A_k\} \vdash t)$.

Two typical examples from the Arrow–Debreu theory have already been met in the discussion of 12.4 on alterations of structure.

The first example has to do with the restriction imposed on the value of normalized prices in the context of the equilibrium existence theorem of the original work – Arrow and Debreu (1954) – and later substituted by a 'free disposal assumption' – see Debreu (1959) and 2.7 in this volume. Hart and Kuhn (1975), Bergstrom (1976) and McKenzie (1981) have since given proofs that competitive equilibrium also exists in structures, the production sectors of which do not satisfy a 'free disposal assumption'.

The second example refers to the dropping from the axiom base of the assumption that consumer tastes are preordered by means of transitive and complete or total preferences. As mentioned in 12.4, Sonnenschein (1971) led a research agenda aimed at producing a proof of an existence theorem dispensing with this classic assumption.

12.6.2 Probing the substitutability of axioms

A situation which is formally different from the one described in 12.6.1 is characterized next.

Definition 12.6.2   Let **t** be a proposition of a theory **L** having the axiom basis $\{A_i: i = 1, 2, \ldots, n\} = A$. One says that a formula $b \notin A$ is a *substitute* of the formula $A_k \in A$ if $A \vdash t$, $\neg\ (A \backslash \{A_k\} \vdash t)$, and $(A \backslash \{A_k\}) \cup \{b\} \vdash t$.

The context of the classical equilibrium existence theorem provides us, again, with an example. Whereas the proof of the theorem by Arrow and Debreu (1954) necessitated a 'survival assumption' (A12.3.8: for each consumer $i = 1, 2 \ldots, m$, $w_i \in R^l$ such that for some $x_i \in X_i$, x_i

$<< \mathbf{w}_i)$, the one of Debreu (1962) was based, instead, on an 'interiority assumption', a sort of 'intersectoral compatibility requirement' (for each consumer $i = 1, 2, \ldots, m$, int$(\mathbf{Y} + \mathbf{w}_i) \cap \mathbf{X}_i \neq \varnothing$), and the proof of Moore (1975) made use of an 'irreducibility assumption' – in McKenzie's (1981) version, it is required, first, that $\mathbf{X} \cap$ int $\mathbf{Y} \neq \varnothing$ and, second, that for any partition $\{A, B\}$ of the index set of consumers $(1, 2, \ldots, m)$, if $\mathbf{x}_a = \mathbf{y} - \mathbf{x}_b$ with $\mathbf{y} \in \mathbf{Y}$ and $\mathbf{x}_b \in \mathbf{conX}_b$ (the convex hull of $\mathbf{X}_b$), then there exists also $\mathbf{y}' \in \mathbf{Y}$ and $\mathbf{w} \in \mathbf{conX}_b$ (the convex hull of $\mathbf{X}_b$), such that $\mathbf{x}_a' = \mathbf{y}' - \mathbf{x}_b - \mathbf{w}$ and $\mathbf{x}_i' \succcurlyeq_i \mathbf{x}_i$ for all $i \in A$, and $\mathbf{x}_i' \succ_i \mathbf{x}_i$ for some $i \in A$.

12.6.3 Extending theoretical coverage

Some analytic experiment simulations – comprising cases that would fit within the categories examined in 12.6.1 and 12.6.2 – may be interpreted as procedures to extend the coverage of theories, in particular, theoretical generalizations. For instance, in relation to current general equilibrium analysis of finite economies, the theory of value for finite economies as presented in Arrow and Debreu (1954) – and the same is true for most theories which historically followed it – did become a special case. At any point in time, 'current theory' is the result of a process of extending the coverage of older theories by a systematic, step-by-step, modification of their axiom base – see the surveys by McKenzie (1981) and Debreu (1982).

12.6.4 Investigating the smoothness of a dependence

In many studies, it is important to probe for smooth changes in the behaviour of the *explanandum* following smooth changes in the behaviour of the *explanans*. Examples include regularity studies in the context of equilibrium determinacy theory – Dierker (1974, 1982) – and the need to guarantee in a non-trivial manner, by means of an appropriate topology, the smooth behaviour of demand relations – Hildenbrand (1974).

12.6.5 Checking the robustness of a result

Theoretical results regarding the properties of a state of a system are often extremely sensitive to very small changes in the conditions and parameters which define the state. For an example, we refer here to the discussion on the determinacy of equilibria of 12.4.3.

12.6.6   Testing for substantive invariance

The current problem is whether a proposition obtained within a language L_1 has an analogous interpretation when the problem is recast in a different language L_2. In other words, the issue is to determine whether the analytic result is language-invariant in the sense that there exist appropriate translations between the two languages that lead to two substantively – that is, economically – equivalent interpretations.

To avoid misunderstanding, a note of caution may be called for here. It is not suggested that given the languages L_1, L_2 and proposition t, the fact that proposition t is both L_1- and L_2-invariant should be taken as an indication, let alone evidence, of the adequacy of L_1 and L_2. Rather, the point that is being made is that *if* L_1 is adequate and t is obtained under L_1, and *if* L_2 is also adequate, then t should be L_2-invariant.

Two examples which illustrate this kind of analytic experiment simulation are described below. They stem, in that order, from the field of perfect competition analysis and from the far more slowly developing general equilibrium analysis of imperfectly competitive economies.

First, as was described in 12.4.1, a perfectly competitive economy is one where the agents are 'negligible' in the sense that their individual actions cannot influence the social outcomes. We recall that for such an imaginary economy the only possible social outcomes are the competitive ones and that this is characterized by the core–equilibria equivalence theorem which states that the core and the set of equilibrium allocations of the economy coincide.

How sensitive is core–equilibria equivalence to mathematical language? Evidence of substantive invariance was given by the fact that analogous equivalence results were obtained by means of a topological sequential approach by Debreu and Scarf (1963); using measure-theoretical and integration-theoretical arguments by Aumann (1964) and Hildenbrand (1974), respectively; in the language of non-standard analysis but following very different approaches by Brown and Robinson (1975) and Anderson (1978); and by the Boolean ring approach of Armstrong and Richter (1984), where postulates requiring a continuum of agents, the σ-algebraic nature of the class of coalitions and the countable additivity of the measure describing allocations could be dispensed with.

Second, as seen in 12.4.6, questions of core–equilibria equivalence – or lack of equivalence – are also raised in the context of imperfectly competitive systems. For instance, in relation to the 'mixed-market' structure previously described, Shitovitz (1973) proved an equivalence result for the case of an economy with a continuum of 'small traders' and one 'large trader' of the same type, that is, having the same preferences and initial endowment as the 'small traders'. This rather counter-intuitive result was shown to be invariant by Jaskold-Gabszewicz (1977) under an appropriately adapted version of the Debreu–Scarf sequence of expanding finite economies.

12.6.7 Probing the adequacy of alternative mathematical languages

In 12.4.2 we commented that there is an important list of problems which can be better studied in relational structures having as domain spaces – specifically, as commodity spaces – not R^l but an infinite-dimensional space. We also pointed out that there is no 'perfect' space for the formulation of all the listed problems and, possibly, even no single ideal space for each problem. It is to be noticed that with each special space there is associated a more or less differentiated functional–analytic language.

In the context of intertemporal allocation analysis, for instance, different descriptions of the consumption process have led to the choice of domains such as the space of bounded sequences of real numbers, spaces of bounded measurable functions, the space of essentially bounded, real-valued measurable functions on an appropriate measure space, and so on.

As another example, this time from the classical equilibrium existence problem, Debreu (1982) distinguishes four general approaches to equilibrium existence, namely, application of fixed-point theorems, use of combinatorial algorithms, application of fixed-point index theory and degree theory of a map, and global analysis. Moreover, within the first general approach, Debreu (1982) distinguishes two further special alternative approaches which he calls the simultaneous optimization approach and the excess demand approach, respectively.

12.6.8 Construction of alternative proofs

Special cases of the situation described in 12.6.7 are the efforts to construct alternative proofs of a known result. A deeper insight into the configuration of a problem is often obtained by this method, which is carried out sometimes within the original mathematical language in which the problem was formulated and other times after it has been recast into a different language.

Two examples of this kind of exercise are the 'constructive proof' of the equilibrium existence theorem for the Arrow–Debreu economy by Mantel (1968), and the alternative approaches to the study of the core–equilibria equivalence theorem for competitive economies – refer, once again, to 12.4.1.

12.6.9 Probing the descriptive power of alternative solution concepts

Core analysis, while successful in the characterization of perfect competition, has been less than satisfactory for the description of imperfectly competitive situations – indeed, as pointed out by Aumann (1973), the core idea may fail to capture adequately key features of monopoly power. Despite partial disappointments, the fact remains that core analysis initiated an approach that is both interesting and promising and that consists in checking the descriptive power of older and newer game-theoretic solution concepts in an economic context.

Such analytic experiment simulations show common patterns among which two steps can be clearly distinguished. In the first step, a 'test' – proof of an equivalence theorem – is carried out for a perfectly competitive structure to serve as a benchmark or reference – usually an economy with an atomless measure space of traders – to ascertain the equivalence between the game-theoretic solution concept in question and the set of Walrasian equilibria. In the second step, the comparison is extended to a framework that incorporates imperfectly competitive features, usually a 'mixed market'. Studies of this type have been made in relation to various solution concepts, including the *Shapley value* – for instance, Mas-Colell (1977a) and Gardner (1977) – and the *bargaining set* – for example, Mas-Colell (1989) and Shitovitz (1989).

12.7 TOWARD EMPIRICAL THEORIES: APPLIED COMPUTABLE GENERAL EQUILIBRIUM

Experiment simulations like those described in preceding sections may be conceived as the construction of new non-intendedly empirical theories by means of analytic operations performed on pre-existing ones. They aim at supplying new, logical – albeit not empirical – answers to the new questions that result from changes introduced to pre-existing theories – for instance, to the Arrow–Debreu theory.

One of the ultimate goals of scientific research is, of course, to produce empirical theories; and general equilibrium analysis is by no means an exception to this rule. On the contrary, it was only natural to expect that some of these chains of analytic experiment simulations would lead, at certain developmental stages, to links resulting in intendedly empirical theories. There is now evidence to support the claim that actual research has already gone beyond mere expectations.

A milestone in the transition from the construction of non-intendedly empirical theories to the development of applied general equilibrium theories has been the work of Scarf (1973, 1982) on the computation of equilibrium prices – for an update, see Kehoe (1991). A discussion of methodological issues and a sample of applications – including such fields as taxation, trade, price rigidities – are to be found in Piggott and Whalley (1985); see also Shoven and Whalley (1992). Evidence of the importance that the field is rapidly acquiring is the recent *Handbook of Computational Economics*, Vol. I, edited by Amman, Kendrick and Rust (1996).

12.8 NOTES AND REMARKS

Stoff (1969) gives a valuable account of 'thought experiments' in science. I am grateful to Professor Bo Gustafsson for making me aware of this work. In the same context and in specific reference to physics, interesting views have been expressed by Einstein and Infeld (1938) and Planck (1970). Regarding 'idealizational' structures of theoretical economics, see Nowak (1989).

A question that might spur the curiosity of the reader concerns the epistemological status – intended or actual – of the original Arrow–Debreu theory. We shall try a tentative answer here, observing that such an answer, whatever its sense, cannot determine or modify our views regarding the central role the theory has played in the development of equilibrium analysis – and, of course, in the configuration of this chapter.

After claiming that the 'investigation of the existence of solutions is of interest both for descriptive and for normative economics', focusing on its importance for the former, Arrow and Debreu (1954) add that

[d]escriptively, the view that the competitive model is a reasonably accurate description of reality, at least for certain purposes, presupposes that the equations describing the model are consistent with

each other. Hence, one check of the empirical usefulness of the model is the prescription of the conditions under which the equations of competitive equilibrium have a solution.

Given the very abstract and succinct nature of the theory, and despite the cautious reference to 'reality' and the mention of 'empirical usefulness', we get the impression that the focus of the authors is on the consistency of the theoretical construct – thus on its suitableness as the nucleus of a relevant research programme, an *ultimate goal* of which is the explanation of reality – rather than on its immediate empirical testability; and, independently of the fact that some of its statements may be satisfied by empirical structures – in the sense that many abstract theories are – the theory does not seem to have been conceived under the restrictive empirical conditions of Definition 4.2.2.

In addition to Volumes II, III, and IV of the *Handbook of Mathematical Economics* (Arrow and Intriligator, 1982 and 1986; Hildenbrand and Sonnenschein, 1991), the reader will find further references to and examples of the methodology discussed in this chapter in the *Handbook of Game Theory with Economic Applications*, Vols I and II, edited by Aumann and Hart (1992 and 1994).

Bibliography

Adelman, I. 'Simulation: II. Economic processes', in *International Encyclopedia of the Social Sciences*, edited by David L. Sills, Vols 13/14. New York: The Macmillan Co. and The Free Press, 1968, reprinted 1972.

Akaike, H. 'Statistical predictor identification', *Annals of the Institute of Statistical Mathematics*, 21 (1969), 203–17.

Alchian, A. A. 'Uncertainty, evolution and economic theory', *Journal of Political Economy*, 58 (1950), 211–21.

Aliprantis, C. and D. Brown. 'Equilibria in markets with a Riesz space of commodities', *Journal of Mathematical Economics*, 11 (1983), 189–207.

Allen, R. G. D. *Mathematical Economics*, 2nd edition. London: Macmillan, 1960.

Amemiya, T. *Advanced Econometrics*. Oxford: Basil Blackwell, 1985, reprinted 1986.

Amman, H. M., D. Kendrick and J. Rust (eds). *Handbook of Computational Economics*, Vol. 1. Amsterdam: Elsevier, 1996.

Anderson, R. M. 'An elementary core equivalence theorem', *Econometrica*, 46 (1978), 1483–7.

Araujo, A. and P. K. Monteiro. 'Equilibrium without uniform conditions', *Journal of Economic Theory*, 48 (1989), 416–27.

Armstrong, T. E. and M. K. Richter. 'The core-Walras equivalence', *Journal of Economic Theory*, 33 (1984), 116–51.

Arrow, K. J. *Social Choice and Individual Values*. New York: Wiley, 1951.

Arrow, K. J. and G. Debreu. 'Existence of an equilibrium for a competitive economy', *Econometrica*, 22 (1954), 265–90.

Arrow, K. J. and F. H. Hahn. *General Competitive Analysis*. San Francisco: Holden-Day, 1971.

Arrow, K. J. and L. Hurwicz. 'Decentralization and computation in resource-allocation', in *Essays in Economics and Econometrics in Honor of Harold Hotelling*, edited by R. Pfouts. Chapel Hill: University of North Carolina Press, 1960.

Arrow, K. J. and M. D. Intriligator (eds). *Handbook of Mathematical Economics*, Vols I, II and III. Amsterdam: North-Holland, 1981, 1982, 1986.

Arrow, K. J., H. B. Chenery, B. S. Minhas and R. Solow. 'Capital–labor substitution and economic efficiency', *Review of Economics and Statistics*, 43 (1961), 225–35.

Arrow, K. J., L. Hurwicz and H. Uzawa. *Studies in Linear and Non-Linear Programming*. Stanford: Stanford University Press, 1958.

Aumann, R. J. 'Markets with a continuum of traders', *Econometrica*, 32 (1964), 39–50.

Aumann, R. J. 'Disadvantageous monopolies', *Journal of Economic Theory*, 6 (1973), 1–11.

Aumann, R. J. and S. Hart (eds). *Handbook of Game Theory with Economic Applications*, Vols I and II. Amsterdam: North-Holland, 1992, 1994.

Balzer, W. 'A logical reconstruction of pure exchange economics', *Erkenntnis*, 17 (1982), 23–46.

Balzer, W. 'The proper reconstruction of exchange economics', *Erkenntnis*, 23 (1985), 185–200.

Balzer, W. and B. Hamminga (eds). *Philosophy of Economics*. Dordrecht: Kluwer, 1989.

Balzer, W., C. U. Moulines, and J. D. Sneed. *An Architectonic for Science: The Structuralist Program*. Dordrecht: D. Reidel, 1987.

Barone, E. 'Il ministro della produzione nello stato collectivista', *Giornale degli Economisti*, 37 (1908), 267–93.

Barten, A. P. 'Consumer demand functions under conditions of almost additive preferences', *Econometrica*, 32 (1964), 1–38.

Barten, A. P. 'Estimating demand functions', *Econometrica*, 36 (1968), 213–51.

Barten, A. P. 'Maximum likelihood estimation of a complete system of demand equations', *European Economic Review*, 1 (1969), 1–23.

Barten, A. P. 'The systems of consumer demand functions approach: a review', *Econometrica*, 45 (1977), 23–51.

Barten, A. P. and V. Böhm. 'Consumer theory', in *Handbook of Mathematical Economics*, Vol. II, edited by K. J. Arrow and M. D. Intriligator. Amsterdam: North-Holland, 1982.

Barwise, J. (ed.). *Handbook of Mathematical Logic*. Amsterdam: North-Holland, 1977.

Basmann, R. L. and G. Rhodes (eds). *Advances in Econometrics*. Amsterdam: North-Holland, 1982.

Battalio, R. C., J. H. Kagel and D. N. MacDonald. 'Animals' choices over uncertain outcomes: some initial experimental results', *American Economic Review*, 75 (1985), 597–613.

Battalio, R. C., J. H. Kagel and M. O. Reynolds. 'Income distributions in two experimental economies', *Journal of Political Economy*, 85 (1977). Reprinted in V. L. Smith, 1990.

Beato, P. and A. Mas-Colell. 'On marginal cost pricing with given tax-subsidy rules', *Journal of Economic Theory*, 37 (1985), 356–65.

Bénassy, J.-P. 'Non-Walrasian equilibrium, money and macroeconomics', in *Handbook of Monetary Economics*, Vol. I, edited by B. M. Friedman and F. H. Hahn. Amsterdam: North-Holland, 1990.

Bénassy, J.-P. 'Monopolistic competition', in *Handbook of Mathematical Economics*, Vol. IV, edited by W. Hildenbrand and H. Sonnenschein. Amsterdam: North-Holland, 1991.

Bergstrom, A. R. 'Nonrecursive models of discrete approximations to systems of stochastic differential equations', *Econometrica*, 34 (1966), 173–82.

Bergstrom, A. R. *The Construction and Use of Economic Models*. London: The English University Press, 1967.

Bergstrom, A. R. (ed.). *Statistical Inference in Continuous Time Economic Models*. Amsterdam: North-Holland, 1976.

Bergstrom, A. R. 'Monetary policy in a model of the United Kingdom', in *Stability and Inflation*, edited by A. R. Bergstrom, A. J. L. Catt, M. H. Peston and B. D. J. Silverstone. New York: John Wiley & Sons, 1978.

Bergstrom, A. R. 'Monetary, fiscal and exchange rate policy in a continuous-time econometric model of the United Kingdom', in *Contemporary Macroeconomic Modelling*, edited by P. Malgrange and P.-A. Muet. Oxford: Basil Blackwell, 1984a.

Bergstrom, A. R. 'Continuous time stochastic models and issues of aggregation over time', in *Handbook of Econometrics*, Vol. II, edited by Z. Griliches and M. D. Intriligator. Amsterdam: North-Holland, 1984b.

Bergstrom, A. R. and C. R. Wymer. 'A model of disequilibrium neoclassical growth and its application to the United Kingdom', in *Statistical Inference in Continuous Time Economic Models*, edited by A. R. Bergstrom. Amsterdam: North-Holland, 1976.

Bergstrom, A. R., A. J. L. Catt, M. H. Peston and B. D. J Silverstone (eds). *Stability and Inflation*. New York: John Wiley & Sons, 1978.

Bergstrom, T. C. 'How to discard "free disposability" – at no cost', *Journal of Mathematical Economics*, 3 (1976), 131–4.

Bewley, T. 'Existence of equilibria in economies with infinitely many commodities', *Journal of Economic Theory*, 4 (1972), 514–40.

Bewley, T. 'Equality of the core and set of equilibria in economies with infinitely many commodities and a continuum of agents', *International Economic Review*, 14 (1973), 383–94.

Blalock, H. M. *Causal Inference in Nonexperimental Research*. Chapel Hill: The University of North Carolina Press, 1964.

Blanchard, O. J. 'Why does money affect output? A survey', in *Handbook of Monetary Economics*, Vol. II, edited by B. M. Friedman and F. H. Hahn. Amsterdam: North-Holland, 1990.

Blanchard, O. J. and D. Quah. 'The dynamic effects of aggregate demand and supply disturbances, *American Economic Review*, 89 (1989), 655–73.

Brock, W. A. 'Overlapping generations models with money and transactions costs', in *Handbook of Monetary Economics*, Vol. I, edited by B. M. Friedman and F. H. Hahn. Amsterdam: North-Holland, 1990.

Broome, J. 'Approximate equilibrium in economies with indivisible commodities', *Journal of Economic Theory*, 5 (1972), 224–49.

Brown, D. J. and A. Robinson. 'Nonstandard exchange economies', *Econometrica*, 43 (1975), 41–55.

Brown, D. J., W. P. Heller and R. M. Starr. 'Two-part marginal cost pricing equilibria: existence and efficiency', *Journal of Economic Theory*, 57 (1992), 52–72.

Bunge, M. *Foundations of Physics*. New York: Springer, 1967a.

Bunge, M. *Studies in the Foundations, Methodology and Philosophy of Science* Vol. 3/I. *Scientific Research I. The Search for System* and Vol. 3/II. *Scientific Research II. The Search for Truth*. New York: Springer, 1967b.

Chenery, H. and P. Clark. *Interindustry Economics*. New York: John Wiley & Sons, 1959.

Chipman, J. S., L. Hurwicz, M. K. Richter and H. Sonnenschein (eds). *Preferences, Utility and Demand: A Minnesota Symposium*. New York: Harcourt Brace Jovanovich, 1971.

Christensen, L. R., D. W. Jorgenson and L. J. Lau. 'Transcendental logarithmic production functions, *Review of Economics and Statistics*, 55 (1973), 28–45.

Christensen, L. R., D. W. Jorgenson and L. J. Lau. 'Transcendental logarithmic utility functions', *American Economic Review*, 65 (1975), 367–83.

Cobb, C. W. and P. H. Douglas. 'A theory of production', *American Economic Review*, 18 (1928), 139–65.

Conrad, K. and D. W. Jorgenson. *Measuring Performance in the Private Economy of the Federal Republic of Germany, 1950–1973*. Tübingen: J. B. Mohr, 1975.

Conrad, K. and D. W. Jorgenson. 'Tests of a model of production for the Federal Republic of Germany, 1950–1973', *European Economic Review*, 10 (1977), 51–75.

Conrad, K. and D. W. Jorgenson. 'The structure of consumer preferences, Federal Republic of Germany, 1950–1973', *Zeitschrift für Nationalökonomie*, 38 (1978), 1–28.

Conrad, K. and D. W. Jorgenson. 'Testing the integrability of demand functions, Federal Republic of Germany, 1950–1973', *European Economic Review*, 12 (1979), 149–69.

Cooley, T. F. and F. LeRoy. 'Atheoretical macroeconometrics: a critique', *Journal of Monetary Economics*, 16 (1985), 283–308.

Davies, D. D. and C. A. Holt. *Experimental Economics*. Princeton: Princeton University Press, 1993.

Deaton, A. 'Demand analysis', in *Handbook of Econometrics*, Vol. III, edited by Z. Griliches and M. D. Intriligator. Amsterdam: North-Holland, 1986.

Deaton, A. and J. Muellbauer. *Economics and Consumer Behavior*. Cambridge: Cambridge University Press, 1980.

Debreu, G. 'Valuation equilibrium and Pareto optimum', *Proceedings of the National Academy of Sciences*, 40 (1954), 588–92.

Debreu, G. *Theory of Value: An Axiomatic Analysis of Economic Equilibrium*. New York: Wiley, 1959.

Debreu, G. 'New concepts and techniques for equilibrium analysis', *International Economic Review*, 3 (1962), 257–73.

Debreu, G. 'Economies with a finite set of equilibria', *Econometrica*, 38 (1970), 387–92.

Debreu, G. 'Excess demand functions', *Journal of Mathematical Economics*, 1 (1974), 15–23.

Debreu, G. 'Existence of competitive equilibrium', in *Handbook of Mathematical Economics*, Vol. II, edited by K. J. Arrow and M. D. Intriligator. Amsterdam: North-Holland, 1982.

Debreu, G. and H. E. Scarf. 'A limit theorem on the core of an economy', *International Economic Review*, 4 (1963), 235–46.

Der Grosse Brockhaus, Vol. 3, p. 733, 16th edition. Mannheim: F. A. Brockhaus, 1953, and *Brockhaus Enzyklopädie*, Vol. 5, p. 825, 17th edition of *Der Grosse Brockhaus*. Wiesbaden: F. A. Brockhaus, 1968.

Diederich, W. 'A structuralist reconstruction of Marx's economics', in *Philosophy of Economics*, edited by W. Stegmüller, W. Balzer and W. Spohn. Berlin: Springer, 1982.

Diederich, W. 'The development of Marx's economic theory', in *Philosophy of Economics*, edited by W. Balzer and B. Hamminga. Dordrecht: Kluwer, 1989.

Dierker, E. 'Equilibrium analysis of exchange economies with indivisible commodities', *Econometrica*, 39 (1971), 997–1008.

Dierker, E. *Topological Methods in Walrasian Economics*. New York: Springer, 1974.

Dierker, E. 'Regular economies', in *Handbook of Mathematical Economics*, Vol. II, edited by K. J. Arrow and M. D. Intriligator. Amsterdam: North-Holland, 1982.

Dierker, E. 'The optimality of Boiteux–Ramsey pricing', *Discussion Paper No. A-159*, University of Bonn. Bonn: 1989.

Dierker, H. 'Equilibria and core of large economies', *Journal of Mathematical Economics*, 2 (1975), 155–69.

Divay, J. F. and P. Meunier. 'Two methods of elaborating input–output tables', in *Compilation of Input–Output Tables*, edited by J. V. Skolka. Berlin: Springer, 1982.

Dorfman, R., P. A. Samuelson and R. Solow. *Linear Programming and Economic Analysis*. New York: McGraw-Hill, 1958.

Dornbusch, R. and A. Giovannini. 'Monetary policy in the open economy', in *Handbook of Monetary Economics*, Vol. II, edited by B. M. Friedman and F. H. Hahn. Amsterdam: North-Holland, 1990.

Douglas, P. H. 'The Cobb-Douglas production function once again: its history, its testing and some empirical values', *Journal of Political Economy*, 84 (1976), 903–16.

Drèze, J. H. 'The pure theory of labour-managed and participatory economies: Part I, Certainty', *Discussion Paper 7422*, CORE, Université Catholique de Louvain. Louvain: 1974.

Drèze, J. H. 'Some theory of labor management and participation', *Econometrica*, 44 (1976), 1125–39.

Duffie, D. 'Money in general equilibrium theory', in *Handbook of Monetary Economics*, Vol. I, edited by B. M. Friedman and F. H. Hahn. Amsterdam: North-Holland, 1990.

Edgeworth, F. Y. *Mathematical Physics*. London: Paul Kegan, 1881.

Einstein, A. and L. Infeld. *The Evolution of Physics: The Growth of Ideas from Early Concepts to Relativity and Quanta*. London: Cambridge University Press, 1938.

Encyclopaedia Britannica, Macropaedia, Vol. 16, *Micropaedia*, Vol. IX, 15th edition. London: Benton, 1977.

Epstein, R. J. *A History of Econometrics*. Amsterdam: North-Holland, 1987.

Farrell, M. J. 'Edgeworth bounds for oligopoly prices', *Economica*, 37 (1970), 342–61.

Fischer, S. 'Rules versus discretion in monetary policy', in *Handbook of Monetary Economics*, Vol. II, edited by B. M. Friedman and F. H. Hahn. Amsterdam: North-Holland, 1990.

Friedman, B. M. 'Targets and instruments of monetary policy', in *Handbook of Monetary Economics*, Vol. II, edited by B. M. Friedman and F. H. Hahn, Amsterdam: North-Holland, 1990.

Friedman, B. M. and F. H. Hahn (eds). *Handbook of Monetary Economics*, Vols I and II. Amsterdam: North-Holland, 1990.

Friedman, J. W. 'On experimental research in oligopoly', *Review of Economic Studies*, 36 (1969). Reprinted in V. L. Smith, 1990.

Friedman, M. *Capitalism and Freedom*. Chicago: The University of Chicago Press, 1962.

Friedman, M. *A Program for Monetary Stability*. New York: Fordham University Press, 1960.

Gale, D. *The Theory of Linear Economic Models*. New York: McGraw-Hill, 1960.
Gale, D. and A. Mas-Colell. 'An equilibrium existence theorem for a general model without ordered preferences', *Journal of Mathematical Economics*, 2 (1975), 9–15.
Gandolfo, G. *Qualitative Analysis and Econometric Estimation of Continuous Time Dynamic Models*. Amsterdam: North-Holland, 1981.
Gardner, R. 'Shapley value and disadvantageous monopolies', *Journal of Economic Theory*, 16 (1977), 513–17.
Gerking, S. 'Input–output as a simple econometric model', *Review of Economics and Statistics*, 58 (1976), 274–82.
Goldberger, A. S. *Impact Multipliers and Dynamic Properties of the Klein–Goldberger Model*. Amsterdam: North-Holland, 1959.
Granger, C. W. 'Investigating causal relations by econometric models and cross-spectral methods', *Econometrica*, 37 (1969), 424–38.
Granger, C. W. *Forecasting in Business and Economics*, 2nd edition. New York: Academic Press, 1989.
Griliches, Z. and M. D. Intriligator (eds). *Handbook of Econometrics*, Vols I, II and III. Amsterdam: North-Holland, 1983, 1984, 1986.
Grodal, B. 'The rate of convergence of the core for a purely competitive sequence of economies', *Journal of Mathematical Economics*, 2 (1975), 171–86.
Hamminga, B. and W. Balzer. 'The basic structure of neoclassical general equilibrium theory', *Erkenntnis*, 25 (1986), 31–46.
Händler, E. W. 'The logical structure of modern neoclassical static microeconomic equilibrium theory', *Erkenntnis*, 15 (1980a), 33–53.
Händler, E. W. 'The role of utility and of statistical concepts in empirical economic theories: the empirical claims of the systems of aggregate market supply and demand functions approach', *Erkenntnis*, 15 (1980b), 129–57.
Händler, E. W. 'The evolution of economic theories: a formal approach', *Erkenntnis*, 18 (1982), 65–96.
Hands, D. W. 'The logical reconstruction of pure exchange economics: another alternative', *Theory and Decision*, 19 (1985), 259–78.
Hart, O. D. and H. W. Kuhn. 'A proof of the existence of equilibrium without the free disposal assumption', *Journal of Mathematical Economics*, 2 (1975), 335–43.
Haslinger, F. 'A logical reconstruction of pure exchange economics: an alternative view', *Erkenntnis*, 20 (1983), 115–29.
Heal, G. M. *The Theory of Economic Planning*. Amsterdam: North-Holland/American Elsevier, 1973.
Heal, G. M. 'Planning', in *Handbook of Mathematical Economics*, Vol. III, edited by K. J. Arrow and M. D. Intriligator. Amsterdam: North-Holland, 1986.
Hicks, J. *Value and Capital: An Enquiry Into Some Fundamental Principles of Economic Theory*. Oxford: Clarendon Press, 1939.
Hildenbrand, K. 'Finiteness of $\Pi(\mathscr{E})$ and continuity of Π', Appendix to Chapter 2 in W. Hildenbrand, 1974.
Hildenbrand, W. *Core and Equilibria of Large Economies*. Princeton: Princeton University Press, 1974.
Hildenbrand, W. 'Core of an economy', in *Handbook of Mathematical Economics*, Vol. II, edited by K. J. Arrow and M. D. Intriligator. Amsterdam: North-Holland, 1982.

Hildenbrand, W. and H. Sonnenschein (eds). *Handbook of Mathematical Economics*, Vol. IV. Amsterdam: North-Holland, 1991.

Hirshleifer, J. *Price Theory and Applications*, 3rd edition. Englewood Cliffs: Prentice-Hall, 1984.

Houthakker, H. S. 'Additive preferences', *Econometrica*, 33 (1960), 797–801.

Hsiao, C. 'Autoregressive modeling of Canadian money and income data', *Journal of the American Statistical Association, Applications Section*, 74 (1979), 553–60.

Hurwicz, L. 'The design of mechanisms for resource allocation', *American Economic Review, Papers and Proceedings*, 63 (1973), 1–30.

Hurwicz, L. 'Incentive aspects of decentralization', in *Handbook of Mathematical Economics*, Vol. III, edited by K. J. Arrow and M. D. Intriligator. Amsterdam: North-Holland, 1986.

Ichiishi, T. 'Coalition structure in a labor-managed economy', *Econometrica*, 45 (1977), 314–60.

International Encyclopedia of the Social Sciences, edited by David L. Sills, Vols 13 and 14. New York: The Macmillan Co. and The Free Press, 1968, reprinted 1972.

Isaac, R. M. and C. R. Plott. 'Price controls and the behavior of auction markets: an experimental evaluation', *American Economic Review*, 71 (1981). Reprinted in V. L. Smith, 1990.

Jackson, R. W. and G. R. West. 'Perspectives on probabilistic input–output analysis', in *Frontiers of Input–Output Analysis*, edited by R. E. Miller, K. R. Polenske and A. Z. Rose. Oxford: Oxford University Press, 1989.

Janssen, M. C. W. 'Structuralist reconstructions of classical and Keynesian macroeconomics', in *Philosophy of Economics*, edited by W. Balzer and B. Hamminga. Dordrecht: Kluwer, 1989.

Janssen, M. C. W. and T. A. F. Kuipers. 'Stratification of general equilibrium theory: a synthesis of reconstructions', in *Philosophy of Economics*, edited by W. Balzer and B. Hamminga. Dordrecht: Kluwer, 1989.

Jaskold-Gabszewicz, J. 'Asymmetric duopoly and the core', *Journal of Economic Theory*, 14 (1977), 172–79.

Jones, L. E. 'Existence of equilibria with infinitely many commodities: Banach lattices reconsidered', *Journal of Mathematical Economics*, 16 (1987), 89–104.

Jorgenson, D. W. 'Econometric methods for modelling producer behavior', in *Handbook of Econometrics*, Vol. III, edited by Z. Griliches and M. D. Intriligator. Amsterdam: North-Holland, 1986.

Jorgenson, D. W. and L. J. Lau. 'The integrability of consumer demand functions', *European Economic Review*, 12 (1979), 115–47.

Jorgenson, D.W., L. J. Lau and T. M. Stoker. 'The transcendental logarithmic model of aggregate consumer behavior', in *Advances in Econometrics*, edited by R. L. Basmann and G. Rhodes. Amsterdam: North-Holland, 1982.

Judge, G. G., R. C. Hill, W. E. Griffiths, H. Lütkepohl and T.-C. Lee. *Introduction to the Theory and Practice of Econometrics*, 2nd edition. New York: John Wiley & Sons, 1985a.

Judge, G. G., R. C. Hill, W. E. Giffiths, H. Lütkepohl and T.-C. Lee. *The Theory and Practice of Econometrics*, 2nd edition. New York: John Wiley & Sons, 1985b.

Kagel, J. H. 'Token economies and experimental economics', *Journal of Political Economy*, 80 (1972), 779–85.

Kagel, J. H. and A. E. Roth (eds). *Handbook of Experimental Economics*. Princeton: Princeton University Press, 1995.

Kagel, J. H., R. C. Battalio, H. Rachlin, L. Green, R. L. Basmann and W. Klemm. 'Experimental studies of consumer behavior using laboratory animals', *Economic Inquiry*, 13 (1975), 22–8.

Kaldor, N. 'The irrelevance of equilibrium economics', *Economic Journal*, 82 (1972), 1237–55.

Kamiya, K. 'The decomposition method for systems of nonlinear equations', *Discussion Paper 87214*, CORE, Université Catholique de Louvain. Louvain: 1987.

Kamiya, K. 'Existence and uniqueness of equilibria with increasing returns', *Journal of Mathematical Economics*, 17 (1988), 149–78.

Katouzian, H. *Ideology and Method in Economics*. London: Macmillan, 1980.

Katzner, D. W. *Static Demand Theory*. London: Macmillan, 1970.

Kehoe, T. J. 'Computation and multiplicity of equilibria', in *Handbook of Mathematical Economics*, Vol. IV, edited by W. Hildenbrand and H. Sonnenschein. Amsterdam: North-Holland, 1991.

Kehoe, T. J., D. K. Levine, A. Mas-Colell and W. R. Zame. 'Determinacy of equilibrium in large-scale economies', *Journal of Mathematical Economics*, 18 (1989), 231–62.

Keisler, H. J. 'Fundamentals in model theory', in *Handbook of Mathematical Logic*, edited by J. Barwise. Amsterdam: North-Holland, 1977.

Keynes, J. M. *The General Theory of Employment, Interest and Money*. London: Macmillan, 1936.

Keynes, J. N. *The Scope and Method of Political Economy*, 4th edition. New York: Kelley, 1955.

Kim, T. and M. K. Richter. 'Non-transitive non-total consumer theory', *Journal of Economic Theory*, 38 (1986), 324–63.

King, R. G., C. I. Posser, J. H. Stock and M. W. Watson. 'Stochastic trends and economic fluctuations', *The American Economic Review*, 81 (1991), 819–40.

Klein, E. 'Economic theories: language, structures, data (a model-theoretic characterization of the notion "empirical economic theory")', *ACEA Papers*, 21 (1992), 10–26.

Klein, L. 'Econometric aspects of input–output analysis', in *Frontiers of Input–Output Analysis*, edited by R. E. Miller, K. R. Polenske and A. Z. Rose. Oxford: Oxford University Press, 1989.

Klein, L. (ed.). *Comparative Performance of US Econometric Models*. Oxford: Oxford University Press, 1991.

Klein, L. and A. S. Goldberger. *An Econometric Model of the United States 1929–1952*. Amsterdam: North-Holland, 1955.

Klein, L., R. J. Ball, A. Hazlewood and P. Vandome. *An Econometric Model of the United Kingdom*. Oxford: Basil Blackwell, 1961.

Koopmans, T. *Three Essays on the State of Economic Science*. New York: McGraw-Hill, 1957.

Kopperman, R. *Model Theory and its Applications*. Boston: Allyn and Bacon, 1972.

Laitinen, K. 'Why is demand homogeneity so often rejected?', *Economics Letters*, 1 (1978), 187–91.

Lancaster, K. *Mathematical Economics*. New York: The Macmillan Co., 1968.

Lange, O. *On the Economic Theory of Socialism*, edited by B. E. Lippincott. Minneapolis: The University of Minnesota Press, 1938.

Lange, O. *Introduction to Econometrics*. London: Pergamon Press, 1959.

Leontief, W. W. *The Structure of the American Economy, 1919–1939*. Oxford: Oxford University Press, 1941.

Leontief, W. W. *Studies in the Structure of the American Economy*. Oxford and New York: Oxford University Press, 1953.

Lerner, A. *The Economics of Control*. New York: The Macmillan Co., 1944.

Lind, H. *Tanken bakom tänkta economier: Om forskningsstrategi i modern nationalekonomi*. Stockholm: Akademeja, 1990.

Litterman, R. B. and L. Weiss. 'Money, real interest rates, and output: a reinterpretation of postwar US data', *Econometrica*, 53 (1985), 129–56.

Lucas, R. E., Jr. 'Expectations and the neutrality of money', *Journal of Economic Theory*, 4 (1972), 103–24.

Lucas, R. E., Jr and T. J. Sargent (eds). *Rational Expectations and Econometric Practice*. Minneapolis: The University of Minnesota Press, 1981.

Malgrange, P. M. and P.-A. Muet (eds). *Contemporary Macroeconomic Modelling*. Oxford: Basil Blackwell, 1984.

Malinvaud, E. 'Decentralised procedures for planning', in *Activity Analysis in the Theory of Growth and Planning*, London: IEA/Macmillan, 1967.

Malinvaud, E. *Statistical Methods of Econometrics*, 3rd edition. Amsterdam: North-Holland, 1980.

Mankiw, N. G. and D. Romer (eds). *New Keynesian Economics*. Cambridge, Mass.: MIT Press, 1991.

Mantel, R. R. 'Toward a constructive proof of the existence of equilibrium in a competitive economy', *Yale Economic Essays*, 8 (1968), 155–96.

Mantel, R. R. 'On the characterization of aggregate excess demand', *Journal of Economic Theory*, 7 (1974), 348–53.

Mantel, R. R. 'Equilibrio con rendimiento creciente a escala', *Anales de la Asociación Argentina de Economía Política*, 1 (1979), 271–83.

Marschak, T. A. 'Organization design', in *Handbook of Mathematical Economics*, Vol. III, edited by K. J. Arrow and M. D. Intriligator. Amsterdam: North-Holland, 1986.

Mas-Colell, A. 'An equilibrium existence theorem without complete or transitive preferences', *Journal of Mathematical Economics*, 2 (1974), 237–46.

Mas-Colell, A. 'Competitive and value allocations of large exchange economies', *Journal of Economic Theory*, 14 (1977a), 419–38.

Mas-Colell, A. 'Indivisible commodities and general equilibrium theory', *Journal of Economic Theory*, 16 (1977b), 443–56.

Mas-Colell, A. *The Theory of General Economic Equilibrium: A Differentiable Approach*. Cambridge: Cambridge University Press, 1985.

Mas-Colell, A. 'The price equilibrium existence problem in topological vector lattices', *Econometrica*, 54 (1986), 1039–54.

Mas-Colell, A. 'An equivalence theorem for the bargaining set', *Journal of Mathematical Economics*, 18 (1989), 129–39.

Mas-Colell, A. and W. R. Zame. 'Equilibrium theory in infinite dimensional spaces', in *Handbook of Mathematical Economics*, Vol. IV, edited by W. Hildenbrand and H. Sonnenschein. Amsterdam: North-Holland, 1991.

Mas-Colell, A., M. D. Whinston and J. R. Green. *Microeconomic Theory*. Oxford: Oxford University Press, 1995.

McKenzie, L. 'Competitive equilibrium with dependent consumer preferences', in *2nd Symposium on Linear Programming. Proceedings*, edited by H. A. Antosiewicz. Washington, DC: National Bureau of Standards and Department of the Air Force, 1955.

McKenzie, L. 'On the existence of general equilibrium for a competitive market', *Econometrica*, 27 (1959), 54–71.

McKenzie, L. 'On the existence of general equilibrium: some corrections', *Econometrica*, 29 (1961), 247–8.

McKenzie, L. 'The classical theorem on the existence of competitive equilibrium', *Econometrica*, 49 (1981), 819–41.

McKenzie, L. 'Optimal economic growth and turnpike theorems', in *Handbook of Mathematical Economics*, Vol. III, edited by K. J. Arrow and M. D. Intriligator, Amsterdam: North-Holland, 1986.

Meade, J. E. 'The theory of labor-managed firms and profit-sharing', *Economic Journal*, 82 (1972), 402–28.

Miller, R. E., K. R. Polenske and A. Z. Rose (eds). *Frontiers of Input–Output Analysis*. Oxford: Oxford University Press, 1989.

Mirrlees, J. A. 'The theory of optimal taxation', in *Handbook of Mathematical Economics*, Vol. III, edited by K. J. Arrow and M. D. Intriligator. Amsterdam: North-Holland, 1986.

Moore, J. 'The existence of compensated equilibrium and the structure of the Pareto efficiency frontier', *International Economic Review*, 16 (1975), 267–300.

Morgenthaler, G. W. 'The theory and application of simulation in operations research', in *Progress in Operations Research*, Vol. I, edited by L. Ackoff Russell. New York: John Wiley & Sons, 1961.

Morishima, M. *Equilibrium, Stability and Growth: A Multi-Sectoral Analysis*. Oxford: Oxford University Press, 1964.

Morishima, M. and M. Saito. 'A dynamic analysis of the American economy, 1902–1952', in *The Working of Econometric Models*, edited by M. Morishima, Y. Murata, T. Nose and M. Saito. Cambridge: Cambridge University Press, 1972.

Morishima, M., Y. Murata, T. Nosse and M. Saito. *The Working of Econometric Models*. Cambridge: Cambridge University Press, 1972.

Mosbaek, E. J. and H. O. Wold. *Interdependent Systems: Structure and Estimation*. Amsterdam: North-Holland/American Elsevier, 1970a.

Mosbaek, E. J. and H. O. Wold. 'Estimation versus operative use of parameters in models for non-experimental situations'. *First World Congress of the Econometric Society*, Rome, 1965. French translation in *Economies et Sociétés*, 4 (1970b), 531–55.

Murata, Y. *Optimal Control Methods for Linear Discrete-Time Economic Systems*. Berlin: Springer, 1982.

Muth, J. F. 'Rational expectations and the theory of price movements', *Econometrica*, 29 (1961), 315–35.

Nadiri, M. I. 'Production theory', in *Handbook of Mathematical Economics*, Vol. II, edited by K. J. Arrow and M. D. Intriligator. Amsterdam: North-Holland, 1982.

Nagar, A. L. 'A Monte Carlo study of alternative simultaneous equation estimators', *Econometrica*, 28 (1960), 573–90.

Nash, J. 'Equilibrium points in N-person games', *Proceedings of the National Academy of Sciences*, USA, 36 (1950), 48–9.

Naylor, H. T. and J. M. Vernon. *Microeconomics and Decision Models of the Firm*. New York: Harcourt, Brace & World, 1969.

Negishi, T. 'Monopolistic competition and general equilibrium', *Review of Economic Studies*, 28 (1961), 196–201.

Negishi, T. *General Equilibrium Theory and International Trade*. Amsterdam: North-Holland, 1972.

Nguyen, H. N. 'Approximate equilibria in an economy with indivisible goods', unpublished PhD dissertation. Department of Economics, Dalhousie University, Halifax, N.S., Canada, 1976.

Nowak, L. 'On the (idealizational) structure of economic theories', in *Philosophy of Economics*, edited by W. Balzer and B. Hamminga. Dordrecht: Kluwer, 1989.

Piggott, J. and J. Whalley (eds). *New Developments in Applied General Equilibrium Analysis*. Cambridge: Cambridge University Press, 1985.

Planck, M. *Vorträge und Erinnerungen*. Darmstadt: Wissenschaftliche Buchgesellschaft, 1970.

Powell, A. P. *Empirical Analytics of Demand Systems*, Lexington: Lexington Books, 1974.

Przelecki, M. *The Logic of Empirical Theories*. London: Routledge and Kegan Paul, 1969.

Quinzii, M. 'Efficiency of marginal cost pricing equilibria', in *Equilibrium and Dynamics: Essays in Honour of David Gale*, edited by W. Brock and M. Majumdar. New York: Macmillan, 1991.

Quirk, J. and R. Saposnik. *Introduction to General Economic Theory and Welfare Economics*. New York: McGraw-Hill, 1968.

Requate, T. 'Once again pure exchange economies: a critical view towards the structuralistic reconstructions by Balzer and Stegmüller', *Erkenntnis*, 34 (1991), 87–116.

Richter, M. K. 'Revealed preference theory', *Econometrica*, 34 (1966), 635–45.

Richter, M. K. 'Rational choice', in *Preferences, Utility, and Demand*, edited by J. S. Chipman, L. Hurwicz, M. K. Richter and H. Sonnenschein. New York: Harcourt Brace Jovanovich, 1971.

Robinson, A. *Complete Theories*. Amsterdam: North-Holland, 1956.

Robinson, A. *Introduction to Model Theory and to the Metamathematics of Algebra*. Amsterdam: North-Holland, 1963.

Robinson, A. *Non-Standard Analysis*. Amsterdam: North-Holland, 1966.

Rogers, R. *Mathematical Logic and Formalized Theories*. Amsterdam: North-Holland, 1971.

Rolleri, J. L. 'La concepción de las teorías empíricas de Suppes', *Crítica, Revista Hispanoamericana de Filosofía*, 15 (1983), 103–37.

Rosenberg, A. 'Are generic predictions enough?', in *Philosophy of Economics*, edited by W. Balzer and B. Hamminga. Dordrecht: Kluwer, 1989.

Roy, R. *De l'utilité: contribution à la théorie des choix*. Paris: Hermann, 1942.

Samuelson, P. A. *Foundations of Economic Analysis*. Cambridge, Mass.: Harvard University Press, 1947.

Sargent, T. J. *Macroeconomic Theory*, 2nd edition. New York: Academic Press, 1987.

Scarf, H. E. 'The computation of equilibrium prices: an exposition', in *Handbook of Mathematical Economics*, Vol. II, edited by K. J. Arrow and M. D. Intriligator. Amsterdam: North-Holland, 1982.

Scarf, H. E. (with the collaboration of T. Hansen). *The Computation of Economic Equilibria*. New Haven: Yale University Press, 1973.

Sen, A. 'Social choice theory', in *Handbook of Mathematical Economics*, Vol. III, edited by K. J. Arrow and M. D. Intriligator. Amsterdam: North-Holland, 1986.

Shafer, W. 'The non-transitive consumer', *Econometrica*, 42 (1974), 913–19.

Shafer, W. and H. Sonnenschein. 'Equilibrium in abstract economies without ordered preferences or free disposal', *Journal of Mathematical Economics*, 2 (1975), 345–8.

Shafer, W. and H. Sonnenschein. 'Equilibrium with externalities, commodity taxation, and lump sum transfers', *International Economic Review*, 17 (1976), 601–11.

Shafer, W. and H. Sonnenschein. 'Market demand and excess demand functions', in *Handbook of Mathematical Economics*, Vol. II, edited by K. J. Arrow and M. D. Intriligator. Amsterdam: North-Holland, 1982.

Shephard, R. W. *Cost and Production Functions*. Princeton: Princeton University Press, 1953.

Shephard, R. W. *Theory of Cost and Production Functions*. Princeton: Princeton University Press, 1970.

Sheshinski, E. 'Positive second-best theory', in *Handbook of Mathematical Economics*, Vol. III, edited by K. J. Arrow and M. D. Intriligator. Amsterdam: North-Holland, 1986.

Shitovitz, B. 'Oligopoly in markets with a continuum of traders', *Econometrica*, 41 (1973), 467–502.

Shitovitz, B. 'On some problems arising in markets with some large traders and a continuum of small traders', *Journal of Economic Theory*, 8 (1974), 458–70.

Shitovitz, B. 'The bargaining set and the core in mixed markets with atoms and an atomless sector', *Journal of Mathematical Economics*, 18 (1989), 377–83.

Shoven, J. B. and J. Whalley. *Applying General Equilibrium*. Cambridge: Cambridge University Press, 1992.

Sims, C. A. 'Money, income and causality', *American Economic Review*, 62 (1972), 540–55.

Sims, C. A. 'Macroeconomics and reality', *Econometrica*, 48 (1980a), 1–48.

Sims, C. A. 'Comparison of interwar and postwar business cycles: monetarism reconsidered', *American Economic Review*, 70 (1980b), 250–57.

Smith, V. L. 'An experimental study of competitive market behavior', *The Journal of Political Economy*, 70 (1962). Reprinted in V. L. Smith, 1991.

Smith, V. L. 'Effect of market organization on competitive equilibrium', *Quarterly Journal of Economics*, 78 (1964). Reprinted in V. L. Smith, 1991.

Smith, V. L. 'Experimental economics: induced value theory', *American Economic Review*, 66 (1976). Reprinted in V. L. Smith, 1991.

Smith, V. L. 'Microeconomic systems as an experimental science', *American Economic Review*, 72 (1982), 923–55.

Smith, V. L. (ed.). *Experimental Economics*. Aldershot: Edward Elgar Publishing Limited, 1990.

Smith, V. L. *Papers in Experimental Economics*. Cambridge: Cambridge University Press, 1991.

Sonnenschein, H. 'Demand theory without transitive preferences', in *Preferences, Utility and Demand*, edited by J. Chipman, L. Hurwicz, M. K. Richter and H. Sonnenschein. New York: Harcourt Brace Jovanovich, 1971.

Sonnenschein, H. 'The utility hypothesis and market demand theory', *Western Economic Review*, 11 (1973), 404–10.

Sonnenschein, H. 'Market excess demand functions', *Econometrica*, 40 (1974), 549–63.

Stegmüller, W. *Structuralist View of Theories*. New York: Springer, 1978.

Stegmüller, W. 'Review' of *An Architectonic for Science. The Structuralist Program* by W. Balzer, C. U. Moulines and J. Sneed, *Erkenntnis*, 33 (1990), 399–410.

Stigum, B. *Towards a Formal Science of Economics*. Cambridge, Mass.: MIT Press, 1990.

Stoff, V. A. *Modellierung und Philosophie*. Translated from the Russian by S. Wollgast. Berlin: Akademie Verlag, 1969.

Stone, R. 'Linear expenditure system and demand analysis: an application to the pattern of British demand', *Economic Journal*, 64 (1954), 511–27.

Stone, R. 'Accounting matrices in economics and demography', in *Mathematical Methods in Economics*, edited by F. van der Ploeg. New York: John Wiley & Sons, 1984.

Suppes, P. 'A comparison of the meaning and uses of models in mathematics and the empirical sciences', *Synthèse*, 12 (1960), 283–301.

Suppes, P. 'Models of data', in *Logic, Methodology and the Philosophy of Science*, edited by E. Nagel, P. Suppes and A. Tarski. Stanford: Stanford University Press, 1962.

Suppes, P. 'Set-theoretical structures in science', Institute for Mathematical Studies in the Social Sciences, Stanford University, mimeo. Stanford: 1967.

Taylor, F. M. 'The guidance of production in a socialist state', in *On the Economic Theory of Socialism*, edited by B. E. Lippincott. Minneapolis: The University of Minnesota Press, 1938.

Taylor, J. B. 'New econometric approaches to stabilization policy in stochastic models of macroeconomic fluctuations', in *Handbook of Econometrics*, Vol. III, edited by Z. Griliches and M. D. Intriligator. Amsterdam: North-Holland, 1986.

Taylor, J. B. *Macroeconomic Policy in a World Economy: From Econometric Design to Practical Operation*. New York: W. W. Norton, 1993.

Taylor, J. B. and H. Uhlig. 'Solving nonlinear stochastic growth models: a comparison of alternative solution methods', *Journal of Economic and Business Statistics*, 8 (1990), 1–17.

Theil, H. 'The information approach to demand analysis', *Econometrica*, 33 (1965), 67–87.

Theil, H. *Economics and Information Theory.* Amsterdam: North-Holland, 1967.

Theil, H. *Theory and Measurement of Consumer Demand,* Vols I and II. Amsterdam: North-Holland, 1975 and 1976.

Theil, H. *The System-Wide Approach to Microeconomics.* Chicago: Chicago University Press, 1980.

Theil, H. and K. W. Clements. *Applied Demand Analysis: Results from System-Wide Approaches.* Cambridge, Mass.: Ballinger Publishing Co., 1987.

Theil, H. and F. E. Suhm, with J. F. Meisner. *International Consumption Comparisons: A System-Wide Approach.* Amsterdam: North-Holland, 1981.

Tilanus, C. B. *Input–Output Experiments: The Netherlands 1948–1961.* Rotterdam: Rotterdam University Press, 1968.

Tinbergen, J. *Economic Policies: Principles and Design.* Amsterdam: North-Holland, 1956.

Van der Ploeg, F. (ed.). *Mathematical Methods in Economics.* New York: John Wiley & Son, 1984.

Vanek, J. *The General Theory of Labor-Managed Market Economies.* Ithaca: Cornell University Press, 1970.

Vind, K. 'Edgeworth-allocations in an exchange economy with many traders', *International Economic Review,* 5 (1964), 165–77.

Vind, K. 'A theorem on the core of an economy', *The Review of Economic Studies,* 5 (1965), 47–8.

Walras, L. *Elements of Pure Economics.* Translated by W. Jaffé from the édition définitive, 1926. Original in French, *Éléments d'économie politique pure,* Paris, 1874. Homewood: the AEA and the RES by R. D. Irwin, Inc., 1954.

Walsh, V. *Introduction to Contemporary Microeconomics.* New York: McGraw-Hill, 1970.

Wang, B., E. Klein and U. L. G. Rao. 'Inflation and stabilization in Argentina', *Economic Modelling,* 12 (1995), 391–413.

Weale, M. R. 'Linear economic models', in *Mathematical Methods in Economics,* edited by F. van der Ploeg. New York: John Wiley & Sons, 1984.

Weddepohl, C. 'General equilibrium theory', in *Mathematical Methods in Economics,* edited by F. Van der Ploeg. New York: John Wiley & Sons, 1984.

Wold, H. O. 'Econometrics as pioneering in non-experimental model building', *Econometrica,* 37 (1969a), 369–81.

Wold, H. O. 'Non-experimental statistical analysis from the general point of view of scientific method', *Bulletin of the International Statistical Institute,* 52 (1969b), 391–424.

Notation Index

The following index lists the various symbols which are frequently used in the book. It registers the first occurrence of a symbol with a particular meaning. This means that if a symbol occurs more than once – for instance the symbol $\mathscr{E}$ occurs three times in the list – it is because it has been given more than one distinct meaning in the book.

Author Index

Subject Index

DATE DUE

			Printed in USA

HIGHSMITH #45230